MAT GU... ...vere allowed, a cat that wo... ...rted Southampton and Sal... ...en about football for *The Football Pink* and *Stand*, as well as on his own blog *Dreams of Victoria Park*. When not fretting about promotion and relegation in the Faroe Islands Football League, Mat enjoys open water swimming and taking part in endurance swims across the country.

Another Bloody Saturday

A journey to the heart and soul of football

MAT GUY

Luath Press Limited

EDINBURGH

www.luath.co.uk

First published 2015
New edition 2016
Reprinted 2018

ISBN: 978-1910745-72-4

The author's right to be identified as author of this book
under the Copyright, Designs and Patents Act 1988 has been asserted.

The paper used in this book is recyclable. It is made from low chlorine pulps
produced in a low energy, low emission manner from renewable forests.

Printed and bound by Bell & Bain Ltd, Glasgow
Typeset in 10 point Sabon by Main Point Books, Edinburgh

Contents

Acknowledgements

THIS BOOK WOULD not exist without the faith and vision of Gavin MacDougall at Luath Press, nor without the support of my long-suffering wife Deb (I mean seriously, who takes a beautiful woman on a second date to see Shrewsbury play Brighton in the Fourth Division!).

Without the painstaking dedication, passion and talent of my editor Juliette King this book would be nothing. Thank you for everything and for putting up with my errant grammar!

My sister Nicky, her husband Nick, their two sons Sam and George, and their dog Reggie have been vital lifelines on a collective journey through traumatic times. They have also been great companions on football adventures far and wide.

Thank you also to Mum for standing in the freezing cold every Sunday morning, having driven me all over the county to play football. Thanks are also in order for patiently waiting for me to finish staring dreamily at empty stadiums, or in club shops wherever we went on holiday.

I am indebted to Kalsang Dhondup, Lobsang Wangyal, Tenzin Dhondup and Jigme Dorjee of the Tibetan National Football Team for their friendship, inspiration and insight, and I am equally thankful to Marni Mortensen, Hannis Egholm and his friend Jacob for their hospitality and expertise on all things football in the Faroe Islands.

To Karma Dorji, Karun Gurung, Chokey Nima and all the other wonderful people from Druk United in Bhutan, I thank you for taking me on an adventure of a lifetime.

Thanks also must go to Dan Seaborne for his friendship, inspiration and honesty. While there are pros like him in the game then we truly have a very special game indeed.

To Keil Clitheroe, Mark Turner, Nick Westwell and everyone else that makes up the Accrington Stanley Family, thank you for your time, friendship, humility and humour. You are what makes football so special.

Thank you to Mark Godfrey from *The Football Pink* and Bill Biss from *Stand* for your support and for publishing a number of articles that I have written. And to everyone that reads the blog *Dreams of Victoria Park*, your interest and support has been the catalyst for this book, and for that I am eternally grateful.

Football wouldn't mean quite as much if it wasn't experienced with friends, so to Emma Townley, who provided a great number of pictures, and even more ludicrous comments, to Greg Joyce, Effie Woods, Will Taylor, Emma Harvey, Russell Guiver, Jennifer Hosking, Tash Davies,

Sarah Bourne, Jamie Burton, Rich Aston and Kieran Rogers, thank you for making life watching football so much fun. Thank you too Margaret King, for your invaluable insights on life, writing and everything in between!

When I was a young boy, Grandad bought me an Airfix kit of a Triceratops for me to do while I stayed with them over the summer. I tried and tried, but got really frustrated at how fiddly it was and pushed it away, saying it was impossible. The only time I ever heard him raise his voice was as I pushed the kit away; his raised voice not necessarily aimed at me directly, but at the thought that I could think things were impossible.

'No, nothing is impossible. Nothing.'

I got up and walked out and sat in the garden in a huff. An hour or two later, when I had gotten bored, I came back inside to find a completed Triceratops waiting for me in the front room. I'm not sure if I got the meaning right away, but it affected me enough to keep that fragile model for a couple of decades, until it fell apart, knowing that it was an important symbol of an important moment.

Now, finally, as I write these words to this book I think I really get what he meant.

So to the man who inspired me and this entire book; a man with an infectious smile, who told tall tales and terrible jokes on long walks and had a positive mentality that taught me so much, to the man who is, was and always will be my hero: this is for you, Grandad.

The original blog which inspired this book can be found at:
dreamsofvictoriapark.wordpress.com

Introduction

THE TWO REASONS I started to write this book remain just as valid now as they did on its initial publication: one was my reaction to the demise of Salisbury City, one of the two football clubs closest to my heart; and two, the sadness that so many other clubs are struggling to keep afloat on dwindling crowds.

Satellite sports packages continue to lure fans away from the terraces. Signing up for a satellite season ticket to watch the world's best players from the comfort and warmth of your front room, rather than standing under windswept skies at places like Hartlepool on a bitter Tuesday night in February, is very tempting.

However, there is so much more to football than what we see on glossy television programmes, so much more to it that the cameras can never capture. This book is a celebration of what it actually means and feels to be part of a crowd, no matter how small, no matter where. It is a celebration of the sights and sounds that watching football at all levels can offer – and that the sofa season ticket holders, and more importantly, their children, are missing out on. And that makes me sad, because my experiences of going to see Southampton (the other love affair) and Salisbury when I was young are some of the most vivid and exciting of my childhood. I was never happier than when sat next to my grandfather watching Salisbury play at the beautifully dilapidated (even back then), long since gone, Victoria Park.

Those experiences are still so real to me now, 30 years on, that I can close my eyes and reach out and touch them: the sound of horns from cars parked precariously behind one goal at Victoria Park, honking every time Salisbury scored; the rallying cry of 'Tally Ho' from an old-timer sat further along the stand we used to sit in; the rich aroma of roll-ups and cigars drifting on the air; the swearing, the humour, the exhilarating play (I've probably over-egged that in my mind); the awful shanked shots that would trouble the corner flag and make my grandfather chuckle (probably far more frequent than my rose tinted non-league glasses recall); the amazing chats with a lovely man who used to work with Grandad called Cyril Smith, who was Salisbury through and through and used to take our admission money on the gate and sell us a programme (one each, carefully stashed under our legs when we sat down, to keep them flat for later reading).

Cyril would always ask how I was getting on playing in my boys team, but he was very self-deprecating and never mentioned that he'd played for Southampton and Arsenal during the war, and later, for Salisbury. Grandad told me. And then Cyril photocopied some programmes from his wartime footballing exploits when he learned from Grandad that I loved collecting them. I've spent years trying to find originals, with some success, and I still have Cyril's photocopies stashed away, like the treasure they are, in programme collection.

Cyril's Southampton career was cut short when his house was bombed during the Blitz. Among the programmes he copied for me was an away match with Brighton that only lasted five minutes – an air-raid siren not long after kick off had players and fans running for cover as German bombers droned over head. The match never got restarted. The coach taking them back home had to inch its way along, unable to use its headlights in the blackout, finally arriving in the early hours of the morning.

Hearing about those experiences really helped me get football, all levels of it, under my skin. The drive to reconnect with those halcyon times took on an extra urgency after it became apparent that Salisbury – the Salisbury that my grandfather and I knew – had disappeared for good.

Ever since my grandfather's passing in 2011, a trip to a Salisbury match, or even knowing that such a trip was possible, would bring moments when the ghosts of a happy past met the present, allowing us to share a terrace once more, the ghosts of Victoria Park, its people, sights and sounds mingling with younger supporters who hadn't even been born when the club left that beautiful old ground for pastures new.

Our last ever game together (though we didn't openly acknowledge it at the time, even though his extremely frail state made getting to the ground, and a seat, very difficult for him), was against York on the final day of the 2007/08 season.

As we sat in the warmth of a late spring afternoon, we talked about the next season and games we wanted to see, even though I think we both knew that it was unlikely we would ever return there together.

But even though that was our last visit to Victoria Park, we still had match reports in the paper to talk about. We had the club. We had something. Even in the dark days of his dementia, we would share lucid moments, looking at the league table, at old programmes.

Maybe it made him feel like he was back to normal for a time.

I know I found value in it, and when he passed away I took comfort looking through those old programmes; the sights and sounds, smells coming back to life of those happy days.

The same thing would happen when I went to a game; that feeling of reconnecting with him once more, with Cyril, the old ground, the ghosts of the past mingling with the present.

And it was that connection, or the loss of having that connection that hit me hardest when Salisbury disappeared and the ground fell into silence.

Not only had I been robbed of a club that meant so much to me and my grandfather, but I'd also lost a way of connecting to those happier times, to him. There was no natural home for these memories anymore.

It didn't hit me just how important that link through time, that connection that our football club had been, was until it was gone. It was as if a door had been slammed shut on those memories, memories that had helped me cope with Grandad's passing, and with other trauma in my personal life, it felt like a kind of bereavement all over again. The only way to regain that precious connection would be to open some new doors and see what could be seen.

On my travels around the country I found myself in some very strange and exhilarating places, visiting old and run-down grounds full of character where I experienced the eccentricities of the people and communities that make up the footballing diaspora. I encountered the amazing characters that keep the true identity of football alive, far from the fame and the millions of the Premier League; the volunteers that have devoted their lives to the cause, the long-time fans providing wit and humour from their usual spot on the terrace; the players, some of whom have amazing stories to tell; . these institutions are struggling to survive.

This book is an attempt to reveal the real love story these people have with real football; a football that exists beyond the television screen.

It is a book celebrating all that is great with the game of football as seen through the eyes of clubs and fans rarely bothered by satellite television cameras and the riches of the elite game. Theirs is a vibrant world of humour, warmth and friendship that has a value beyond price.

These are the clubs struggling to stay afloat in a world where new generations of football fans aren't getting to experience anything other than television punditry, who may never get to witness a non-league manager climb into a stand and offer a supporter who had been haranguing him his money back, on the promise that he 'f*ck off'.

This is why I felt compelled to write a diary of a season travelling around the backwaters of football – to find a way of reconnecting with the ghosts of Victoria Park and my grandfather, and also to inspire others to turn off their remotes every now and then, and give a random game a go. You never know what you may see and find.

This may be a book describing my adventures during the 2014/15 season, but in the characters it describes, the love and devotion it discovers, the rich wealth of warmth, passion, history, and community that it uncovers, it could be any season, past or present. And let's hope, through the singular dedication of a small band of fans, volunteers, and underpaid and overworked staff, these wonderful institutions remain vibrant for many more seasons to come.

It is a great place to find friendship, humour, captivating sport and the true soul of football; and with our support, long may it continue.

Mat Guy, September 2016

1

13 July 2014. Bangor City v UMF Stjarnan
Europa League First Qualifying Round Second Leg

NIGHT GAMES ARE always special. I'll never forget my first night match: Southampton v Hull in a Milk Cup match in September 1984. The clack and clatter of the turnstiles, programme sellers barking "ogrammes, come and get you 'ogrammes' into the darkening skies, the glow of the floodlights visible from far away like a call to prayer. I remember heading up the old wooden steps of The Dell, pausing at the top in awe at the pristine playing surface below, shimmering a perfect emerald green beneath the lights, at the stands, slowly filling, rising up on each side, at a marching band playing in one corner while the players warmed up. The atmosphere, to an 11-year-old boy, was intoxicating and thrilling beyond words.

Night games are special. I go to as many as I can, especially towards the start of any season, like that first match against Hull. This is why I found myself driving to Bangor to watch a Europa League first qualifying round second leg match between Bangor City and Stjarnan of Iceland. I was wondering if the mid-July fixture, combined with the early kick-off time of 6.45pm, would have any effect on the night game feeling, not, as possibly more rational people might, questioning why I was driving from Southampton to Bangor and back on a Thursday night to see a second leg match of a game already out of Bangor's grasp?

I was thinking about this to distract myself from the fear that was creeping up on me in two waves. The first was that I'd eaten too many Skittles and Starburst for any one human being, the result being that I felt like a saucer-eyed Hunter S Thomson caricature hurtling across the country, completely out of control. The second fear was that I was going to lose my mind if I had to hear any more of the twisted 'logic' of Emma, my regular companion on these long trips (who had provided all the sweets that were causing my mania and was therefore, in my mind, Dr Gonzo to my Hunter ST). It was the topic of time travel that seemed to keep returning to blight hours of tedious motorway driving.

'But I don't get it? If you get on a plane in Australia and fly to England, which takes a day, but arrive on the same day that you left – surely that's time travel. You've gained a day in your life, right?'

'We've gone over this so many times, you haven't gained a day. You've just travelled through many time zones over the course of day, resulting in you arriving in another country technically on the same date as you left. That's not time travel.'

'But, you've gained a day. That day you left, you can do what you want with it, again, since you used the first day to fly, surely?'

'No,' I shook my head. 'That's not how it works. Time is linear; hours, minutes and so on are a construct of man to document the passing of seasons. You have to be on a plane for a whole day for you to fly from Australia to England. An actual day. Just because it's the same calendar date, due to the many time zones that cover the world so lots of people don't have to live their waking life in the dark, doesn't mean that it's time travel. It's just travelling while time is happening.'

'But… you get an extra day…'

I lost my cool. 'Jesus f*****g Christ Emma! You don't get an extra day and it's not time travel! It's just how mankind measures the passing of lunar cycles; you don't go back in time by flying from Australia to f*****g England!'

She shook her head. 'No.'

'What do you mean "No"? That's not a response, you can't just say "No".'

'No.'

There was silence for a little while. I ate some more Skittles.

'What if you kept flying west, like, refuelling the plane as you went? You'd definitely be going back in time doing that, wouldn't you?'

I could feel my eyes beginning to bulge.

'We're stopping at these services up ahead. I need some fresh air.'

I'd been to two early qualifying rounds of European competitions before, but this one felt like a proper fixture between teams that would have no chance of bothering the group stages, let alone the final in ten months' time.

I'd been to Anfield to watch Liverpool play FBK Kaunas in the second qualifying round of the Champions League the season after they'd won the thing. It was an amazing experience, with the Kop singing 'You'll Never Walk Alone' and the memorials to the Hillsborough and Heysel tragedies. It was spine-tingling stuff.

The second match was between Fulham, then a long-established Premier League team, and NSÍ Runavik of the Faroe Islands in 2011, when Fulham had qualified through the fair play league. There was intense stuff at Craven Cottage on a warm summer's evening on the Thames too, though not from the beautifully antiquated ground but from the Michael

Jackson statue that was so bad it had my friend in absolute awe. I had to gently lead him away to watch the match. I think he would have been quite happy to spend his entire time at the lovely old ground studying that gaudy, plastic horror show in the corner. This, thankfully for the Fulham faithful, has now departed.

Both grounds and clubs were big time, stuck in the early qualifying rounds by chance: Liverpool because UEFA let them defend their title even though they hadn't qualified through the league, controversially at the expense of their city rivals Everton, and Fulham because they had started the least amount of fights.

But Bangor City, of the Welsh Premier League, and Stjarnan of Iceland... this was the sort of match that typifies the early qualifying rounds, the sort of match I'd been dreaming of for years.

Every July, I'd find myself looking at the opening round draws, wondering how long it would take to drive to Luxembourg and back. Every July, I'd disappoint myself with the realisation that 16 hours and two channel tunnel trips to watch FC Dudelange might constitute insanity. (Might. I'm still thinking about it.) But North Wales and a paltry ten hours in the car to watch a Welsh semi-pro team take on a club from the suburbs of Reykjavik, well, that wasn't so bad.

In fact, it was well worth it when we were confronted by the scenery of the north Wales coastline: wind farms (I like them) faint on the horizon out to sea; the mountains of the Snowdonia National Park rising up inland to our left; signposts to Llanberis proof that Snowdon and its stunning views were within reach. It had been bright and sunny all the way up, but the mountains reared up as we approached Bangor and clouds began to snag among them. The silence as we took it all in was interrupted just the once.

'If they were low enough, could you punch a cloud?'

Bangor is a picturesque town of 16,000 inhabitants, topped up by another 8,000 students who attend the university. It sits on the banks of the Menai straits overlooking Anglesey and we headed straight to the pier (I love piers) to stretch our legs and take in the view. Even people who don't get excited by piers, something I don't understand but appreciate can happen, would find Bangor pier enchanting; the perfect antidote to a long motorway drive. It was quiet, save for the cries of a gull skittering away between the stanchions below from a couple of men in waders harvesting mussels from little eddies of water that snaked through the vast mud flats of low tide.

'Does your friend want to come in and take some pictures?' The lovely official on the gate asked when he noticed Emma's camera. 'The ground is nice and quiet just now.' It was about three hours before kick-off and we'd just collected our tickets.

'Really? Is that ok?' I asked.

'Of course it is,' he said, opening the turnstile, 'have a good look round now.'

The Book People Stadium was opened in 2012 and is a beautiful place to take in a football match. Through the fence and trees on the far side of the ground you can see down to the Menai Straits, and if it hadn't been built in a little dell surrounded by trees you would be able to see the mountains beyond Bangor as well.

The flags of Wales, Iceland and UEFA fluttered on either side of the main stand which looked like it could hold maybe 700 people. A few people were tending to things around the ground; the pitch was pristine on what was, for Bangor, the first day of the home season. As Emma took her pictures I watched the people working. You could see the sense of pride, as you could in the lovely official on the gate, as they worked; pride in their club, their stadium, the community it stood for and the fact that they were back in Europe. I felt excited to be there to witness it.

It's amazing how quickly all the fatigue of a long drive just falls away once you get to a ground, especially one so warm and welcoming as Bangor's.

Pictures done, we headed for a bite to eat at The Antelope pub right on the corner of the Menai Bridge. Like everything else here the bridge is beautiful in its design, and links the mainland to Anglesey. At The Antelope we saw our first Stjarnan fans wearing specially made tour shirts to mark their first ever excursion into European football. There were three of them and we later discovered that they made up one tenth of the away fans who had made the long and expensive trip.

I'm guessing that there was some UEFA stipulation that Bangor could only sell tickets for the seated areas of their ground, which meant that as the 6.45pm kick-off approached it didn't look very busy. However, the tannoy announced that the attendance was 805, 150 or so less than the total number of seats available. Not too shabby really for a match pretty much out of Bangor's grasp already.

As the players warmed up one of the locals, an old-timer who looked and sounded not unlike Ricky Tomlinson of *Royal Family* fame, motioned to the Stjarnan keeper.

'Hey keeper, do you speak English?'

Ingvar Jónsson stopped his warm up and nodded, approaching the barrier.

'Good. Could you let in four goals please?'

Jónsson stopped, shook his head in slight disbelief and went back to warming up. The old-timer chuckled to himself, then carried on round the ground to one of the two small stands on the far side of the pitch.

'Do you speak English?' had been a good shout, as it quickly became apparent that my flippant comment in the car about 'why spend so much money on signs in Welsh as well as English if no-one speaks it?' had been well off the mark. There were lots of people talking in Welsh, at the pub and in and around the ground, and arguably they outnumbered those speaking English. It had a soft, lilting sound to it and reminded me a lot of the Faroese language I heard when I went out there (another chapter entirely), and indeed the Icelandic we could hear being spoken from one small corner of the main stand.

It also helped to answer another question that I had been thinking about in the car, nonsensical Emma-isms notwithstanding, namely: 'why do some teams prefer to play in the Welsh Premier League, rather than in the larger English pyramid system, like Colwyn Bay just up the road, with more opportunities potentially to move up into bigger professional leagues against bigger name sides?'

The answer was all around me as I watched the stands begin to fill: because the people of Bangor are Welsh, a lot of them speak Welsh, their community and identity is clear, their league is theirs and is perfectly fine to satisfy their desire for good, competitive football. If you do well you have a chance of playing in Europe, of winning the league and being the best team in Wales. They are the epitome of why I wanted to start this book in the first place: because life doesn't revolve around the English Premier League, and this match, this stadium, this atmosphere of simple pride in their culture and identity proved that.

We found a couple of seats in front of the old-timer who had been bothering the Stjarnan goalie and sat in raptures as he and three of his friends, all, like him, in their 70s, talked and ranted about a controversy raging at their local bowls club.

'They should have kept it in house, rather than forward it to the league,' said one.

'Yeah, now the only way they'll lift his life ban is if he apologises,' added another, 'and we know there's no chance of that happening.'

'He's going to be hard to replace,' the third man sighed.

'We shouldn't have to; it's all a load of rubbish from the league. We should write back and tell them to f**k off,' the goalie-botherer replied.

'F*****g idiots,' the second man muttered.

I wanted to ask them what their friend had done to warrant a life-time ban from crown bowls, but at that moment the teams came out and that answer will forever remain a mystery. I like to imagine some fist fight over a septuagenarian lady bowler, false teeth flying as a jack smashes into the face of the bowler getting a little too fresh with another's squeeze.

From the kick-off you could tell that Stjarnan were just sitting back on their 4-0 first leg lead, absorbing some incisive attacks from Bangor's wide men in Jamie McDaid and man of the match Sion Edwards, supported by some decent play from Damien Allen in midfield. Every now and then Stjarnan upped the pace and looked very dangerous, cutting through Bangor at will, however the match remained goalless through a cagey first half that was lit up by one of the weirdest chants I had ever heard. It rose up out of nowhere from the main stand, in English, and to the tune of The Pet Shop Boys' 'Go West':'Shoes off if you love Bangor, Shoes off if you love Bangor, Shoes off if you love Bangor, Shoes off if you *love* Bangor,' and lots of the fans duly obliged; took off their shoes, and started waving them in the air.

I have no idea how or why this came about, and I didn't ask. Some things are better left a mystery. They were selling t-shirts in the club shop with a picture of a shoe beneath the slogan 'Northern Sole'. I'll leave it at that.

In the second half, Stjarnan slowly began to ramp up the pressure, which finally told midway through with a worldie of a goal from their defender Martin Rauschenberg screaming an unstoppable shot from well outside the box into the top right hand corner. Bangor heads dropped a little, with the exception of Sion Edwards who was immense, running himself into the ground and attacking almost singlehandedly until the final minute.

Gaps began to appear, and Arnar Már Björgvinsson helped himself to two goals as Bangor were cut apart. Right at the end, Atli Jóhannsson scored a tap-in through more incisive passing.

4-0, 8-0 on aggregate seemed a little harsh on a decent Bangor team, but this and the first leg were their first games of the season. Stjarnan were a little under halfway through their Icelandic Premier League season, and were unbeaten in second place. This may well have contributed to the score; one team being ring rusty, the other finely tuned, and maybe if these matches had been played in October, after Bangor had had a few months under their belts, things would have been a little closer. We'll never know. I got the feeling that Stjarnan just had a little bit more about them, and probably would have no matter when they played. We would see how they got on against Motherwell in the next round.

Without wanting to sound like a clichéd fool, the score-line didn't really matter too much, as on the day football was the winner. (Jesus!)

However, it is true, for a number of reasons: the standing ovation the main stand gave the Stjarnan fans, who had to leave early to catch the last bus back to Wrexham where they were staying, singing and waving their shoes in the air as they headed out the ground. The exhausted Sion Edwards, leaning against the barrier that ran around the pitch apologising to the Bangor fans as they filed out. (Many of them told him: 'You've got nothing to apologise for. You were outstanding.') The warmth and honesty of Bangor City FC; from their officials, to their fans, to the players, who clearly knew a lot of those that had been in the stands cheering them on.

Football has won the day again when you leave the ground and know that, forever more, you'll be keeping your eyes out for the Welsh Premier League scores during final score; because, yet again, another club has gotten itself under your skin, (dug in even deeper from reading in the programme – three pounds, solid effort – that beloved ex-Saints manager Nigel Adkins had managed Bangor the last time they played Icelandic opposition). Through knowing its simple and humble place in the firmament; that it is there for the community it represents, that it is there because of the community it represents, it becomes a bit of everyone, and everything, as vital as the Menai Bridge, as unifying and synonymous with the town as the pier.

I just hope that in the coming weeks we can say the same thing about the local bowling community, that sanity prevails, and no-one needs to receive a letter telling them to 'f**k off'. My arse.

PS. Despite it being a 'night game' the floodlights weren't needed. In fact it was still light long after we set off for home.

2

21 July 2014. Swindon Town v Southampton
Pre-season Friendly

PRE-SEASON FIXTURES can often be tedious affairs for those of us in the stands. They are a great work out for the players and useful for the manager in developing things practiced on the training ground, but for the fan the edge is missing with nothing riding on the outcome, and the players are not really at the blood and thunder levels expected of them come mid-August.

I do however enjoy the feeling of just being able to sit back in the warmth (hopefully) of a summer's evening and watch your team play, knowing that the result doesn't matter. It is a feeling that brings back happy memories of Victoria Park as a young boy and hot, humid, carefree pre-season summer nights sat in the stands with Grandad, batting at mosquitoes, the rich smell of freshly cut grass thick on the warm breeze as we watched Salisbury take on the reserve sides of Bristol City, Southampton and tonight's hosts, Swindon Town.

Maybe, if you're lucky, you can catch that feeling at the end of the season too, at midweek games crammed in to get all the fixtures done on time. I remember as a boy Blackfield & Langley's Hampshire League matches being played out beneath failing light with midges starting to circle and bite beneath the branches of big old oak trees that lined one side of Blackfield's recreation park pitch on balmy May evenings, full of the promise of a hot summer to come.

However this feeling, predominantly, is the preserve of pre-season and is a feeling that I like to call 'Susan Sarandon'. Susan Sarandon, the feeling, is named after Susan Sarandon, the actress, for her role in *Bull Durham*, a film about a minor league baseball team in the middle of anywhere America. Her character sits in the stands every match and tries to help one player every season with her own special kind of coaching. It's a great film and you should check it out. It captures Susan Sarandon, the feeling, or the notion I have of what it must be like to watch small town baseball at the height of an American summer, with hot, balmy evenings, the chatter of families and friends in the bleachers lazily watching the play below, the crack of ball on bat, ripples of applause, organ music drifting up into the floodlit night sky between innings. It seems idyllic, at least that is how it is portrayed in the movie, and that is how I gauge if a pre-season football match is any good: if I am feeling all Susan Sarandon.

Even with the possibility of feeling Susan, I rarely go to friendlies. It is good to see players playing with a total freedom, trying little things knowing it's not the end of the world if they don't work. That's all good, but more than one a season and their lack of edge, and sometimes their lack of Ms Sarandon if it is belting it down with rain, and I start to feel a bit unfulfilled.

However this friendly was worth the relatively short trip for three reasons: to see a dear old friend who we didn't get to see enough of, to watch a match in a lower league stadium and to see the remnants of a very successful Saints team, now decimated by manager and player departures, try and shape itself up for a new campaign.

Ronald Koeman, our new manager, in reaction to what seemed like every single player wanting to leave the club, had come in with the revolutionary (or just pragmatic, given the amount of empty seats on the team bus) tactic of fielding a six-a-side team in the Premier League the coming season. The hope was presumably that a rush goalie system used in school playgrounds the length of the country would bamboozle some of the world's great tacticians and lead to an unorthodox first Premier League title. With respect to our hosts, Third Division Swindon Town, Koeman decided to pad out the team to a full 11 with academy players, not wanting to show his hand too early on. Keep them guessing Ronald, I like it.

For Saints fans, the new season was almost something to dread. We had lost one of the best young managers in the game, who moved to Tottenham, we had lost our captain and most creative player to Liverpool, our talismanic striker, also to Liverpool, and we were about to lose our best centre back, to cocking Liverpool! Our latest in a long line of 18-year-old wonderkids had gone to Manchester United, and Arsenal, Tottenham and many others were circling around another five of our players.

This was happening because last season we played some of the most attractive and attacking football the Premier League had ever seen outside the top four teams. And those big teams wanted a little of the magic dust we had spent years creating and honing. Such is life spent supporting what is seen as a 'small' club.

I'm not bitter, I'm really not; we don't have the financial clout to reach the Champions League, so sometimes the most talented players need to move on, to challenge themselves. (Though I may seem bitter after the first game of the season, away to Liverpool, if three certain players all score!)

It's going to be a tough season; an impossible season if we compare it to the high water-mark of the last. We just have to hope.

But back to my list of three reasons why we were rocking up at the County Ground, Swindon on a Monday night in July. Number one: Effie.

I met Effie when she came to work where I do. She is a delightfully wonderful and lovely, caring human being. We all need an Effie in our lives and hopefully you all have one. However, no matter how lovely she was, when she arrived at work to help fund her studies at university she was not a football fan.

I discovered this due to another work colleague pulling out of an away trip to Walsall in December 2009, back when Saints, fresh from being saved from oblivion by sadly now passed Markus Liebherr, were still in the relegation zone at the foot of the Third Division, battling to overcome a ten point penalty for going into administration the season before.

We had the four tickets, Greg (another long time away travels companion) and I. A third ticket was filled by an Emma (not the Emma already mentioned). So what to do with the fourth ticket? Walsall away, December, bottom of the Third Division; it was such an attractive proposition, that ticket should have flown out of our hands, but it hadn't and we had run out of football friends to ask. But there was Effie, sat at work, and as a joke, knowing we had never even really had a conversation about football before, I asked her if she would like to come.

'Yeah, alright,' she replied, to my considerable surprise.

'But it's tomorrow,' I warned her.

'That's fine. Can you pick me up?'

From one throwaway comment doth a freakin' monster grow! Effie quickly fell in love with the atmosphere, the passion, the camaraderie and everything else that is associated with following a lower league football team. She went to every game she possibly could, come rain or shine, sleet or snow. She fell hook, line and sinker, heading every ball, celebrating every goal like she had scored it herself, hurling abuse that would have made a docker blush at every injustice. It was wonderful to watch.

Seeing her experience her first night match, home wins and losses, away wins and losses, terrible refereeing, and amazing goals was like having an out of body experience, watching myself as a young boy going through it all for the first time. No-one made her like it. It just captivated her all on its own.

They had a nickname for me when Greg, Effie and I set off from work across the car park to another Saints game – Gandalf, the cheeky shits. Because I was much older and much taller than the other two, it looked like I was leading a couple of Hobbits off on another adventure, which, I suppose, I kind of was. I often felt like such a comforting figure as Gandalf when Saints lost, looking down at the two forlorn faces either side of me, trying to cheer them up.

However, it could have all been so different if Effie hadn't had something clarified to her in the away end at the Bescot Stadium, Walsall, on that cold December afternoon. After the kick-off Greg and I quickly became engrossed, and didn't really see the concern, almost horror, spreading across Effie and Emma's faces. Saints were shooting towards us in the first half and every goal kick by Trinidad International Clayton Ince was greeted with the traditional chant of 'YOU FAT BASTARD AAAAHHHHHHHH!'

Although annoying, it was actually quite funny, because either the Walsall goalie had a very unflattering shirt on, or he was in fact getting on for a right old pie of a man. I don't think it was the shirt. It wasn't until midway through the first half that I caught the girls' concerned expressions after another goal kick.

'I can't believe it,' one of them was saying.

'Are they really allowed to get away with that?'

Emma shrugged.

'Get away with what?' I asked.

'Calling him that,' said Effie.

'But,' I said 'but... he is?'

'Yeah, I know, but Jesus. It's the 21st century. It's disgraceful.'

'Wait a minute. What do you *think* they're singing?'

'Well, I really don't want to say it, but... aren't they singing "you black bastard"?' Effie blushed.

'*Fat,* Effie. They're singing "you *fat* bastard".'

Emma and Effie digested this information for a moment, then fell away into fits of hysterical laughter which led to them pretty much missing the rest of the half.

'Ohmygodithoughttheyweresingingblackohmygodwellthatsfairenough heisprettyfat.'

Had Effie not asked the question there is a very good chance neither she nor Emma would have ever set foot in a football ground again. They would have probably avoided me and Greg as well, seeing our chuckles as tacit acknowledgement of BNP membership.

The second reason for an evening out in Swindon was the enjoyment to be gained from watching football in a lower league ground, albeit a pretty large one. I'd been to a number before, mainly with my old mate Russ who was a Brighton supporter back when Brighton were homeless and hovering above the relegation zone in division four in the late '90s. I'd loved the trips to Darlington (twice), Exeter, Southend and Shrewsbury, because they felt like 'proper' football matches at 'proper' grounds. Southampton had been a top flight team pretty much all my life. I'd never experienced relegation out of the big division until 2005 and as such you get a little bit pampered watching the best of the best all the time in big stadiums. However lower league football offered me a step back in time to the feelings of watching Salisbury in the southern league in the '80s, watching matches in great little grounds bursting with character; I mourn the loss of Darlington's old Feethams ground even now. It's sad that no-one else can enjoy its wonderfully ramshackle charm.

I didn't see much to be positive about when we slipped into administration in 2009, quickly followed by relegation into division three. I felt particularly glum on one miserable trip to Sheffield Wednesday Greg and I took in April 2009, the week after we'd been put into administration. We lost 3-0, were truly awful and had to stand, on the 20th anniversary of the Hillsborough tragedy in the Lepping's Lane end (where those terrible events occurred), in front of 96 empty seats, each one with a bouquet of flowers for every lost soul that day.

No, there was not much to feel positive about.

What followed, however, turned into the best five years of supporting the Saints I had ever had: a Wembley win in the Johnstone's Paint Trophy, successive promotions, followed by stabilisation, then significant progress back into the top flight. What beat all of that, hands down, were the two seasons in the Third Division watching a completely different set of teams week in, week out. Smaller clubs from smaller towns, with fans even more dedicated than those from Premier League teams, as these sides had little chance of glory ever. The football was great; these teams really tried to play and it felt more like football back when I was growing up, before the financial explosion of the Premier League.

Both Greg and I were really getting into watching Saints play Exeter, Hartlepool, Orient to name but a few. It was good honest stuff, between honest teams, supported by honest, passionate fans. We wanted more, so we started to go to away games, to places like Wycombe, Yeovil, Walsall (as you know) and Bristol Rovers. I screamed like a little girl when Morgan Schneiderlin, my hero, scored his first goal for the club. While everyone else was cheering and shouting as his dipping, long range shot smashed into the net, I found myself screaming 'MORGAAAAAAN' at the top of my lungs, much to Greg's amusement. Even now I get a barrage of texts spelt much like that every time he scores!

Third Division football was a blessing and a joy, and enabled me to delve into another side, a more honest and believable side to modern football in England, taking in grounds full of character and soul, rarely troubled by success. In our second and last season in the Third Division I went back to Walsall with Effie, as well as Brentford (the only ground with a pub on each corner), Carlisle, and on a cold Tuesday evening in February, to Hartlepool. It seemed like glorious serendipity as I got off the coach outside Hartlepool's ground, after a seven hour journey, to see 'Welcome to Victoria Park' written across a sign at its entrance. It was love at first sight; that little ground, which, although obscured by the night, overlooked the town centre, the harbour and the North Sea beyond.

I bought two programmes that night; one for me and one for Grandad, and I wrote to him on the long coach journey back home how I'd been to Victoria Park once more. I had gotten into the habit of buying an extra programme for Grandad the year before. He was in the advanced stages of dementia by then and we were looking to find ways to keep him stimulated. I had thought of programmes.

We had always gotten a programme each wherever we went to see football together, and as a boy I would, from time to time, get the odd programme through the post from him whenever he had gotten one from one of his workmates, who knew I loved them and would bring them in for me if they went to a match. The excitement I felt when a new little parcel with a Salisbury postmark fell through the letterbox was intense. Where was this one from?

To this day my favourite programme, of a collection exceeding 1,200, is an old and battered Hampshire League one from Downton in 1984 that had clearly been folded up and forgotten about by Bobby Andrews, Downton forward and work colleague of Grandad, after a match that he had played in. After some time being battered about in his work coat he noticed it again and gave it to Grandad, who handed it on to me almost apologetically, stained and beat up as it was.

I loved it. It smelled of oil, but I loved it; the red cover, the logo of a Robin on the front (their nickname is the Robins), the erratically typed notes inside, the name of Bobby Andrews on the team sheet in the centre pages. I was in awe, an actual player had given this to Grandad, who gave it to me. An actual player! In the 30 years since, books, programmes, all sorts of stuff have been become misplaced or lost. But not that programme. No way. It's too precious.

Nan said that after I'd started sending Grandad programmes he would sit quietly and study them from cover to cover, like he used to. How much he was actually taking in wasn't really the point. He would sit there and pour over them, giving Nan a bit of time to herself.

I don't know how much he comprehended of that Hartlepool programme and what it meant to me; all those wonderful times that we'd shared at our own Victoria Park and other little non-league grounds that I still cherish so much. I like to think that he knew the significance.

We had driven to Cheltenham, where Effie lived and had returned to once her studies were over, much to my annoyance. There, we met up for some lunch and spent a few hours relaxing on the hills above the pretty town while we waited for her boyfriend Wills, a lovely, funny bloke, to finish work, so we could head off to the match together.

The journey was relatively uneventful, until we came to Swindon. Roundabouts. What the hell?! There were so many, everywhere. It's like the place where roundabouts from all over the world come to die. Next to the County Ground there was one large roundabout and on it there were five smaller ones! It was total carnage and insanity and we had to cross it three times as we tried to find somewhere near the ground to park.

Ah Susan, sweet, sweet Susan Sarandon! *It's going to be a good evening*, I thought, as we took our uncomfortable seats in the away end. The country had been basking in a mini heat-wave for a couple of weeks and you could feel it in the air, even long past seven in the evening; the crowd relaxing in shorts, shielding their eyes from the sun to look out at the players warming up. It was glorious; if you listened closely you could hear the faint crack of bat on ball echoing about the stands, organ music playing in between innings. It was so warm, even in the shaded away stand, that when the sprinklers came on to water the pitch just before the kick-off the faint spray drifting on the air felt refreshing and welcome.

The County Ground consists of two decent size stands running the length of each touchline, a shed end behind one goal and some uncovered seating behind the other. Technically it was a lower league ground, albeit a lower league ground that had hosted Premier League football for a short time in the '90s. It certainly wasn't a lower league ground in the way that Hartlepool or Exeter's are, which is in no way a slight on either. In fact I'd say it's a compliment.

As we walked around the 'CG', as the programme calls it, I noticed a picture of the stadium with six or seven different club badges they had used over the years across the top. I recognised one as being on the cover of a Swindon programme from the '80s that Grandad had sent me and was therefore my favourite of them all. Surely changing your badge that many times must be a record?

The match, as I had expected, was pretty nondescript; the first half spent trying to work out the names of the many youth team players Saints were fielding. Harrison Reed I recognised as he'd played a bit last season, but there were a few that had me and most of the away end scrabbling along the team sheet in the programme for clues. Whoever they were, they could play pretty well, which was good to see.

The relaxed nature of the whole event had me drifting off from time to time, looking out across the uncovered seating to our left, watching small clouds wander by, the far floodlight stretching up into blue sky that gradually began to tinge with red and as the sun began to set the shadows of the players on the pitch lengthened toward the far touchline. One by one, as dusk fell, the floodlights flickered into life, replacing the natural shadows of the players with the familiar floodlit shadow that seemed to stretch out in three different directions from each player.

I then had a brief physics moment, trying to fathom how four floodlights, one in each corner of the ground, cast only three shadows. After deep thought, I remembered that I was useless at science and had no idea, which settled the issue and the whole thing was filed in the ever bulging 'it's good not to know everything' section of my brain.

The second half followed the same pattern as the first, with Saints dominating play and Swindon creating the odd moment of pressure around our box. But it was Saints' Jos Hooiveld who scored the only, pretty scrappy, goal of the game, before one of the greatest substitutions I have ever seen.

With about 25 minutes remaining Ronald Koeman made nine changes at the same time, causing great distress to the tannoy announcer who had already struggled through the Saints players names once at the start of the match. The name of our sub goalie, Paulo Gazzaniga had been the highlight, as he stuttered:

'Um... Paul... io... Gazzy... ahgingingia...'

Unimpressed by Koeman's antics he just said: 'Substitution for the Saints,' then, realising there were nine, he muttered something, paused and then just turned the microphone off.

At the final whistle everyone seemed happy enough; the players had got what they needed out of it and the 3,000 or so supporters had signalled the end of a long off season by getting back into the stands.

'I can't wait for the new season to start after that,' Wills said, seeming to articulate what everyone was thinking. The ball was now rolling and the clock was ticking. The fixtures were out and waiting to provide joy and misery to millions across the country and we were just itching to get amongst it.

But as we headed off into the Swindon night, I looked back at the County Ground, at the floodlights burning into the darkening skies and nodded to my summer lover.

Goodbye Susan Sarandon. Until next pre-season...

3

27 August 2006. HB Tórshavn v Skála
Faroe Islands

I KNOW, 2006 doesn't sound like it took place during the 2014–15 football season. It didn't. So I should explain why this is included. 2006, for me, was the year where I took a chance and decided to try and follow some of my dreams in the hope they could develop into a career or, at the very least, become a constructive way to spend my free time. I had decided to head out on some football adventures in the hope I could write them up and possibly get into sports journalism, as I'd enjoyed writing from a very young age and wanted to try my hand.

2006 saw me take in a World Cup match in Berlin (Ukraine v Tunisia, 1-0, voted the worst match of the whole tournament), a trip to the Faroe Islands in August and a week out in North Cyprus in November to watch the Tibetan National Football Team take part in the ELF Cup, an unofficial tournament mostly populated by nations/regions not recognised by FIFA or the United Nations. As a result of that final experience (which will feature later on) in February 2007 I became an intern at the Free Tibet Campaign offices in London, travelling up on my days off.

All these new doors were opening to me, new possibilities and options unfolding here, there and everywhere. However life very often gets in the way of all our best laid plans, and my father taking his life in March 2007 soon had all those new doors slamming shut once more. The need to look out for my loved ones and then dealing with the mental and emotional fall-out of it all, took precedence, and kept them closed for quite some time.

But looking through the handwritten 'notes' I had made at the time (they're like the scratchings an epileptic spider having a seizure might make, brought on by falling into a pot of ink, then trying to make its way to spider hospital via a blank piece of paper), I realised that all the issues and topics raised then are just as relevant now, eight years later. So I thought that I should include them here in this book, if for no other reason than to make me feel like I have reclaimed what seemed for many years to be lost time and wasted opportunities.

I'm going to sneak them in during the book at roughly the same dates in the season as they originally occurred.

The 2006 adventures weren't my first or last excursions abroad to watch football. There had been Le Havre v Sochaux in the '90s (that's as specific as I can get – it was part of a trip to play for a local team against a club I had become friends with. They plied us with Pernod. All I remember is nearly whiting out on the pitch as a result of all the alcohol).

There had also been La Roche-sur-Yon v Les Sables-d'Olonne, a French Derby at the sixth tier of the national football pyramid. My sister married one of my best friends in 2002 during the World Cup (as they married, Germany beat Saudi Arabia 8-0) and my wife and I went with them and their first child Sam on holiday in 2005.

That match featured a number of notable highs and lows:

Low: There was no programme. Devastated.

High: They sold red wine.

High: Trying to translate some of the home supporters' shouts of encouragement: *'Allez les Blancs, Mange les Vertes.'*

High: Trying to start our own chants, in French, by roughly translating English ones:

This one aimed at a tubby Les Sables-d'Olonne player in the hope of ingratiating ourselves with the home faithful –

'Qui mange beaucoup flan? Qui mange beaucoup flan? Tous gross bastard [we didn't know the translation so just went with it] *Tous gross bastard. Tous mange beaucoup flan.'*

Low: The realisation that our French was awful and that 'Who ate all the pies?' chants don't cross language barriers well.

In 2010 Nick, his second son George and I also caught Servette v SC Kriens in a Swiss Second Division match.

High: They did a programme, albeit a very simple one, and it was free!

Low: The bloody heathens tore up their programmes to use as footballing confetti, throwing it in the air every time Servette scored.

High: They sold baguettes that had some kind of mustard in them that was like crack cocaine to my taste buds. I find myself twitching a little just thinking about it.

High: George, not even four at the time, wanted to sit next to the Servette Ultras and he would marshal the chants, the flag waving, everything. George is pretty hard-core. He had his first Southampton season ticket at the age of three!

Low: The Kriens goalkeeper getting sent off early on and his very young replacement shipping six goals then leaving the pitch in tears.

High: Spending our last remaining Swiss Francs before heading back into France, where we were staying, on the largest Toblerones I have ever seen!

But back to 2006 and the Faroe Islands. And why the Faroe Islands, the third smallest nation in UEFA, in the first place?

There was an article, ironically published in *The Guardian* two days after the HB v Skála match, by Kevin McCarra under the headline: 'Andorras of the world are wasting everybody's time'. It was basically suggesting something that many journalists and pundits had been saying for a while: that the smaller football nations should have to have a pre-qualifying tournament to get into the qualifying tournament for World Cups etc with the 'big boys', so that only the best worst teams would insult the 'larger' teams with their presence.

In the cold light of day it could be seen as a logical argument, if only it didn't go against everything that made football so special and made these qualifying tournaments the best part of the whole thing: that school teachers and postmen from Liechtenstein and Luxembourg could come up against the World Champions, that non-league teams could play Manchester United in the FA Cup. Football is universal, for everyone to play, and that universality means that there needs to be a fluidity between all abilities. Take that away, or dilute it, and you dilute the romance and one of the fundamental joys of football: that it's for everyone and everyone can have their day.

I think the cynical hacks are just fed up of having to go to San Marino and the like and I think that professional cynicism; doing the same thing over and over again for years and years, has ground them down and blinkered them to the simple romance of the game that probably inspired them to become sports writers in the first place.

I loved the idea of giant killers and the underdog; I guess a lifetime of supporting Southampton and Salisbury gives you that edge. This is why the thought of exploring the Faroe Islands and Faroese football was an exciting one to me, something to look forward to with expectation rather than dread, and by delving into this rarely visited place I knew I would see first-hand how football is every bit as vital there as in Spain, Brazil, or any of the world's traditional hot-spots.

I wonder whether Kevin McCarra *et al* changed their minds when watching Tahiti play in the 2013 Confederations Cup. Yes, they lost, quite heavily. But the way they attacked these champions of World football with pure abandon was a joy to watch and they were by far and away the highlight of the whole tournament. Did he appreciate that joy? Could he see through that hard bitten journalist shell and remember the feeling his inner child had when Ronnie Radford scored that screamer for Hereford against Newcastle in the '70s?

I really hope so. Because that doesn't happen every day, and for every

Ronnie moment you need 100 matches where the bigger teams turn over their non-league or smaller nation opponents with ease. But there is always the possibility, and that's what makes football so captivating, so spellbinding to so many, and if you take that away, or dissolve the opportunity for magical and unexpected things to happen on a football field, then you surely dissolve the magic of football full stop?

If Tahiti are prevented from playing in the Confederations Cup, if Gibraltar are prevented from possibly being drawn against Germany in a qualifying tournament then what are you left with? Uniformity? Not romance, that's for sure.

The Faroe Islands seemed a great flag bearer for football's 'Minnow' community in Europe, as, unlike many of the mainland small fry, it was remote and therefore a little bit more mysterious and unknown. This assumption was aided by the flight there, as the trip from Stansted, resulted in all but 20 or so of the passengers of what had been a full flight getting off when we stopped in Lerwick in the Shetland isles on the way.

Maybe just to stretch their legs?

No. The doors were closed once more and the ghost plane began to taxi away for take-off.

Mystery and the unknown became reality, sat in an eerily empty plane as we approached the Faroes, when, after some time looking out on the North Atlantic through gaps in the thick cloud, the seatbelt signs came on and we began to descend.

I have loved adventure stories, stories of mystery and intrigue, monster movies and spooky films, ever since I was a young boy. And it seemed like we had become part of one, the '78 *King Kong*, I thought, as when out of the cloud and ocean, as if from nowhere, huge dark jagged cliffs loomed out of the mist. Hundreds of feet tall, with rough seas crashing against them, this first view of the Faroes was overwhelming and for a moment I felt what I used to as a young boy watching those old monster movies; a surge of excitement coursing through me. I blinked once, twice at this bleak, unfathomable, awe-inspiring sight rearing up out of the ocean. Then it was gone, the plane skirting narrowly over the cliff tops, plunging into more cloud, the pilot looking out for the lights of the runway, somewhere out there in the mist.

The Faroe Islands are a dormant volcanic archipelago comprising 18 islands, 17 inhabited, situated between Iceland to the North and Scotland and its outlying islands to the south. Looking at a map of the North Atlantic they are quite easy to miss, just a little dot in a vast expanse of turbulent sea. In keeping with their volcanic geography and location the Faroe Islands are beautiful and rugged. Mountains dominate, their tips often lost in low lying cloud, while small communities nestle at their feet, seeking shelter from the elements.

I am a country boy. I love rugged. I love what other people may see as desolate. *I am in the right place*, I thought to myself, as the shuttle bus weaved its way along the coast. Mist-shrouded silhouettes of mountains rose up above and the vague shadow of an island out to sea loomed in and out of view amongst the fog.

The capital, Tórshavn, population 17,000, is on the island of Streymoy and is to all intents and purposes a small port town, with its harbour the main focus. It is a pretty capital, its architecture much like that of Scandinavia to the east, with brightly coloured warehouses dockside and neat, Nordic-looking wooden framed houses stretching up and away from the waterfront. The only pub that I found, Café Natúr (serving beer from the locally brewery *Föroya Bjór,* which is amazing), is one of a number of buildings on the Faroes that has a grass covered roof. It looks beautiful and adds to the impression that even in the nation's capital, one is never far from nature.

It was a Friday night and the game I was here to see wasn't until Sunday afternoon. I decided to take a walk around Tórshavn, along quiet, neat, pretty streets with pretty houses, and up into a park above the town where narrow pathways weaved and forked between thick trees, opening up occasionally on a bench, a duck pond, a natural rock formation jutting out of the ground. Gurgling and sputtering streams zig-zagged over rocks and stones around it all. I carried on up to the park's highest point, where a statue of a sailor stood looking out across the ocean, commemorating all those who have been lost at sea.

Moored beyond the harbour were three large fishing vessels that looked suspiciously like whalers to me. I didn't ask anyone, but I did look a little anxiously at the very chewy, almost blubbery 'fish' I got with my fish and chips from a small kiosk in town. *It's probably just some variation I haven't tried before*, I thought, not really convincing myself.

As I discovered, Café Natúr is the best local in the world, with friendly bar staff, good beer and a nice atmosphere that makes even a lone stranger feel comfortable. It's a great place to watch Faroese life pass by and listen to the soft, lilting Faroese language in action.

This is a sweeping generalisation, especially as it was a Friday night, but everyone seemed very laid back and happy as did I after a few pints of the local beer (black like stout, but as light as ale). Head-swimming stuff. I headed back to my guest house before I could be tempted by more, as the following day I planned to catch a bus to Klaksvík, the most northerly and remote town in the Faroes with a football team in the Formuladeildin, the top Faroese League, and I didn't want to turn up sick as a dog.

I don't know exactly why I felt the need to track down bus times and the like to get to the remotest football outpost in what was already a very remote country. It has sort of become ingrained in me to look for these spots, wherever I go. Could it be some mid-life crisis? Well I was 33 back in 2006, which doesn't seem to fit that stereotype. And my compulsion to visit the smallest, supposedly least glamorous and quirkiest footballing venues I could, can be traced as far back as my childhood.

I couldn't have been more than 11 or 12 when I begged my parents as loudly as a painfully quiet child could to take a detour into Luxembourg while driving down to a Euro-camping holiday on the French/German border, to try and track down the municipal stadium that was home to the Luxembourg national team. Somehow they agreed, and before too long mini-me found himself pressed against the gates to the home of Luxembourgian football, taking in the part of the pitch I could see, the small section of stand, with fascination.

I didn't argue when Mum or Dad politely suggested that I'd been standing there for long enough and that we should go, but I did take (badly) a few pictures with my little manual wind-on camera before I left. I still have them now. They look like an excited 11-year-old took them.

To my sister's credit (she is four years younger than me), I don't recall her complaining too much that day, so it's quite possible that this could be a genetic issue. This is backed up by a trip in 2000 that me, sis, her soon-to-be husband Nick and his mate Fingers went on, on a cold February day that threatened snow, from Southampton up to Newcastle to watch a match that we could have caught on the telly. After a seven plus hour journey, Saints were 4-0 down after 12 minutes and Alan Shearer missed a penalty in that time. It ended 5-0; I remember the few hundred Saints fans that were there jumping like we'd won the Champions League when we got our first lame shot on goal in the last ten minutes of the match, a few snowflakes trickling from the ashen skies.

Did I mention that Fingers was a Newcastle fan? It made the seven plus hour journey back hone just that little bit more unbearable...

The bus journey to Klaksvík was spectacular; every turn on the exposed coastal road provided another breathtaking view of stark, sheer mountains staring out on the North Atlantic, the shadows of islands off shore mostly hidden by cloud.

It just kept coming.

The main cropping of islands on the Faroes are linked by tunnels beneath the Atlantic. The bus wound its way from Streymoy, Eysturoy, and finally Bordoy, passing through tiny communities that looked like mini Tórshavns in their architecture. The bus passed a couple of football grounds as we crossed the islands, ÍF Fuglafjørður and GÍ Gøta, both of the top division. Both grounds, no larger than a small non-league stadium in the UK, lined an artificial pitch; the subarctic climate making it impossible for a grass pitch to survive the rigours of the weather and a full season of football.

There are two grass pitches on the Faroes: the Tórsvøllur Stadium in Tórshavn and the Svangaskarð Stadium in Toftir on the island of Eysturoy that are used for international matches and European club competitions, as neither are allowed to be played on artificial surfaces. They can just about survive the limited football played on them.

Klaksvík is the second largest and one of the most northerly towns on the Islands. With a population just shy of 5,000, this tiny community is dwarfed by some of the biggest mountains in the country that tower over it (breathtaking, even by Faroese standards), and the Atlantic Ocean, on either side. The town centre straddles a narrow strip of land that looks out on the ocean to the east and the west, and as the bus pulled up and I stepped out I finally felt satisfied that I had come to the end of the road.

As the cloud descended I listened to what sounded like hymns, or maybe folk songs, drifting from the PA system on top of an old bus parked on the far side of the small bus station. I walked over, but there didn't appear to be anyone around. There didn't appear to be anyone anywhere.

I stood there for a time, listening to the frail, beautifully haunting vocals that trail up into the heavy sky, and taking in the town that is overlooked by a large church built like an ancient Norse hall. The rest of the town, like all the others, is built in the same style as in Tórshavn. Tradition is cherished here, it would seem.

The home of KÍ Klaksvík, like everything here, was within earshot of the music, and I wandered in and watched some children having a training session on the far side; the first signs of life I had found. The 'Injector Arena' consists of one small neat stand with ten or so rows of seats and is probably, in any other setting, a decent size, but here, like everything else, it is dwarfed by the scenery looming over it. I wondered how they can concentrate on anything while surrounded by such stunning views; it must be difficult even after years of living here. At least, that's how it felt to me.

As with every small town I passed, and with Tórshavn as well, it was clear that the football club is one of, if not the only, focal point for the community. On a notice-board by the main stand were lists of times and days for training for different boys and girls teams: three senior men's teams, two women's and a veterans' side. It must be hard to find a household in the Faroes where one of the family isn't playing for their local club.

I didn't stay long in Klaksvík due to the bus schedule, but it was long enough to get a feel for the place and wonder how a team from such a tiny community could compete against the relative might and resources of teams from the capital. It is a place I will never be able to forget. For a fan of the forgotten, the hidden, this place is nirvana, and as I left, with echoes of angelic voices from the mystery bus growing fainter, I decided that one day I'd come back and take in a match here.

Skansin Fort overlooks the bus station and harbour in Tórshavn; the small island of Nolsoy tiny and vulnerable on the vast and still Atlantic. The Faroe Islands feel remote and cut off at the best of times and I wondered what it must be like here during the vast winter storms that rage from Newfoundland right the way across to Norway. I also wondered whether I had enough time to head on up to Gundadalur Stadium where, if my scribbled notes from home were correct, I should just be able to catch a match in the Third Division between B36 Tórshavn's reserves and KÍ Klaksvík's third team. *It would be rude not to*, I thought, and set off.

Gundadalur stadium consists of two artificial pitches, the second of which has no stands around it and sits in the shadow of the main complex of the National Tórsvøllur stadium, where the match I had come to see was taking place.

These two pitches are the home for the two main local rivals: B36 and HB Tórshavn, who have two men's teams each, a women's team each and countless youth teams from the age of eight years old up. Gundadalur also has to find room for Fram, a lower league team and all its subsidiaries. It's just as well the pitches are artificial, as two grass pitches back home would struggle under that workload. Thankfully the subarctic climate, and therefore the need for artificial pitches, has helped overcome the Faroes biggest problem, in that there just isn't enough flat land to create any more football pitches, so even if they could turn to grass it just couldn't happen.

The match was entertaining enough for the dozen or so souls who joined me in watching, however I kept getting distracted by the statue in the park on the hill beyond which cut a lonely figure as it faded from view behind ever thickening hill fog and mist. Then the low cloud above began to trail heavy veils of rain behind it and the island out to sea slipped from view as it swept in. The air became very cold, very quickly.

Not wanting to get too wet (you have to accept in the Faroes that getting wet is inevitable, it's just up to you how wet you allow yourself to become before you seek shelter), I decided to make for the main stand of the main pitch beyond as, one, I would get out of the weather, and two, I hadn't had a good look around it yet.

There were two smaller stands opposite, one holding the clubhouse and changing rooms for HB, the other for B36. Behind one goal was a steep grass bank that had little wooden benches dotted about on it for spectators to perch rather precariously on to watch the matches below. It looked pretty risky to try to get to them, especially as the grass was wet. The stand I stood in was a large wooden structure that stretched two thirds of the pitch. It was a comforting place to hide from the rain, as it drummed on the roof.

And it is here your opinion of me may change forever, as I wandered along this grandstand waiting for the rain to stop. What I did next probably reflects just as badly on you as it does me, depending on your reaction, so just remember that if you think what happened next is rational, even vital, as I did. (I am in denial of course. In reality I appreciate that the overwhelming majority of you will, depending on your levels of compassion, consider me in need of some life coaching/therapy/electro convulsive treatment.)

At the front of the stand were large barrel shaped bins, half full with disposable coffee cups and the like, and as I passed one something caught my eye. My football programme spidey senses flickered into life. There, wet, coffee stained, mostly buried in rubbish, was a football programme. A B36 programme from a couple weeks earlier, I discovered, as I fished it out. My heart began to race, as I imagine the heart of that feller who discovered the pharaoh's tombs did when he saw what he had before him; treasure, just lying about. Treasure!

I flicked through the sodden pages, some of which were stuck together, then stuffed it into my back-pack. *If there was one, there might be others*! The stands opposite had their bins at the back of the seating, rather than at the front like in this one, where they had gotten rained on countless times over the past month. Could there be any there? Could there? Forgetting about the rain all of a sudden, I hurried round and began scouring through bins, under seats, everywhere, like a man possessed.

They were just lying there. I'll say it again because you probably can't quite believe what you've just read. They were just lying there... multiples of four different programmes from recent B36 games. Some were in decent nick, they weren't even covered in bin juice. I mean, I did scoop them up tenderly and stick them in my bag even if they were, but I stashed the clean, intact ones in the front pocket, so they didn't get contaminated.

I didn't appreciate it at the time, but am prepared to admit it now, that the looks on the faces of passing dog walkers were at best quizzical and most were likely somewhat troubled. I didn't care. I'd just hit the jackpot in programme terms and was more concerned with getting back to my room so I could try and dry some of the more damaged ones off on the radiator.

I bloody love football programmes. I don't know what it is about them specifically, other than they let you into the world of the club you love, or any club you happen to visit; the team sheet on the back giving you the power of knowledge when anyone nearby who didn't buy one asks:

'Who's the number ten?'

They are football, in printed form, often with pictures and everything!

Later that night there was a solemn burial in the waste bin for those that didn't quite make it; that despite being dried out had pages that were still stuck together, or had torn when trying to prise them free. But even after all that I was still left with four good ones and a few not quite so good swapsies. Now, that is pretty decent by anyone's standards. And, unlike that feller that discovered the Pharaohs tombs, the British Museum could jog on.

As it would have been plain sad if I just sat in the room watching them dry (I'm married, you know, somehow), I went for a walk around quiet and dusky Tórshavn; the narrow streets near deserted even though it was Saturday night. I popped into a sports shop that seemed to be open much too late for a Saturday evening and asked if they sold football shirts of HB or B36.

'What? No,' the bloke behind the counter said incredulously, apparently amused by the notion that anyone would want to buy one.

I guess it was a stupid question to ask. With such a small population, almost everyone must have a link to their club, either as a player, ex-player, or the like. They probably have the shirt they play or played in to wear to games if they want.

After a couple of quick *bjors* I decided to head home, as I wanted to be ready for the next busy day. I had arranged to meet people from both HB and B36, either side of the game and I was anxious to appear at least a little bit journalistic, rather than the wide-eyed kid scampering here and there, which I knew had been my default appearance up to that point.

Marni Mortensen, webmaster and ex-secretary of HB walked me around the HB stand and clubhouse proudly, showing off pennants of European fixtures against Motherwell, Tromsø of Norway and FBK Kaunas of Lithuania in 2005 (who I saw in the following round at Anfield against the European champions), among others.

'The ground and the clubhouses for us and B36 are council owned, but we get to use them for free. We just have to keep it up and running. And there is always something that needs doing.

'All of us, from the Chairman down are volunteers. We have to fit everything in around our day jobs. There is lots of work to be done and it is a struggle, but it's a labour of love. We sometimes complain, but we always turn up.'

Those like Marni take it in turns to handle different aspects of the club. Marni has been secretary, chairman and is now the webmaster, as well as having represented the first team for a couple of years in the '80s.

We wandered along the rows of seats in the HB stand looking out at the stadium and a match between B36 and NSÍ Runavík's (of 2011 Craven Cottage, dodgy statue fame) women's teams (5-0 to B36, who were a decent side playing good passing stuff). I nodded further down the touchline at the B36 clubhouse and stand, which were identical to HB's.

'So what's it like, having your biggest rivals right on your doorstep?'
He shrugged.

'No, it is a rivalry I suppose, but a healthy one. It's all just words. I think they might hate us, but we don't mind them.' He chuckled.

B36 Tórshavn were formed in 1936 because there were too many players wanting to play for HB (formed in 1904). Right from the start, HB were seen as the bigger club, because B36 had to start with the players deemed not good enough for their neighbours.

As the women's match ended, Marni nodded at the pitch.

'The artificial grass is getting worn; it needs to be replaced soon. It should have been done years ago but it costs so much.'

He went on to explain that the two pitches in the Gundadalur complex were used by a huge number of teams; as already mentioned, B36, HB, Fram and all their feeder sides played here Thanks to a brilliant little book called *Ronaldson's Directory Of Faroese Football*, which is just amazing, I knew that a fourth team with all its subsidiary teams called Undrid played here as well, battling for the title of third best team in Tórshavn with Fram. When Marni said that the pitches were in pretty much constant use every evening and all weekend, he really wasn't kidding.

But they were being used even more than my research had suggested.

'You see that island out there?' Marni nodded beyond the harbour.

'What, Nolsoy?'

'Population around 250,' he said 'but even they have a club, called Nólsoyar Ítróttarfelag, and they have two teams, they play in the lower divisions. There is no pitch over there, so they play all their games here. This place is so important for so many more teams than just us and B36. It's the centre of the community here. Everyone knows someone who plays here.'

'With it being so busy you must look forward to being able to use the grass pitches I guess, if only for European games?'

He laughed.

'No, those pitches are terrible. The grass can't grow well in this climate, it's horrible and bobbly. They plant grass seed all the time, to try and improve it. But there is no full-time groundsman and whenever they do, the geese come along and eat it all. There's no-one to stop them!'

There is no groundsman and no money in Faroese football. Clubs are getting a little more professional, offering contracts to players with a little money, and more often than not giving them an apartment to live in rent free and expenses, and so on. However, all the players need a day job too. As Marni says, you can't make a living from football alone here.

'The contracts are getting better,' he said, 'and players move about between teams more because of it. It always used to be that players stayed with their home clubs. Now it's getting a little more like other leagues.'

'But I think this is as professional as our league can get. There is no money to take the next step and we have the constant problem that our best young players go abroad, mainly to Denmark, to study. If they are good they stay and play over there, where you can make a living from the game.'

Marnie didn't look too downbeat at the thought, however.

'I'm not,' he said. 'It would lose why football is so special to me if it did become more professional. This standard, this is it for us, this is what I love. We have a good competitive league here and it is exciting to watch. There is no money to chase an impossible dream and I'm glad in a way. Football clubs are meant to reflect where they are from and I think we have that here in the Faroes.'

With bigger and better contracts, by Faroese standards at least, there had been a few issues that annoyed Marni, especially with the attitudes of some of the first team players. Part of their contract is that they must be a referee at some of the children's matches during the season.

'It's not like every week, maybe two or three times a season. But they don't turn up,' he shook his head. 'Because they play for HB they are suddenly too good to turn up. It never used to be like that. When I was a boy there was never a problem, they would always come.'

'What about foreign players?' I asked. 'Do you ever get them coming over to the Faroes?'

'Yes, we do. At the moment HB have two and B36 have three. However we don't need them too much, as most of the talent on the islands that doesn't go abroad ends up in Tórshavn, as they have a better chance of winning things, getting to play in Europe here. It's more the smaller teams in the remote areas that use them, as they sometimes don't have enough players. But some of them that come over,' he shrugged, 'they are no better than what the clubs already have.'

'To be a foreign player and play for B36 or HB, they need to be much better than what we already have. Even then they still aren't on a full-time contract; they need a day job. The club often finds them one, so they can pay their bills.'

We watched the two women's teams trudge off the pitch at the end of their warm down, activity slowly ramping up around the ground as the main match of the weekend – HB v Skála drew closer.

'No, the standard we have right now, that is good enough, it's probably as good as we can achieve. If we can just get a new surface for the pitch, maybe next year they say, then that's all we need.'

It's clear that football here is rooted in the community and that clubs are far greater than just the first team. Everyone, with the exception of those few on contracts, are volunteers and work for their club because they love it. Because of that, there aren't really any egos, Marni explained.

'Everyone is the same here on the Faroes, in football, in life. Yes we get the odd player not turning up to referee matches [which clearly does grate with him, especially since he works so hard for nothing, and is dedicated to the cause] but by and large things are like how it was when I was playing for the first team, there is no class system. Everyone is equal. Nothing much has changed and in this case that is good.

'Yes, players move around clubs more now and don't just play for their home team. But people move around in life, they come to Tórshavn for work, or studies. It's hardly the mercenary attitude of players in other leagues moving for money. Here players move to try and better themselves on the pitch, not at the bank. And I guess that is fair enough.'

As more supporters decked in red and black started to fill the HB clubhouse I could tell Marni was itching to get amongst it, so we began to finish up. Marni looked at me a little suspiciously when I asked him to take a couple of pictures of me perched on one of the benches on the grass bank behind the goal. My facade as a journalist slipped a bit when I pulled out an old disposable wind up camera for him to use (it looked less hi-tech than my old manual one I used in Luxembourg 20-odd years earlier!).

'Here,' he said, pulling a digital camera out of his pocket and taking a few shots, 'I'll email them to you.'

As the players came out to warm up, a couple of air horns sounding off from somewhere among the support, Marni shook my hand.

'I hope you like the match and that you understand it's not like the English Premier League here. But it's a good standard, good enough to keep the league exciting and competitive every year.' He looked back across Gundadalur, at the nearly full HB clubhouse and wistfully, much like the Colonel in *Apocalypse Now* when he admits that someday the Vietnam War will end, said, more to himself than for my benefit:

'This is it for us. It's HB, it's our club.'

We shook hands and he headed off to take his place in the stand, looking over his shoulder one last time.

'You're meeting Hannis from B36 tonight, yes?'

I nodded.

'Well,' he said, kind of smiling, kind of serious, 'don't let him turn you into one of them.'

The HB support was too raucous for me, so I headed round to the main Gundadalur stand where the 50 Skála fans who had made the trip from Eysturoy had gathered in one corner and were trying to make themselves heard. They didn't really stand a chance. A voice that sounded suspiciously like Marni's started off a chant that was picked up by the entire clubhouse and a woman down the front started banging a tambourine with all her might, turning a little manic as the players came out.

Skála just weren't at it in the first half. They could barely get near the ball with HB's impressively neat passing game running them ragged and it was no surprise when HB scored with a simple cross and shot having got behind the Skála defence for the umpteenth time. The only real surprise of the first half was that HB didn't score any more, but, as Marni suggested, it was good to watch. I sat back and enjoyed the game.

There is always something slightly different about every foreign game that I've been to, something that separates it from the standard British experience.

At La Roche-sur-Yon it was being able to get your wine tumbler topped up, at Servette it was that amazing mysterious mustard, and here it was the loudspeaker system that seemed to be in constant use as its operator relayed goals from around the country as they went in. The groan from the HB stand and the muted cheers from the B36 clubhouse that housed maybe 20 or so spectators, suggested that B36 had scored in their away fixture on the most southerly of the Faroe Islands.

Football, eh? A game of two halves, eh?

This one most definitely was. Having gone in lucky to be only one down, Skála came out like a team possessed for the second half, playing high tempo stuff, passing it about, looking hungry. HB by contrast had come out like a side who had thought the game was already won, and by the time the equaliser came (tambourine paused for ten, 20 seconds or so before it started up again), they had still to find their earlier rhythm.

With a point on the cards Skála began to step off the gas too and the match became a bit of a stalemate, though still punctuated with some decent passing football and it came as no surprise to anyone when the ref blew his whistle and both teams finished with one point. It was apparently more appreciated by Skála, given the celebrations on the pitch in front of their fans; a good day's work in the capital.

As if the concept that these pitches were for everyone hadn't been displayed enough, both goal mouths were filled with little kids trying to emulate what they had seen before the senior players had even got into the dressing rooms. If only that could happen at Old Trafford!

I met Hannis Egholm, secretary of B36 Tórshavn, and his best friend Jacob, lifelong HB fan at Café Natúr, later that evening. They hadn't long got back from the ferry, having travelled down to the island of Suðuroy to watch B36 beat VB/Sumba 2-0. I asked how their friendship worked, being on opposite sides of the football divide in Tórshavn.

'No, the rivalry is good, it's just words and is usually good natured,' Hannis said. 'I mean B36 beat HB 6-0 recently, but all the HB fans went straight home after the match, you couldn't see any of them anywhere, apart from one who sat in the corner here in a daze.' He pointed over my shoulder to a small empty table tucked mostly out of sight. 'You should have seen his face; there really wasn't any point in ribbing him about the score!'

Hannis and Jacob then spent quite a time trying to get one over on each other: which team had won most league and cups, the first team to win the league, the last team to win the league! Hannis won, I think, with the fact that B36 are the only club from the Faroes to ever progress past the first qualifying stage of any European competition (they had recently lost to Fenerbahçe in the second round). During the one-upmanship it was always friendly, always funny.

'Of course, if we disagree I always let Hannis win because he is big and strong,' Jacob said, giving Hannis a playful clip round the ear.

Hannis was big and strong; a burly man with a shaven head, in his 40s with four children. Jacob, by contrast, was a slight figure, a chain smoker with shoulder length grey hair who mentioned one daughter.

When they talked about rivalry they never mentioned trouble, or fighting. In fact it only occurred to me at this point that there were no police at the match between HB and Skála; much like non-league football back in the UK.

Hannis talked very fondly of the Fenerbahçe club and fans, who he said were very friendly and respectful; the Faroes and Turkey had warmed to each other very quickly.

'Why would there be trouble? We all get along here. It's just not how we do things. Our society is not like that, everyone is equal and there is no class issue or ego. Members of our Government live next door to shop workers; everyone is on the same side. We are all Faroese, we just support different clubs. Hooliganism is unthinkable really.'

When I explained how rivalry can work in the UK, between Rangers and Celtic in Scotland for example, or West Ham and Millwall in London, they both looked confused.

'But if you live close by you should be more friendly, not less?' Hannis asked shaking his head. 'Surely people would have more in common?'

Jacob then talked about Denmark. His daughter, like lots of Faroese students, had studied in Denmark. Jacob was out there at the same time for a while and was given tickets to see FC Copenhagen play Brøndby, a top match in the Danish league. He took his daughter but there was trouble right away, with Brøndby fans trying to attack the home support. Jacob shook his head.

'Terrible.'

He and his daughter left. They couldn't believe it.

When it came to football in the Faroes, Hannis echoed Marni in almost everything; the country was too small to develop the game much more, lots of footballing talent went abroad to Denmark to study and if good enough didn't return, there wasn't any money to take the game further.

'We like our standard of football. There is good skill, it's good to watch. The league is competitive, maybe more so than in places like Scotland or even England. We love our teams and the games are often close and exciting, but,' he said, 'it is separate from the rest of football. We watch our teams at Gundadalur and other places and we love it, then we go home and watch the rest of the world play on the television and we love that too – our teams could never compete. There are two kinds of football: Faroes football and rest of the world football, and we love watching both. Some of the skill you see on the TV… It's just amazing.'

He went on to mention a few teams over the years who had come to the Faroes while on tours of Europe. He saw Athletico Mineiro from Brazil in the '80s.

'Technically unbelievable, it was incredible to see. There is Faroes football, then there is the rest of the world,' he repeated. 'That's it. It's good.'

Jacob nodded in agreement.

'But maybe our national team could compete a bit more if it wasn't hampered by clubs abroad bullying our players.'

He mentioned one Faroese player who was top scorer for FC Copenhagen in the Danish Premier League for five seasons in a row, but the club wouldn't allow him to play for the national team in case of injury.

'To them our national team is not seen as important enough, so they put pressure on our players. Our national team could be better if we had all the players available like other countries do.'

The national team had been punching above its weight for a long time as it was. For the third smallest UEFA nation their results were decent. From Skansin Fort, if the weather is right, one can just see the vague outline of the most southerly tip of Eysturoy island, and from there it's not far to the small town of Toftir and the second grass pitch at the exposed and desolate Svangaskarð Stadium, the site of some solid results. Then World Champions Italy came away with a narrow 2-1 win in 2007, while a few years earlier Scotland left having clawed a point in a thrilling two all draw that, by all accounts, the Faroes dominated.

Hannis went on to tell the story of B36 and how it was formed; his tale was exactly the same as Marni's. There was no elaboration, no ego trying to make their club seem other than it is.

'But despite being the team with the players not deemed good enough to play for HB, we are now equal in stature. We won the league last year, which is why we got to play Fenerbahçe in the Champions League.

'We have three foreign players this year: Alex José dos Santos is from Brazil, and Obele Okeke Onyebuchi and Amed Davy Sylla are Africans. You have to be much better than our home grown players to get a contract in Tórshavn, and even then they need another job because the contracts are so small. Alex is very good. He's been with us for three years now and is the best defender in the league.'

Despite their love for their respective clubs both Hannis and Jacob seemed to think that EB/Streymur, a small team from the north of Eysturoy Island, would win the league in the upcoming year.

'They are a small team who have never won it before. But they have good young players and the right spirit. They would deserve to win it. They have played very well this year.'

'I doubt they will repeat it too often though. It's too small a place to keep developing more players, or to attract them. It's a bit of a crazy, one-off situation this year, where everything has fallen into place for them. I expect them to fall back a little bit once this current team has broken up.'

Hannis and Jacob both looked tired. The trip down to Suðuroy to see B36 play had worn them out. From the map, and having studied the state of the ocean since I'd been on the Faroes, it looked like it would have been a long and rough ferry trip there and back, especially for Jacob, who didn't even support B36. Hannis went to all the games and he used to take his kids when they were little.

'They have seen all parts of the Faroes. They were the only kids in their school who could name all the towns and villages, because they had been to them all! But now,' he said, 'I have to take him instead!' He chuckled and dug Jacob in the ribs.

As we talked, a crowd of lads sat around a long table upstairs got drunker and noisier.

'That's B36,' Hannis explained. 'The players have been given the week off because of the international break.'

Every now and then a couple of them came downstairs for more *bjór* or the toilet and stopped to talk to Hannis, giving him big hugs or a handshake. It was clear that he was well liked and respected, and that the players are just a part of the community, getting drunk, as friends do, on a Saturday night. It just felt nice.

As we drank, and got drunk ourselves, it was great to witness the amazing bond between Hannis and Jacob; they were life-long friends, who would happily travel the length and breadth of their country to watch their mate's football team play. As they said goodbye and left, I felt very happy to have met them, as they epitomised the Faroes for me: warm, friendly people who made you feel very welcome in their country.

Just as they were leaving, Hannis offered me one final fact.

'Wherever you go in the world to watch football, you'll probably never find as eccentric a league as ours. Where else would you have a top league of ten teams, who play each other three times, so some teams will have home advantage over others twice in a season?' He laughs. 'It's crazy! But that's our league. It couldn't happen anywhere else in the world but the Faroes, I think.'

With a wave, the two friends headed off into the night. I walked back up to Skansin Fort and took in the lights of Tórshavn; the distant chants of drinking games from the B36 players drifting on the quiet night, the ocean dark and still. I knew that I would miss this place; its football, its people and its scenery, which was just as stunning on the bus trip back to the airport as it was on the way out, the tunnels beneath the ocean interrupting mountain views and clouds, a shadowy island a little ways out to sea.

The Faroe Islands is a special place; hidden away from the rest of the world, lost in the north Atlantic and populated by warm and proud people, proud of their culture and traditions, their architecture, their classless society where everyone is seen as equals. They are not entirely cut off from the rest of the world, but they can appreciate the benefits of it as well as the attraction of everything that lies beyond. I think they view everything much like Hannis and Marni explained their views on football:

'There is the Faroes and then there is the rest of the world.'

It works.

By the time we reached the airport visibility was virtually zero, as the cloud and fog descended over everything. It seemed fitting that, as my 30 or so fellow passengers and I boarded the plane, we'd be leaving the Islands in the same way as we arrived; shrouded in cloud and mystery.

Postscript

EB/Streymur didn't win the league that season. They faded at the last and were pipped by HB to the title (I can just imagine the ribbing Hannis got from Jacob for that!). However EB did win it in 2008, where they got to play the new billionaires of world football, Manchester City, in the qualifying rounds, losing 2-0 home and away. Since 2006, HB have won the league three times to B36's one in 2011 and HB also equalled B36's record of qualifying for the second round, managing it four times. Finally, and for me very happily, *Ronaldson's Directory of Faroese Football* (Google it, then buy it) has questioned my belief that KÍ Klaksvík's ground is the most picturesque, by publishing that Leirvík stadium in Leirvík, home to the relatively newly formed Víkingur club's reserve team, is in fact the most stunning venue to watch football in the Faroes.

Challenge accepted.

4

21 August 2014. Wales Women v England Women
Women's World Cup Qualifier, Cardiff City Stadium

THERE ARE SOME players, and not necessarily just those at the very pinnacle of the game, who can turn football into poetry. Players who can make what is already a sweeping, flowing game into art, who can use sublime skill to wriggle out of a seemingly impossible position, who can make a breath-taking pass where no-one else could see it, who can score a goal that no-one else thought possible.

These players can be found throughout the vast football pyramid (some people get the breaks, others don't), though if they don't appear in the Champions League or the Premier League they are often ignored by the mainstream media (I remember Lee Trundle doing stupendous things for Swansea in the third and Fourth Division, largely unnoticed); and I travelled to Cardiff in the hope of finally, finally being able to see once such player. In the end, I left having stumbled across another one.

Kelly Smith can do things with a football that simply baffle me, and leave me in awe and wonder. In the 2014 Women's FA Cup final she found herself marked by two or three players, facing the touchline, no Arsenal team-mate close by; but instead of knocking it out of play she turned, jinked, dummied with the ball at her feet and left those opponents behind to set up another Arsenal attack. It was simply amazing. And she has done it her entire career; goals, passes, pieces of skill that make your heart race.

Yet I doubt she appears near the top of many armchair football fans list of players of the 21st century and I doubt many of her awe-inspiring moments have been captured by TV cameras. Why? She is a woman, and the women's game is not given the time of day or the respect that it deserves in this country.

Things are certainly improving; BT Sport now broadcast Women's Super League games and the BBC show England Women's international matches. But maybe this slight increase in exposure has come too late to offer Kelly Smith's unbelievable talent to a much wider audience, as the multiple injuries that she has suffered throughout her long career have made her body less receptive to niggling knocks.

It is a combination of bad luck and work commitments, along with these injuries that prevented me, despite numerous attempts, seeing Kelly play in person. But with two days to go before England played Wales, with only a point needed for England to qualify for the 2015 Women's World Cup in Canada, and with Kelly Smith having been named in the squad with no injury news reported, I was quietly confident that this might be the match.

It was not the match.

Kelly pulled out with an injury.

Damn it!

It is not just her abilities that draw you to Kelly. If you read her autobiography you find a shy, likeable person; an ordinary person blessed with extraordinary talent. Her problems are your problems, her self-doubts are yours. She is the child we all were, playing football religiously, anywhere, anytime, only she made it and was thrust into the professional sport of Soccer in the USA, where the women's game has often been more popular than the men's.

It is heart-breaking to read of her struggles with self-confidence and the self-destructive coping mechanisms that crippled her for a long time; there for the grace of God, and talent of course. But she came out of it the other side and has had a glittering career. It's just a pity it isn't more widely recognised, as she must be ranked as one of the ten most gifted players this country has ever produced. That is where I put her, at least, and one day, hopefully sooner rather than later, I will be able to say 'I saw her play'.

Despite Kelly not playing I was still very excited to be going to the qualifier in Cardiff for a couple of reasons; to see the two best teams in their qualifying group go head-to-head and also to tick off another Football League ground visited from the 92. The Cardiff City stadium was number 40. It could have been more, but I have a knack of visiting teams that then get relegated out of the Football League, as if they don't even appreciate how damaging that is to my mean average. It had taken ages to get to 40; Bristol Rovers, Torquay United, Aldershot, Darlington I am looking at you!

You may consider 40 to be excessive and very sad or a badge of honour, depending on your outlook. Either way, there are plenty of people to have done all 92 that make my efforts seem very trivial.

For this trip I was in the company of Tash and Jen, without whom I wouldn't have even known the match was being played. They were my finger on the pulse of the women's game. Having been to see England play out in Germany at the last World Cup, and being regulars at Arsenal Ladies matches, there isn't much that they don't know. They got me a ticket to my first England Women's international in September 2013 (one of the first World Cup qualifiers, where they beat Belarus 6-0 and where Kelly Smith was injured).

I didn't drive across to Bournemouth with them for that game and I turned up late and with England already winning 2-0 due to Emma being late picking me up, no doubt lost in thought at a petrol station somewhere, wondering 'if you drive in the direction that the planet is rotating do you save petrol' or something like that. She couldn't be with us on this occasion due to pressing house moving demands, so I was philosophy-less in the back of Jen's car as we headed for Wales.

Jen and Tash are archetypal women's football followers, in that they are women and the sport is followed predominantly, though by no means exclusively, by women and girls. Tash explained that she has in the past and still does from time to time, go to see Southampton play, and I am guessing that many of the people that make up the crowd at the Cardiff City stadium watch men's football too.

But I got the sense, the same one I felt at Bangor and in the Faroes, that for Tash and Jen and the rest of the crowd, like Hannis and Marni in Tórshavn and the shoe-wielding Bangor fans, the women's game is theirs, is number one, and is everything. Their real sense of belonging to it and of it proudly belonging to them, after years and years of effort, dedication and support, of helping to mould it into what it is today, leaves the Premier League and everything else as merely an entertaining side show.

Wonderfully, refreshingly, just like football in the Faroes, it has its own set of unique qualities that you rarely find in the Premier League.

There is a theory which states that even if a lion could speak English, you would still not be able to understand what he said, as you would have no common frame of reference to build your communications upon. In my opinion, Faroese and Women's football are akin to this theory, as although they are technically the same game as the mainstream sport, they are also entirely different.

For example, the atmosphere is different; completely free from the spectre of hooliganism that plagued the men's game when I was growing up and still lingers every now and then, to the point that I was a little shocked to see Jen wearing an England hoodie in Cardiff. When I asked if she and Tash weren't worried about wearing it they looked at me a little blankly and said:

'No, should we be?'

Sadly, I explained that on all my travels to watch Southampton play away with the exception of going up on an official coach, where you get dropped off right outside the away end, then get picked up again, I just simply wouldn't even consider wearing a top or scarf walking to an away ground. Watching football in the '80s had cured me of that need. It must be lovely to never even have to consider it.

The atmosphere on the pitch seemed to be different as well, as during the entire match there wasn't one bad tackle or intentional foul. Yes there were fouls and thundering tackles, but the match seemed untroubled by the cynicism of the men's professional game, with no play-acting, trying to get people booked (there were no bookings in the whole match), and no professional fouls breaking up play. The match seemed to flow with a simple spirit of fair play; even long after Wales were well beaten (spoiler alert, they got well beaten) they just got on with it, trying to get the ball into dangerous areas. There were none of the niggling tackles that can creep into some matches when one team is being soundly beaten, even when the pitch became slippery toward the end after some rain.

Like trying to explain the concept of ownership to a lion, the basic need to stop an opponent by any means necessary seemed to be completely absent, and thankfully seems not to have become a part of the DNA of the women's game as it has in the men's. As in the Faroe Islands, the Women's game exists in an environment most supporters of Premier League teams would be envious of. It is something they should be very proud of.

And why not feel that way, when one can interact with the players, either on Twitter or in person? After the match, Lianne Sanderson and a number of the England team came into the stands to meet and talk to some of the 1,500 or so England fans, chat to buddies or relatives and celebrate with everyone qualifying for the World Cup. The humility, friendship and kinship between players and fans, fans and players, is intoxicating and special, and creates that bond which produces such passionate support.

This passionate support nearly burst my ear-drums as, after parking up at the stadium hours before kick-off, Tash, who had always seemed a quiet and friendly soul, started screaming as a car drove past:

'Oh my God that's Faye f******g White! Faye f*****g White is in that car! Jen!' Jen was outside of the car looking at a parking notice and the windows were up. 'Jen! Faye f*****g White! JEN!'

That is why football is so special and why it has become vital around the world. It's a game that captivates and is spellbinding to so many. So much so that, sometimes, you can't help yourself screaming at the former England and Arsenal player Faye f*****g White (I've checked, it's not her middle name) when she drives past.

We arrived very early, which I like, so we spent some time wandering around and getting something to eat; some of us staring more intently at cars and their drivers as they roll into the stadiums car park than others. In a way, the Cardiff City Stadium was a perfect venue for this match and a perfect allegory for why football outside the Premier and Champions League bubble is in many ways more honest and of the people, for the people, than the football bloated with money of the rich for the corporate events market.

Cardiff City had always played in blue. They were nicknamed the bluebirds. Blue was their colour. Then along came a Malaysian multi-millionaire owner, whose lucky colour was red. Red was also apparently more marketable around the world than blue. The blue shirts became red; the bluebird became a red bird. History, belonging, meaning, were ditched in favour of increased worldwide revenue. Finally, despite all of that, Cardiff's promotion to the Premier League was followed by relegation back into the Championship at the first attempt. Ridiculous.

So now Cardiff play Championship football, in red shirts, in a stadium full of blue seats (excepting a red band of seats high up in one stand that depict the famous Cardiff Ayatollah salute, played out with white backed seats) for a stadium full of fans wearing older, traditional blue shirts.

The women's game really couldn't be any further from this bloated corporate football charade; mainly because the FA and Premier League clubs don't put much money into it. The Women's Super League, populated by Chelsea, Arsenal, Manchester City, Liverpool and so on, doesn't have a single full-time professional women's team. Every English and Welsh player on show, excepting the few who play in America, is part-time. I believe there are some central contracts from the national football associations as well, but when you consider that the weekly wage of any one of the big clubs leading male players would probably fund an entire squad and backroom staff in the women's game for a number of months, it does suggest that allowing the women's sides to go full-time, despite the money available to these monster clubs, is not very high on their list of priorities. This is a real shame, as there was some amazing talent on show, and who knows what even greater heights they could reach if they were allowed to dedicate their time and efforts to it.

As it was, the football was captivating, with England passing the ball fast and incisively across the pitch, probing the Welsh team for weakness. Despite the vast majority being semi-pro their control and ability on the ball was immaculate. Steph Houghton and Laura Bassett were dominant in defence, Fara Williams (an inspirational character who had risen to the top despite enduring homelessness as a youth) bossed the midfield and made the team tick along at a high tempo with always accurate passes sending the exciting Lianne Sanderson and Eniola Eluko up front on another attack.

After 15 minutes or so of constant pressure the floodgates opened and

England goals started to flow. Karen Carney scored direct from a free kick way out on the touchline and Laura Bassett prodded in from close range, again from a defence dissolving set piece. But the two goals that stood out in the 4-0 win were quite simply very special and would be worth an entrance fee far, far greater than a fiver. Eniola Aluko's volley into the top left corner after controlling a high ball on her chest would have been beamed across the world if Lionel Messi had done it, and Lianne Sanderson's diving bullet header would have done the same.

Both goals were moments that instinctively lift you out of your seat, that get a crowd to rise as one at a piece of mind-boggling magic. It's just a shame that there weren't more than the 3,500 spectators there to witness them. At least it was being screened on BBC Three, and hopefully plenty of boys and girls were able to see those goals, and be inspired by them; inspired by a dominant display full of excellent passing; the kind of display that helps to make football sing to a potential Lianne Sanderson, Kelly Smith, Fara Williams of the future.

There was not much to be cheerful about if you were a Wales supporter; their team was outplayed from start to finish, only getting some kind of foothold in the second half once England had switched off a little, feeling comfortable enough to cruise home with a four goal lead.

Jess Fishlock, Wales' captain and the only Welsh player to play professionally in the US, was outnumbered in midfield and couldn't get a passing game going, which inevitably lead to long balls from the Welsh defence being mopped up by England, who could set off on another attack. But even amongst all that, amongst the siege-like hold England had on the ball, there was one shining light in a Wales shirt, creating something out of nothing, running almost single handed at the English defence with sublime skill; a small, slight figure creating opportunity, just like Kelly Smith, from apparently impossible situations, the ball seemingly stuck to her boots. Sarah Wiltshire with the ball at her feet made your spirit soar, and her intricate footwork as she tried to break through the English defence turned sport into an art-form, and made hour upon hour staring out of a window on the motorway to get there to see it seem a trifling inconvenience.

It allowed me to forget my disappointment at Kelly Smith's injury for a time. Sarah's efforts had helped light up a match that, despite being watched by only a few thousand people, had been a wonderful advertisement for the drama and craft women's football can offer. As the game came to a close, it seemed fitting that a rain storm of almost biblical proportions began to fall from the night sky. Cascading from the lip of the stadium's roof like a waterfall, shimmering in sheets beneath the floodlights before falling onto the touchline a few rows in front of us. It was a dramatic and theatrical finale worthy of the skill on offer. As the players and the stand beyond grew faint and indistinct, lost beneath the deluge, the rainstorm signalled the end to a thoroughly entertaining evening's football.

As the England players celebrated on the pitch at their qualification for the Women's World Cup in Canada, the dejected Wales team stood in a huddle, listening to their manager hopefully offering them words of consolation and encouragement, as qualification was still open to them through the play-offs.

I for one will be hoping that they do it; for the sake of Jess Fishlock's determination and her never-say-die attitude, even when out-gunned and outnumbered.

Also for the sake of Sarah Wiltshire, because a talent like that deserves to play at the World Cup. You never know, if they made it they could even get to have a rematch against England, and Kelly Smith and Sarah Wiltshire on the pitch at the same time really would be something to see.

Postscript
The day after England's qualification was secured, the FA announced a showcase friendly in November between England and Germany at Wembley stadium. Jen told me that this would be the first time that England Women's team play an international match at the national stadium, decades after it was formed.

Better late than never is one way of looking at it and let's hope there is a decent crowd to watch it, because whoever does go will not regret it.

5

30 August 2014. Cowes Sports v Yate Town
FA Cup Preliminary Round

THIS MATCH WAS one of 162 at the stage of the competition that aren't even a part of the 'official' qualifying rounds for the FA Cup. There are four of these that non-league teams need to traverse in order to get to the first round proper. From the first round, it's then just another seven victories to the final.

For Cowes Sports and Yate Town there was some work to be done to even reach this first qualifying round. Cowes had already battled through an extra-preliminary round to get them into this preliminary round, which would determine who would qualify for the qualifying rounds! (These start a good eight months before the final.) So, in front of a crowd of roughly 100, in a tiny ground overlooking the Solent from its lofty perch on the Isle of Wight, two teams, two of 736 who had entered this year's competition, went at it with a determination, almost desperation, to make it into that first qualifying round draw.

A lot of people may ask: Why? Why try so hard – in fact why even enter a competition that you have absolutely no chance of winning? This is a question that could in all likelihood be asked of 730 or so of the 736 entrants.

In the cold light of day, it's almost an impossible question to answer. Why would Yate Town travel all the way down from Gloucestershire and cross one of the most expensive stretches of water per mile in the world, to play Cowes Sports, a team three divisions below them in the football pyramid? Like all teams at this embryonic stage of the competition, it all boils down to one little phrase: 'The magic of the FA Cup'.

This phrase has grown a little muddy in recent years, verging on the obsolete if your FA Cup consumption is largely made up of watching from your armchair as jaded TV commentators, having been old enough to have grown up during its glory days, speak of it with a complete lack of conviction and even sadness at its fading from the elite levels of the professional game. The FA haven't treated what was the most important competition in the world with enough respect in recent years; the final, which once was the focus of an entire days' worth of analysis and programming, has spent a number of years having to compete with often title-deciding Premier League games with their worldwide appeal on the same day.

With that shifting relevance away from history and toward high finance, many of the top clubs have used the FA Cup as an opportunity to 'rest' more senior players for more 'important' league or European fixtures, and many of the teams near the foot of the table now do the same, preferring to prioritise Premier League safety above FA Cup progression. Even Championship sides fighting to get in among the play-offs have started to field weaker teams, the lure of the big time now the be-all and end-all. This results in a tournament that seems to have had its legs taken out from beneath it at the top reaches of the sport.

Thank God therefore for the non-league sides and the sides from Leagues One and Two, for whom the FA Cup can often be the only way to inject some of that magic into their season, along with some much needed income that can keep the wolf from the door in an otherwise financially frugal, hand to mouth existence. These teams keep the magic of the FA Cup alive, the opportunity for glory, for giant killing, for part-time or amateur players to have a chance of playing against those much higher up the food chain in grounds much greater than they are used to. And it needn't be getting drawn against Manchester United that makes a season; for clubs and their fans at the preliminary round stage, getting drawn against a top Southern league side would be amazing and would bring in some much needed publicity and money. For a Southern league side there is the opportunity of pitching up against someone from the Conference, maybe one of those ex-league clubs. And all of this is even before the first round proper when Leagues One and Two join in.

A couple of seasons ago, I watched AFC Totton of the Southern League play Bristol Rovers, then of League Two, in the second round proper. The ITV cameras were there, it was a full house, and a club surviving on the support of a couple of hundred fans found themselves with a 3,000 plus crowd, TV money, and for a couple of hours on one Sunday lunchtime, they were live on ITV.

Later on it is the turn of the lower league professional sides, going at it against the top boys; journeymen players finally getting their shot against Liverpool or Arsenal. The FA Cup gives them the opportunity, for one match, to live out their childhood ambition. And every now and then, among it all, an upset can occur.

It is these situations, these opportunities that confirm that there still is magic to be found in the world's oldest football competition, It's just a pity that the vast majority of the magic is now long gone by the fourth round and the large portion of it is played out in front of small crowds in the qualifying and early rounds, often going completely unnoticed by the TV armchair Champions League football fan.

The thought of the early qualifying rounds of the FA Cup remind me straight away of Victoria Park and trips there with my grandfather. It also brings back memories of other non-league gems such as Andover's characterful and now long gone Walled Meadow ground; Brockenhurst in the heart of the New Forest, a ground that needs a cattle-grid to prevent ponies, donkeys and cows wandering in; and a defunct ground near Lymington that used to be the home of Wellworthy Athletic, my grandfather's works team and therefore his favourite little ground (excepting Victoria Park).

As a young boy the warmth and charm of these grounds and those that populated them were very appealing: cackling old-timers sharing their bag of boiled sweets and jokes with strangers in the stand. The whole experience being completely devoid of the fear of hooliganism was just the icing on the cake.

Cowes Sports' Westwood Park sent me drifting back the best part of 30 years to those old grounds and faces as it resembled Victoria Park in many ways; a quaint old stand dotted with spectators, some sheltered terracing running alongside it, voices echoing about them both, competing with the crackling tannoy playing tinny music, the whole place buzzing with excitement and anticipation; because, for the supporters and players of Cowes and Yate Town, it was FA Cup weekend.

It's hard not to feel at ease at places like Westwood Park, a ground hidden away at the end of a residential cul-de-sac, where children run about unattended and play behind the goals while the teams warm up, a rope swing dangling from a tree near one of the corner flags positively encouraging it. It is a very relaxing and enjoyable way to watch football.

As a child, sat alongside my grandfather, Victoria Park and the rest felt so much safer than The Dell in the mid- to late-'80s, where after 30 minutes or so into the second half of a match all I could ever think about was how me and Dad, or family friend Colin Worthington, or whoever had taken me, were going to get safely home as the tension between home and away fans ramped up. The spectre of dodging running battles through the narrow streets around The Dell was a very real concern.

Back then my non-league trips were a place where I could really enjoy football and my grandfather's company, the space and quiet of half empty stands allowing time to breathe, to take everything in. That safety net came to my rescue many years later in 2007, after my father took his own life.

Probably due to the turmoil in my head that results from such an experience, along with a claustrophobic funeral service attended by what felt like far too many people for the size of the chapel, I began to struggle with noise and crowds; so much so that I couldn't go to St Mary's to see Southampton for well over a year. Weddings were a nightmare, as were parties or functions of any kind; shops, so many places you take for granted, they were just too much.

But one place I found myself returning to, instinctively rather than consciously, after many years absence, were football clubs like Downton, Vosper Thornycroft, Brockenhurst and Hamble of the Wessex League (a league near the foot of the non-league pyramid), where you could quietly sit and watch a game, read the programme and breath out for a while. (Unfortunately Victoria Park was long gone by then, otherwise it would have been top of that list.) Those places were a real respite from everything, where you could find some space and time and comfort, reminding me of happier times with my grandfather, who by now was far too frail to join me, but always seemed to be there anyway.

Walking into Westwood Park with Emma I felt that warmth and comfort, that familiarity, even in a place that I'd never been to before. It was there, in the rickety old stand, the jovial old chap on the turnstile taking gate money with a joke and a wink, old-timers leant up against the barrier by the tea hut sipping tea from mugs. This seemed to blow Emma's mind.

'They serve it in mugs? This is amazing!'

It seemed obvious where to start introducing a first time visitor to the lower reaches of the game: with the ritual of a cup of tea and a chocolate bar. This is basic, an ingrained experience of my non-league childhood, adhered to religiously by my grandfather (who sometimes used to cheat and bring chocolate from home) and Terry, dad of one of my oldest friends, who would also take us to games, who would head straight for the tea hut with a certainty which implied that there could be no other possible option.

Mugs in hand, I suggested we should wander round the perimeter of the pitch and take it all in. Emma looked a little nervous.

'What... we can take the mugs away?'

'Yeah, we just bring them back when we're done.'

She shook her in amazement.

It's amazing how different an experience like a preliminary round match looks and sounds when compared to the larger, professional leagues. For one, you can hear every word the players say as they chat to one another while warming up and you can hear the thudding of boots on grass as they jog by, balls pinging from player to player sounding heavy and hard. You lose all this in cavernous stadiums surrounded by thousands of supporters; you lose these fundamental truths.

Mugs safely returned to the tea hut, we took our seats in the stand and waited for the game. Cowes Sports, from Wessex League Division One, were one of the lowest ranked teams left in the competition after the extra-preliminary round; Wessex One being the lowest point in the non-league pyramid (six promotions away from the Football League) where you can take part in the FA Cup.

As though coming here didn't feel like a trip back in time for me enough already, as we sat and waited for the teams to come out a deep, booming drone began, growing louder, until an old Lancaster bomber came into view, flying low across the island. For a moment everyone seemed to stop and watch, giving one of the symbols of the Second World War the respect it deserved. There was an air show on further along the coast, we overheard someone explain, and it reminded me, again, of my grandfather, sitting out in my grandparents' back garden in a tiny village near Salisbury Plain, watching different planes from the RAF base at Boscombe Down fly past. He knew them all and would explain what they did, giving a special reverence to those that were used during the war.

As the teams came out and lined up, the PA announcer read out the player's names and I sat up a little as the Yate number ten was announced: Lewis Haldane. *Really? Could this be the same Lewis Haldane who was in the Bristol Rovers squad that beat Southampton 3-2 with a last minute screamer in Saints' first season down in League One, back in 2009?* A quick flick through the programme to the visitor's player pictures confirmed that it was him, a veteran of over 200 Football League games for Rovers and Port Vale.

What on earth is a player of that calibre doing here? As I read on, his profile revealed that a serious knee injury had finished his professional career. *Fair play*, I thought, as he walked out to a smattering of 100 or so souls lining the pitch; a far cry from the thousands he would have become used to playing in front of during his pro days. Clearly he just wanted to continue playing the game he loved, and if injury meant he couldn't in the pro leagues, he would drop down as far as necessary in order to do so.

The game kicked off and quickly developed a pattern, with Yate Town dominating possession and Cowes Sports defending resolutely, trying to set up attacks on the break. The difference between a semi-pro team in the Southern League and a team of amateurs from the lowest rung of the senior non-league pyramid was clear to see. However, even with Yate's dominance, the magic of the FA Cup that had been bubbling along beneath the ebb and flow of the match almost boiled over when Cowes' number ten, thanks to a rare slip up by the Yate defence, found himself with the ball dropping on a half volley about 40 yards from goal, the keeper off his line. He didn't think, he just went for it, and if his shot had only been a few inches lower it would have sailed into the top left hand corner.

Regardless, you could tell from the look on his face that this moment would last forever. Tonight, and for many more nights after, he would regale anyone down the pub who would listen about the time he nearly scored a screamer in the FA Cup. Even though it didn't go in it was a little bit of magic; FA Cup magic.

Emma had also picked out Cowes' number ten for attention, not being the thinnest player you would ever see. The lowest standard of football she had seen before this match was a Conference match at Salisbury, where the players were all full-time. This was her first experience of amateur football and she seemed transfixed by his 'everyman' build. I reasoned that Cowes playing in stripes wasn't helping his physique, not being that flattering to a larger man, but I suspect she wasn't listening, absorbed by him as she was.

I must confess that I got a little caught up in her awe and amusement at 'the fat lad up front,' and found myself, after the Yate centre back won yet another header, saying:

'He hasn't missed a single header all game, much like your feller,' pointing to Cowes' number ten, 'clearly hasn't missed a single meal his whole life.'

It brought a laugh, but I immediately felt bad. I knew I had said it out of spite, out of jealousy and with a begrudging respect brought on by the fact that in my playing days I wasn't good enough to appear in the FA Cup, preliminary round or otherwise. I would never have a story to tell of when I nearly scored a worldie in the oldest football competition of them all.

No matter what you think, or what you think you think, about Wessex league football, or southern league football, or these early rounds of the FA Cup, there is one thing I can guarantee, and that is you and your mates who maybe have a kick about down the park would, just like me, be well out of their depth on this Westwood Park pitch. Both sets of players could play a bit and it was entertaining stuff to watch, unlike your kick about (most probably).

So here I am, apologising to Cowes' number ten: Jared Wetherick, you were, are and always will be a better player than me, and I am sorry for joking about your weight.

As the match wore on the semi-pro side started to turn the screw, with the front three, spearheaded by Lewis Haldane, creating more and more opportunities. Despite a resolute display by the home team and a man of the match performance by their centre back Aiden Bryan, a winner for Yate finally came, courtesy of Haldane, with 15 minutes to go. With that, Cowes threw everything at them, even bringing on the wonderfully named substitute Sergio Castellano to try and nick a draw, but it wasn't to be. At the final whistle it was Yate who were heading into the first qualifying round. Both teams were given a warm round of applause as they trudged, exhausted, from the pitch, the announcer on the PA system wishing Yate all the best for the next round.

The changing rooms were just on the other side of the main walkway that lead from the stand to the exit, so while the players were heading in a couple of officials held back the spectators to let them through. There were pats on the back all round. The referee and his linesman were last to go in, and were dawdling on the pitch chatting. The two officials holding the spectators back were getting a little fidgety about how long they were delaying everyone when, from somewhere ahead of us, an old, broad country accent bellowed:

'Bloody hell ref, hurry up. I want to get home for my tea.'

Sheepishly, they scurried through and the officials released us into the wild. As we headed through the gates and down to the ferry, I took a quick look back at the old stand slipping from view. Who knows when I might next get to slip back in time again, to revisit those happy afternoons with my grandfather, remember those good times and deal with the bad? I don't know when it will be, but I hope that it isn't too far away.

Postscript

Ironically, this preliminary round weekend, which was first drawn to my attention by a Salisbury programme sent to me by my grandfather for a cup game against Marlow in 1984, was the weekend that the Wessex League refused what was left of Salisbury City FC entry into their set-up, being unable to admit a club still fighting in the courts over who owned it, with no manager or a single player. This last rejection signalled the end for Salisbury, at the very least for the season.

It's winding up order in the high court on 1 September (the date of that Marlow programme) was suspended for two weeks. The agony of Salisbury's slow death continued a little while longer, before the inevitable became reality, and Grandad's team slipped from the face of the earth.

6 September 2014. Accrington Stanley v Tranmere Rovers
League Two

IN A WEEK that began with the insanity of a player being paid £250,000 a week to play for Manchester United on transfer deadline day, it seemed perfect serendipity to end that week in the company of a team at the foot of League Two (Division Four in proper money); a league where most clubs live a frugal, hand to mouth existence from one set of gate money to the next; a league where the transfer window being open or shut is often an irrelevance, save for the odd free transfer coming or going.

For them the loan market, which opens a week after the transfer window ends, is where most of their dealing is done, trying to bolster threadbare squads with a few youth or reserve team players from higher up the leagues who are looking for a bit of Football League experience. In that sense, visiting Accrington Stanley offers a typical lower league experience, but Stanley are not a typical lower league club. Returning hero Andy Proctor (a free transfer from Bury and a veteran of more than four hundred games for Accrington in his first spell with the club) said it perfectly in his interview in the programme when he called the club, even in a league populated by other clubs running on tiny budgets, 'unique'.

It was that uniqueness, or my understanding of it, that was the catalyst for a 500 plus mile round trip to Lancashire on the last day of the season to see them play another great lower league success story in Wimbledon. The story of both clubs is well documented: Wimbledon suffered the horror of being the first Football League club to be relocated some 60 miles up the road to another town, then having their name changed (the modern day Wimbledon is a club which started from scratch at the foot of the non-league pyramid and worked its way up into the professional game).

For Accrington, the road back from extinction took far longer after going bust in 1962, with over 40 years spent working their way back through the non-leagues. These years were interspersed in the '80s and '90s with a playful, but ultimately patronising and insulting, milk advert that suggested that if you didn't drink lots of it you would only be good enough to play for Accrington.

Back in May, having never been to Accrington, the trip was made largely on the basis that it might be good fun and a nice way to round off what had been a great season watching Southampton tear up the Premier League. As a season ticket holder at St Mary's it was hard to get to many other matches besides the odd Salisbury match, and a few others watching the homeless Coventry City play over at Northampton (a story for a later chapter), so an old-school road trip like the ones we took in Southampton's League One days was very much in order. But unlike those trips, this one ended with the host club getting completely under my skin, in a simple and organic way. This was possibly helped by staying over for the night, but was confirmed while wandering around the ground before kick-off, by walking past a conversation between Stanley's manager and ex-Saints player, James Beattie, and a couple of elderly fans: 'Would you like to come in and have a look round? Come on then,' he said, and ushered them inside.

Outside an amazing pub called The Crown, which is right on the corner of the steps leading down to the ground, an old feller with a walking stick and a badge on his suit lapel that said 'Director' alongside the Stanley crest stopped us and said, in a broad Lancashire accent:

'Hello, are you here to see Stanley?' He spoke with a humility and almost incredulous intonation which I imagine people working for clubs that operate on a shoe-string must have ingrained in them, where nothing can be taken for granted. When we both nodded, he smiled and as he walked past slowly he said 'Well, thank you. Enjoy the game.'

Accrington won 3-2 and played with the freedom of being long since safe from relegation, dominating possession and covering every inch of the Crown ground's (now known as the Store First Stadium's) pitch with attacking intent. Wimbledon were also happily well above the dreaded dotted line and their fans were in a relaxed mood even though their team were being dismantled. By describing them as relaxed I really mean, for a significant section of them, shit-faced, balls out drunk, having travelled up from London hell-bent on enjoying being safe for another season.

Not only were they enjoying themselves, they were also keeping up the tradition, quite possibly unfathomably bizarre to those outside the football family, of dressing up on the last away trip of the season. It's kind of like getting to bring in games and wear your own clothes on the last day of school term, or possibly some kind of beer fuelled and extreme version of an office dress down day.

From the home end where we stood we could see a couple of Franciscan monks, Mario from Mario World, countless builders in high-visibility vests and hard hats, a sort of dinosaur (God knows, I genuinely have no idea what he was meant to be) and various other characters weaving to and from the toilets across the exposed away terrace.

We got to check them out up close and personal in The Crown pub after the match. Mario and a couple of builders tried to start chants about different teams as they watched the final league tables appear on the large screen TV, waiting to see which League One teams had been relegated and would therefore be destinations for them the following season. Groans were quickly replaced by an almost resigned chant of: 'If you're all going to Carlisle clap your hands,' when it was revealed that the team just south of Scotland had gone down. Once they'd digested that information they turned to a game that had been instigated by Fred Flintstone, who had brought in a traffic cone from outside, and in the saloon they took it in turns putting their heads on its top, spinning around it ten times before trying to run out into the beer garden through an open door. Most missed, and instead slammed into the wall either side or fell through the door into the ladies toilets.

Mercifully, the landlord put a stop to that after a few efforts. At last they filtered out into the late spring evening to find whatever mini-bus they had come up in for a five plus hour drive home that must have been an absolute joy for their poor, sober driver.

Amongst it all Emma and I sat drinking the best beer known to man, called The Pride of Pendle, in our Accrington Stanley club hoodies that she had bought us for the trip and watched in incredulity as almost the entire Stanley team wandered in for a pint and to hang out with the supporters. It was a blissfully fun experience and one that we felt a part of, even though it was our first time among it all. Looking back now, it is clear that the catalyst for this book came from that weekend in the company of the fans and players of Accrington Stanley FC.

With the sun shining and the season successfully completed, it had been a heady, happy atmosphere back in May; a real contrast to the drizzle and gloom of the early September morning as we drove back to Accrington, storm clouds building all around. It was a fitting metaphor for the poor start Stanley had produced in the new season; six defeats out of seven in all competitions, a draw with Luton the only point on the board that left them rooted to the foot of the fledgling League Two table. Last season they had started off with 12 games without a league win, which meant they had been stuck in a relegation battle for all but the last three weeks and it was clear that no-one would wish to go through that again.

Yet for Accrington it was almost an inevitability that runs like that can and will happen. The reason for this brings us back to Andy Proctor's description and the new-found understanding that Accrington Stanley genuinely is unique.

Even among the modest surroundings of the Fourth Division, Accrington are minnows; operating on home attendances that average around the 1,500 mark they are at a distinct financial disadvantage to nearly every other club in the league. Indeed, Portsmouth operate on gates often ten or 11 times the size of Stanley's and a host of other clubs work to a budget based on gates five or six times larger. Even the poorer relatives in the league can often double the attendance that Accrington receives. This is the reality that the club must operate within and it is a miracle that every season they not only keep their heads above the line, but on occasions make a real assault on the play-offs.

But why is there such a gulf? To the outsider it might be hard to fathom why they suffer such low attendances, especially to someone like me, who grew up on the south coast in a one team town. It's only when you drive up that you realise why.

Beneath the menacing skies on the motorway I could count at least ten signs for towns and cities that contained other Football League clubs within a 25 mile drive of Accrington, including Manchester United, one of the world's biggest clubs, to Manchester City, their rivals and current champions of England, and two other sides, Premier League Burnley and Championship Blackburn Rovers, who were literally within spitting distance of the Crown Ground. All these teams were well within the distance it takes to drive from Southampton to either of our local rivals in Portsmouth and Bournemouth.

With such neighbours it is understandable, especially when you couple that with the reality that Accrington just isn't that big a place. To their credit, the club does try to make a strength out of having so many higher league teams so close by, by offering supporters a 'flexi-ticket', which is kind of like a season ticket for Burnley, Blackburn, or any other local team's fans who might see Stanley as their second team. With the flexi-ticket you can attend Stanley matches throughout the season at a discounted price. Judging by the number of Burnley shirts in the crowd for the Wimbledon match, it clearly works and they clearly do have a set of 'second team supporters', over and above the two idiots that drive up from Southampton to watch them.

Once you understand why attendances are so low, the next question is how on earth can a club with a tiny playing budget in comparison to their peers not only simply survive, but even end up in mid table like last season? This is where part of the unique nature of Accrington Stanley comes to the fore. As the sign that welcomes the players out onto the pitch at the Crown Ground proclaims: 'This is Stanley, the club that wouldn't die.'

Accrington; the players, the board, the fans, everyone, appreciates the enormity of their task, season on season, to survive in the Football League. And without any fuss or bemoaning their lot they do just that, in style on the pitch, and with passion on the terraces and in the boardroom. Witnessing it in action, it is easy to see why fans of other local clubs gravitate towards them when their team is in some other far flung part of the country. In a way it is the ultimate romantic underdog story in English football and, like many before me, I found myself falling in love with it back in May. Driving up for a second encounter, I was looking forward to falling in love all over again.

We arrived at our hotel an hour and a half before kick-off and checked in. We were little freaked out when the receptionist recognised us from our last trip.

'Hello again, are you back to see the football?' Either she had some kind of photographic memory of all the guests that have visited the Sparth House Hotel, or the sight of two people driving up from the south coast to see Accrington play is ludicrous enough of a notion to have us labelled as 'eccentric' guests the first time around.

As we walked to the ground the rain started to get a little heavier and Emma, who forgot to bring a coat, began to get wet.

'The funny thing is, I have at least five coats.'

When I asked why she hadn't brought one she just shrugged, then her eyes brightened.

'Do you think they sell them at the club shop?' *Jesus, here we go again.*

Emma is a magpie, a consumer. She loves 'stuff' and has managed on our football travels to find something to buy at pretty much every place we've been. Don't get me wrong, I absolutely have to get a programme at each match, but Emma can take it to another level. For example, we went to Wembley in May for England's last World Cup warm-up match to say goodbye to three Southampton players who would all be coming back from Brazil to sign for other teams. While I queued for a mushroom burger (only at Wembley) Emma came back from a stall laden with an England shirt, two flags and a bag with God knows what else inside. Even at Cowes Sports recently she spied a small club badge behind the bar and bought one.

Well what do you know; in the small club shop next to the main stand they had one large, three-quarter-length bench coat for sale, a snip at £60. The bloke behind the counter even said he could do it for £55 if she was interested. Sold. Meanwhile I picked up a combined team poster and fixture list and asked how much it was.

'Oh, they're free, help yourself.' Boom! Free treasure!

It was too late to stop in The Crown for a pint of Pride of Pendle so we wandered about a little before taking the steep steps by the pub down to the ground. On our first visit we had stood on the home terrace behind the goal, and it had been a good view, so we made for there again. We looked out on the compact little ground with genuine affection, at banners draped across the back of our stand celebrating the club's resurrection back in 1968, after a six-year vacuum, and beyond the open away terrace steep hills loomed, smothered in mist and cloud. It felt good to be back. The only negative was the appearance of Winstanley, the mascot, striding down the pitch toward our stand. (I think he is meant to be a bulldog, but his eyes are so wide open and his lower jaw so pronounced that he looks more like a seven foot hell dog on PCP.) Disturbingly he noticed Emma trying to take a picture of him and stopped and stared. I quickly checked for the exits just in case, then waved, hoping to diffuse the situation.

Thankfully Winstanley gave us the thumbs up, then continued on his mission to terrify the adults in the crowd. The kids didn't seem to be aware of his menace and innocently gathered round to have their pictures taken. One day they will stumble across those photos, and shudder.

Winstanley isn't even the scariest mascot I have ever seen. That honour goes to the Yeovil Town mascot, who I can best describe as a green, eight-foot-tall top-hat-wearing monster with a demonic grin. He should be in those public awareness films they make for children warning them against talking to strangers, or getting into strangers' cars. Terrifying.

As kick-off drew near the terraces began to fill up. Thankfully, Winstanley made himself scarce, leaving the pitch clear for the players. Tranmere had brought such a large following that the small, ramshackle stands lining the far touchline were allocated to them as well as the away terrace behind the far goal, meaning that to all intents and purposes the away fans occupied at least half the ground. It really brought home the gulf between Stanley and some of the other sides in League Two. Tranmere had been relegated along with Carlisle on the last day of last season and were a club used to playing higher up the football ladder in front of much larger crowds; players like Jason Koumas and Matt Hill having played at the highest level during their careers.

The match quickly fell into a predictable pattern of the club with a bigger playing budget and larger squad to choose from pressurising Stanley's goal and their 19-year-old keeper, Joe Lumley, who was halfway through a month long loan from Premier League Queens Park Rangers. Nineteen is an unbelievably young age for a goalkeeper to be playing first team football in the Football League, but for Stanley needs must, so Joe it was who had to concentrate on wave after wave of Tranmere attacks, while dodging a lone fire-cracker hurled by one of the away fans behind him and peering through a haze of blue smoke from flares that plume outwards from among the visiting masses.

It seemed obvious which way this game was going, but Stanley stuck at it and, in the traditional underdog fashion, on a rare attack towards us Kal Naismith was brought down in the box. Penalty to Stanley!

It was at this point I noticed a young boy, possibly ten or 11, stood a step behind me, craning his neck to see through the crowd. Emma and I had pitched up on one of the barriers behind the goal to get a good view, and looking back at this boy quietly trying to watch the game through a sea of adults reminded me a little bit of my first experiences of The Dell. I remembered how I would be manoeuvred by the supporters around me so as I could see the pitch a little better. It seemed good karma to keep that friendly tradition alive, so I asked him if he'd like to stand where I was. He nodded and thanked me, and was in position in time to see James Gray plant the penalty high into the Tranmere net. 1-0 Stanley!

'Thanks pal,' the boy's father said, smiling.

'Not a problem, though I'm in your way now,' I joked.

'No, you're alright.'

The goal seemed to settle Accrington's nerves a bit and they started to press more and more as the half wore on; the boy's father cheering for them as the team battled for a second. It turned out that both he and his son were Rochdale fans, with Stanley their occasional second team. They hadn't fancied the long drive down to Crawley to see them play, but kept up to date with their score via the father's phone. There were muted high fives all round as each of Rochdale's four goals went in.

The half ended with Accrington on top; with Piero Mingoia and Kal Naismith looking dangerous on the wings, and the defence, led by the impressive Tom Aldred, becoming more and more confident in the handling of Tranmere's attack. The boy's father observed that it was looking good, and he was right. Despite the tiny squad, Stanley were fighting harder, working more ferociously, bound together by their underdog status. Intoxicating stuff.

What happened right from the kick-off to the second half was a real body blow; Tranmere upped their passing game and their tempo, cutting open the Stanley defence with devastating accuracy. The one time Salisbury player Abdulai Bell-Baggie was left with two one-on-one opportunities against Joe Lumley right in front of us – 2-1 Tranmere, who then went on to control vast swathes of the half. Stanley shoulders on the terraces sagged as the realisation spread that six defeats in seven looked likely to become seven from eight. The boy's father leaned across:

'Who have Stanley got on the bench that can go up front? We can't get a shot in on goal.'

Damn it! I thought as I looked down at the team sheet on the back of the programme. I hadn't heard the subs being read out. I didn't know! I was going to be found out as a charlatan, a lightweight two-time visitor to the Crown Ground, and I wanted so dearly keep the feeling I had felt standing on the terraces: one of them. I remembered Josh Windass being a late sub with some real attacking flair at the Wimbledon game and I'd spotted him warming up for most of the second half. Against all the odds, just like the club I was watching, I went for it.

'Josh Windass?' I said.

He shook his head. 'No, he's powder-puff. Gets knocked off the ball too easily.'

Damn it! Bloody shitting bollocks! I'd been rumbled, my southern accent suddenly sounding very conspicuous.

It was then, as time was starting to run out, that two wonderful, Accrington Stanley-sized slices of magic occurred. The first, with about 15 minutes to go:

'Substitution for Stanley; Coming off number 24 Andy Proctor, coming on number eight Josh Windass.'

The boy's father shrugged and nodded, deferring to my 'greater knowledge' of the Stanley team. A look of hope spread across his face.

Slice of magic part two: Windass started to link up play between midfield and the attack, and Tranmere, who had begun to switch off, comfortable and content with their day's work, began to get edgy. And with that new energy Stanley pulled off one of those wonderful Hollywood underdog stories that happen ever so rarely in the real world. On 78 minutes, and as the pressure built, a ball got whipped into the box and there was James Gray to divert it into the bottom left hand corner. The place went nuts!

It was that unique Accrington Stanley factor, that never say die, all in it together, underdog against the world element, in action, right before our eyes. In a game that, in the cold financial light of day, they had no right to get anything from, here they were, yet again, proving the world wrong.

Then things got really special on 82 minutes, when Stanley pressed and pressed, launching ball after ball into the box, until one fell just out of the reach of the Tranmere goalie, who tried to catch it as he dived for it, but spilled it as he hit the floor into the path of Kal Naismith, who belted it into the net to make it 3-2.

Delirium on the terraces! They were in front! They were going to do it! A first win of the season!

Goalkeeper Joe Lumley went in for a 50-50 ball outside of the box, clearing it with inches to spare but getting clattered by the striker. He was a slight figure and was only on the team for a month, but he had clearly fallen under the Stanley spell and didn't hesitate to put his body on the line, getting back to his feet and retreating back into his goal. Defenders and midfielders hurled themselves in front of Tranmere shots. Forwards chased back 80 yards to try to prevent crosses into the Stanley box. The Stanley ultras to our right banged their drum and chanted and sang, roaring the team on, then went ballistic at the final whistle.

Players dropped to their knees, exhausted but elated, and the roof got lifted off this fantastic little ground as though they had just won the FA Cup, rather than move from bottom to fourth-from-bottom in Division Four.

Who am I kidding? Emma and I went mental too. How could we not when confronted with such an unbelievable attitude and love for something that would never amount to anything, if you were naive enough to compare it to a club like Manchester United just down the road.

To top things off, the PA announcer gave the attendance at 2,100 and something, a good 600 more than usual, which was a welcome boost to the coffers. And they hadn't even had the time to factor in Emma buying a £55 coat as well! All in all, it had been a fantastic day for the Stanley and as we filed out I couldn't help but pause to take one last look out at the pitch, the emptying stands, at where the lower league magic happens, and I hope, really hope, that it won't be too long before we get to come back and enjoy it again.

'The Crown?' I said to a beaming Emma. 'Pride of Pendle?' Like there was ever any doubt!

Like some glorious football symmetry, we spent the next few hours watching away fans, this time despondent, getting hammered in The Crown; the three closest to us swaying on their feet by the fruit machine and looking out the window as the Tranmere supporter's coaches went past. One of them pointed as they trundled away with a very drunk finger that seemed to suggest a little uncertainty as to whether or not they should have actually been on one of them.

Either way, after a time the Tranmere fans headed home and the pub thinned out, leaving the Stanley fans to revel in the league table as it popped up sporadically on the big screen TV in the corner. This revealed a second slice of coincidence for Emma and me, when the score from the

Carlisle v Wimbledon match came up.

'Jesus,' I muttered, as it dawned on me that our second trip up here had fallen on the same day as Mario, Fred Flintstone and that dinosaur had probably made their way up to the most remote point on the League Two map, as they had drunkenly boasted right before our eyes in this very pub back in May.

'JESUS!' I proclaimed, when I saw the score-line: four all, with Wimbledon scoring a 94th minute equaliser. That would have made any trip, no matter the distance, worthwhile. However it was hard not to pity whatever pub had let them in afterwards, especially if they were carrying a traffic cone. They probably wouldn't be able to even begin to imagine the carnage they had opened themselves up to.

The magic in League Two wasn't reserved for Stanley alone, and Wimbledon and their travelling fans had just discovered some far from home. I was pleased for them, but I was more pleased, or possibly just blissfully content, in a haze of amazing ale, to have cemented Accrington – unique, unbelievable Accrington – as my second spiritual football home.

7

20 September 2014. Northampton Town v Accrington Stanley
League Two

THIS MATCH WAS never meant to be a chapter in the book, coming so soon after our first Accrington visit of the season. Even though a lot had happened on and off the pitch in the fortnight since the Tranmere match it still didn't seem to warrant another chapter quite so soon, with any experiences here to be kept for the next planned Stanley trip in December. This day out was always meant to be a simple experience of enjoying a game of football, nothing more.

However, some games, indeed, some clubs, compel you to change your plans, and this remarkable game at Sixfields Stadium, Northampton, featuring the remarkable club that is Accrington Stanley, did just that.

It had been a crazy few weeks, both for Stanley and for our blog, *Dreams of Victoria Park,* that became the backbone of this book. A few days after the Tranmere win the manager, James Beattie, left the club, seemingly completely out of the blue and, to an outsider at least, at a time when the team had gained some serious momentum and was ready to push on into the season. Despite that upheaval, they won their next match 1-0 at home to Wimbledon before losing in midweek away to Oxford, with leading goal scorer James Gray getting sent off.

Then came the news that talismanic ex-boss John Coleman, who managed the club from 1999–2012, and who steered the club back into the Football League, was returning as the new manager. Just a standard ten days or so at Accrington Stanley!

While all this was going on, my blog post on the Tranmere game was published and something happened: people started to read it. There must be a million different blogs and magazines, newspapers and fanzines out there, about so many things, and because of all of that we had no expectations at all when we kicked off yet another one back in July. It was always meant to be a simple little thing with a simple message that pretty much acted as an online scrapbook of a season's travels, and if anyone happened to read it along the way, then that would be great. The idea of 1,000 people visiting it over the course of the season seemed a plausible one and one we seemed to be heading for that, with 40 or so hits for every chapter that went up. But then along came Accrington Stanley and, like with everything to do with this club, expectations and preconceptions were thrown out of the window.

Two hundred or so views in the first day, well in excess of 400 views within a week and some very kind comments later, it was clear that the chapter had struck a chord with some of the online fans of Accrington Stanley. It was amazing to receive that kind of attention and positivity, even though I remain adamant that all I did was write down our experiences which were generated by those same Stanley fans. I am a football romantic, I admit that, but in this instance the warmth of affection in the writing was simply a reflection of the warmth we received when we were there.

The response was humbling – it still is – and if nothing much ever comes from the blog, and now this book, then the kindness and friendship generated by the Stanley fans is more than enough to consider it a success.

Despite all of this, the plan for the Northampton trip was still just to enjoy the game and remember anything interesting that happened for possible inclusion in a Stanley entry in December. This was blown out of the water when, at around ten in the evening the night before the match, my phone rang.

'Hello, this is Mark Turner from Accrington Stanley Football Club, are you alright mate?'

It was Accrington Stanley. On the phone!

Football has thrown up plenty of gloriously surreal experiences in my 30-plus-years of watching the game, but this! The conversation was a bit of a blur, but the upshot of it was that the club wanted to thank me and Emma for the blog post by giving us a pair of tickets for the following day's match. Unbelievable is a word I have used an awful lot when describing Accrington Stanley, either in this book, on the blog, or to anyone who would listen. I see no reason to change now, as it is entirely appropriate. Unbelievable! What a wonderful gesture, and it is further evidence of the unique nature of the club. The two hour journey up to Northampton was a breeze.

Sixfields Stadium will always have happy memories for Emma and me, as we came up a number of times last season to watch a friend of ours, Dan Seaborne, play here for Coventry during their season long exile from The Ricoh Arena. How we came to be friends with Dan is another story entirely and one for a later chapter. For now, all that matters is that it was no hardship to find ourselves back here again, this time however searching for the away end ticket office where we picked up our tickets that had been left for us by Mark.

Emma wasn't feeling well and in truth probably shouldn't have come out, but when I sent her a text the night before about the free tickets and the phone conversation I knew she would make it to the game come hell or high water. With her tucked up inside the Stanley coat that she had bought at the Tranmere match we headed into the ground to see if a cup of tea and a pie might help her feel any better.

If the tea didn't help, then the friendly smiles and waves from the few Stanley fans already inside certainly did. A few had known we were coming up via Twitter and the like, and their kindness and warmth towards us as the team came out to warm up was yet another humbling experience in a fortnight littered with Stanley-sized humbling experiences.

One feller, a school teacher with a kind smile and a soft voice, and his mate, told us that they had planned to come down on the supporters coach, but had been told on Wednesday that it had been cancelled as only 16 seats had been taken. The majority that had booked onto it, he said, would be coming by minibus, but he didn't think there would be too many other away fans.

The problems of local, higher-league competition that Accrington faced in getting decent home attendances obviously applied with even starker effect on away attendances, where the lure of Manchester United and City, Burnley and Blackburn, and the host of other clubs nearby limiting the numbers that might travel. Add to that the time and money needed to come all the way down from Lancashire to countless Fourth Division matches at the other end of the country and you could fully appreciate the dedication that the smattering of souls that began to file into the away end possessed.

Our school teacher friend also informed us that they had been down to Northampton three or four times before and not once had they seen Stanley win, draw, or, in fact, even score a goal. The dedication of him, his friend and the other away fans was truly unfathomable, and far beyond impressive.

'I've only not been to two of the grounds in League Two,' he said. 'Portsmouth down your neck of the woods being one. We went down two seasons ago but it was called off at the last minute and James Beattie managed to sort us out with some tickets to see Southampton play Burnley instead.'

Despite Beattie having left their club and the frustration or resentment that would obviously cause, there was no denying that that was a very nice thing to do, and would only really be done by players and boardroom members who truly appreciated what their small band of supporters went through in the name of the club. I have no doubt that larger clubs do equally nice things for people, but it definitely feels more special coming from a club with precious little in the way of resources or money; these gestures made with a simple thanks and camaraderie, far from the eyes of the media.

As kick-off approached, the minibus finally arrived, swelling the away gate to over 50, and we looked on as the two home stands in use (one was being redeveloped), began to fill up ominously with nearly 5,000 home fans.

This is probably something the Stanley players and fans are very used to; this enormous imbalance of support and relative wealth that they have to face both home and away at nearly every game they play. But for someone watching Stanley away for the first time it really did hit home the seemingly impossible odds the club have to cope with, and as someone not used to it I couldn't help but wonder just how those 11 out on the pitch and the small band around us in the stand could ever possibly hope to survive, let alone compete, in an environment that is so heavily stacked against them such as this. The referee blew his whistle to start the game and both Stanley players and fans proceeded to show us just how they did it.

From the off, Northampton went at Accrington, probing their backline, surging down the wings to try and find their weak spot, exactly as Tranmere did a fortnight before. And just as in the Tranmere match, Stanley absorbed the pressure and looked to hit Northampton on the break, feeding the ball out to their two new teenage loan signings John O'Sullivan and Sean Maguire to see what they could do.

And, while the team tried to gain a foothold on the pitch, the cluster of mini-bus ultras did the same in the stands. For every Northampton chant aimed at the away end of 'Is anybody there,' the ultras sent back in a heartbeat 'We've got more stands than you'! Brilliant! It was a wonderful part of the football crowd experience, this chorus of humour that seemed to rise up organically, a group of individuals morphing into one very quick-witted mind.

As the sparring continued across the stands, something amazing began to happen on the pitch. Despite having a squad half the size of Northampton, judging by the team sheet on the back of the programme, Accrington started to press and the two new signings began to turn the Northampton defence inside out. From a Stanley corner their centre back Rob Atkinson planted a diving header past the Northampton Goalie. 1-0 Stanley!

Among the delirium I looked round and spotted our school teacher friend, who had seemed resigned before the match to the reality that 'we never score at Northampton', jumping around in pure joy, looking to the sky with a nod of thanks to the footballing gods, who very rarely come to your team's rescue but must be thanked nonetheless.

Four minutes later it was one all. Northampton's centre forward found some space and planted a header past young Joe Lumley. The 5,000 home fans erupted, making those in the away end feel very few in number for a moment. Or two minutes, to be specific.

Sometimes the very thing that can be perceived to be your weakness can turn into a moment of pure genius. That Stanley need to bolster their tiny playing squad with young, untried teenagers from other clubs could be seen as a disadvantage, especially if those players turn out to be not quite ready for first team football. However sometimes, just sometimes, a club like Stanley can put their faith in a couple of kids and have that faith repaid with some priceless performances. What happened next, I am sure, exceeded even new manager John Coleman's wildest dreams.

Straight from the kick-off Stanley attacked, a long kick out by young Joe Lumley finding the equally young John O'Sullivan who won the 50-50 tackle for the ball and proceeded to outrun the entire back four, round the keeper and shoot into an empty net! 2-1!

Behind us, the ultras went crazy; shirts were ripped off and hurled about and small sea of topless men danced around wildly. From one of them I heard:

'If we score again the pants are coming off!'

3-1!

This time it was the other new boy, Sean Maguire, causing Northampton all sorts of trouble, and from the resulting corner big Rob Atkinson did it again. I looked around nervously, half expecting trousers and pants to come flying over my head. I caught our man looking about him sheepishly, just in case anyone had remembered what he had promised; thankfully for him, me and everyone else they seemed to have forgotten, and he could continue to celebrate an unlikely half time score without having to break any obscenity laws!

Now, this was only my third Accrington match, the first two having ended in 3-2 victories, so being 3-1 up at half time wasn't such an outlandish notion to me. However, remembering years of watching Southampton play away, and going two years without even seeing a draw, let alone a win on the road, I fully recognised the wide-eyed disbelief among the Stanley faithful. Even for a team that has to produce little miracles every season in order to survive, this score-line against a team that won 5-1 at home the previous Tuesday was more than they had ever dared hope.

Amazingly, things didn't get any more believable in the second half. Northampton kept attacking and Stanley kept defending, trying to feed

O'Sullivan, Maguire and their third youngster up front, Marcus Carver, for the occasional break away to relieve the pressure. It was on one of those breakaways that the day truly turned surreal. In the first half Stanley were attacking the far end, so all three goals were seen from a distance and these Stanley fans deserved to see a goal up close and personal.

Accrington always looked dangerous on the break, but as O'Sullivan set off after a ball, pretty much the only Stanley player in Northampton's half; this one didn't look to pose any real threat. He took a look up to see the situation, a sea of claret Northampton shirts, brought the ball under control out wide, then, realising he had nothing to lose, he drove at the defence, dropping his shoulder, feigning a shot and, running into the box he paused, picked his spot and lashed it into the net. There is that word again: Unbelievable!

How does a team with no victories, in fact no draws on the road this season, find themselves 4-1 up away at one of the form sides in the league? Were it any other team it could possibly be attributed to luck, or maybe to a poor performance by the home side. But I had seen enough of Stanley by this point to know when that unique nature, that against-all-the-odds attitude, was in full swing. Is it something that could be sustained every game, with a tiny squad, for a whole season? Probably not. But when it works, well, it really does work.

And when Northampton pulled a goal back, what did Stanley do? They scored a fifth! Sean Maguire guided a clever solo effort into the bottom right hand corner to top off an outstanding debut. At that point Northampton threw on two large substitutes and launched everything they had at Stanley. Just like against Tranmere, the Stanley players ran themselves into the ground trying to stop crosses into the box, throwing their bodies in the way of goal-bound shots, and despite Northampton scoring another two goals right at the death, the day was Stanley's, as were the points. For the first time in my life, after over 30 years of going to football matches, I was applauding a team off the pitch having won 5-4!

As the fans filed out into the night, we shook hands and said farewell to our friends that we had met, safe in the knowledge that their long drive back home would be made with a smile on their faces, having been part of something quite remarkable; something that, despite the 5-4 score-line, would only be worthy of a couple of column inches in the mainstream newspapers the following day. But those of us who were there, we knew differently. Whether the minibus ultras ever found their shirts again, or whether they had to go all the way home topless I guess we will never know. But one thing I do know is that a visit to see Accrington Stanley play is most definitely worth the effort.

8

11 October 2014. Aldershot Town v Bristol Rovers
Conference Premier

GOING TO A match alone has never been a problem for me. For some, watching football is embedded in a shared experience; with friends, with your father or grandfather, and the thought of going without that faithful band of brothers or sisters, without that social element, is a hard one to reconcile.

I once heard of a man who went with his best friend. They had season tickets together for decades, until finally his friend passed away. He never went again. He just couldn't go without his friend. I can appreciate his thinking; when my grandfather became too ill to go and see Salisbury play I really struggled to go by myself. The feeling that a large part of the experience was missing was exacerbated by the club having moved from Victoria Park to a new ground which held no real memories for either of us.

Had they stayed at the little ramshackle ground that I basically grew up in, I think I would have gone more, even without Grandad. I can't help but feel that the welcoming embrace of childhood memories drifting about the place would have been a comfort; helping to keep Grandad well and far away from the clutches of dementia; much as thinking about those days now does for me.

I guess I never truly feel alone when I go to a match by myself anyway, as I can't help but remember those that took me when I was young and helped get me hooked. While many around me look on despairingly at the thought of a trip to Hartlepool on a cold Tuesday night in February, I can imagine our family friend Colin Worthington and my grandfather nodding quietly in approval from somewhere out there; kindred spirits that understand.

Going on your own can be, in fact, quite a liberating experience, especially if you are quite happy in your own company like I am. You can just wander around and observe the idiosyncrasies of a club, a stadium and the fans that populate it virtually unnoticed, just like in one of those old memories. I used to use solitary trips to football matches as a form of therapy after Dad took his own life; the space and quiet of being alone, the anonymity of not knowing anyone gave me time to breath, to think, to see, in a familiar, safe environment. But these days these lone trips and the quiet cover they afford really allow me to get a feel for a place, especially at such an old venue as full of character as Aldershot Town's The Recreation Ground.

I had been to see Aldershot play once before, also on my own, during a busy Christmas and New Year period a few years ago. That match, v Hereford United, had been a Fourth Division match. Three and a half years later, neither club remains in the Football League; Aldershot, a community-run club, suffered administration and relegation a year after Hereford went down, though at least in the case of Aldershot they have since managed to settle down and are now on a sound footing, looking up rather than down.

For Hereford, relegation was only the beginning of their troubles; like every lower league/non-league club, falling attendances, in part due to the recession, maybe partly to do with shiny satellite packages and the saturation of Premier League and Champions League matches on the television, caused Hereford havoc. Unsustainable playing budgets and financial miss-management soon had them tumbling toward relegation once more.

The hard-line stance taken by the football conference about financial rule-breaking saw them, along with Salisbury, ejected from the conference in the summer and relegated two divisions into the Southern Premier League, where they played surrounded by fan protests over ground ownership and suspicion about those who controlled the club. Worse was to follow when the club folded entirely, their record expunged, though at least the fan-run phoenix club that emerged in the wake of it all is something for them to hold on to.

It was very sad, especially after having spent a cold January afternoon beneath skies threatening snow in the away end at Aldershot, in the company of a number of long-suffering and well-travelled Hereford old-timers, seeing them go through the emotion of watching their team play. For whatever reason, following Hereford home and away, trekking all across the country on a Saturday after them had become their life. I couldn't help but feel sad that this outlet for them was left clinging on for dear life in the Southern League amidst continued stadium ownership disputes and the looming financial woe that finally did for their club. It was, to quite a number of those I stood with that cold afternoon, their lives, and I couldn't help but hope that the new phoenix club became all that it needs to be for them.

I don't know why I always used to go in the away end at matches where I was the neutral; possibly because it can be quite an adventure in itself. At the Recreation ground the away turnstile is, or at least was back, in 2011, located at the end of a densely wooded park, with small paths winding their way between the trunks of gnarled old elm trees, the canopy of branches and heavy snow cloud above casting thick gloomy shadows about them, making it seem more like the setting of a ghost story than a football match.

It reminded me of Darlington's now long gone Feethams ground, where the away end could only be reached by weaving through a string of narrow alleys between the fenced off back yards of tightly bunched terraced houses. Neither entrance felt much like the beginning of a day out at the football. With the away end syndrome long since cured, the home end entrance, once past the turnstile, opened out beneath a sunny sky onto a small stretch of gardens. Tall trees and neatly planted shrubs lined a stretch of grass with some picnic tables dotted about, where at half time small children would have a kick about. Is this the only professional football club to have a garden inside its gates? It definitely beats a soulless concourse.

From the very off this felt like a club deeply rooted in the local community; from the kids playing on the grass to the small memorial garden for supporters who had passed away, The Recreation Ground felt, much like a lot of lower league grounds, to have those that frequent it ingrained deep within its buildings and terraces, its programme shop and tea hut.

This is what makes smaller, older football grounds so very special to visit, because it is easier to see that hopeless love affair between a person and a football club. You can sense the band of volunteers who helped to touch up the paint on the barriers on the banks of terracing during the close season, who tidied up the main stand, who forever keep this old ground vibrant despite its years. It feels like so many other lower league or non-league grounds. It feels right, and good.

The Rec has been around for a long time. The old-school floodlights perched on towering pylons at each corner of the ground and its aging stands attest to that. They must have seen some amazing football matches back during the Second World War when Aldershot could call on the many great players of the time, who had been conscripted and were stationed in the town, to guest for them in the Wartime League.

This game promised to be a good one too, with Bristol Rovers as the visitors, who were coping with the opening few months of their first ever season outside the Football League quite well, starting the day in the play-off positions.

No-one expected a club the size of Bristol Rovers, with the significant support that they had, to have been in any real danger of relegation in the last season and in fact the only day they were one of the bottom two teams in the Fourth Division just so happened to be the only day that it really mattered: the last day.

To the disbelief of all, Rovers were duly relegated out of the Football League and had to start thinking about life playing Eastleigh and Alfreton, when only five seasons earlier I had witnessed them score a last minute screamer at St Mary's to beat Southampton 3-2 in front of a crowd of 20,000.

On the Saints team that day were Adam Lallana, Rickie Lambert and Morgan Schneiderlin, all of whom progressed up the leagues with the Saints to become Premier League players while their victors that night in September slid downwards, and as Rovers began to deal with life in the conference, those three players headed off to Brazil to play for their nations at the World Cup. It's quite breath-taking how fortunes can change and teams so close in ability one year can seem a world away just a few short seasons later.

But all was not doom and gloom with Rovers, as a new talisman, or, more specifically, a feature of said talisman began to emerge and lead them back toward the light.

I knew Stuart Sinclair from his playing days at Salisbury, where he would pick up man of the match and player of the season awards with his infectious and heroic midfield displays. Rovers snapped him up after the demise of Salisbury in the summer and anyone who had seen him play knew that he would be a hit for them. What I didn't know at the time however, was that his beard, which is as impressive as his playing style, had a personality all of its own.

This season I have been following the mini phenomenon that is 'Sinclair's Beard' on Twitter, following its forewarnings of doom to Rovers' next opponents, celebrating the resultant three points, basking in the self-proclaimed title of 'best beard in football' (it is an amazing beard, which describes itself as '826 strands of golden fibre'!), and I was looking forward to seeing it in full flow.

But as with all my best laid plans, I felt myself slump into the crush barrier on the North stand terrace when the teams were read out; No Sinclair, no beard. Not even on the bench. Its Tweets leading up to the match had been their usual self-assured and confident style, warning Aldershot that 'the beard' was coming for them and three points. Maybe there had been some last minute horrendous barbers' incident? Had he met someone called Delilah? I supposed that was for Twitter to reveal in the fullness of time.

Disappointment absorbed, I flicked through the programme as the growing crowd waited for the teams. A quick look at the Conference league table revealed an institution that was more a halfway house than anything else, populated by teams on the up, teams rebuilding and teams in real trouble.

The conference has been and probably always will be, in reality, a good thing for clubs relegated out of the Football League. The supposed trap door into obscurity is actually a very competitive league that offers crisis clubs the chance to rebuild and to eradicate the often crippling financial bill left by boardroom mismanagement. The Conference's stance on financial stability is pretty harsh when your team is involved (Salisbury have been forcibly removed from the league twice in four years) but you can't help but appreciate that it has generally been good for clubs in the long run.

Teams that have tumbled out of the Football League suddenly find themselves up against well-run non-league sides who have moved up through the football pyramid and are often in a far better position than themselves. For a year or two they have the chance to go one of two ways; to either sort themselves out, lick their wounds and build on a more sustainable level for the future, or to find the heart of their club torn out by financial blundering, with consolidation in the conference as far a fanciful dream as staying in the Football League was.

It is a harsh lesson for proud old clubs like Stockport County and Hereford United, but one that hopefully, eventually, will have them set for a brighter future. It has worked for many of the clubs in the conference and teams that have tumbled just as far such as Halifax and Chester can be beacons to what can lie ahead.

Rarely, very rarely, things can go spectacularly wrong, as with the sad demise of Darlington, for whom I will always have a soft spot due to two enjoyable trips up to their old Feethams ground with a Brighton buddy of mine in the late '90s. But even here there is a little hope, with a reformed club climbing slowly upwards from the very bottom of the football pyramid.

Ultimately, the teams that have moved up from the non-league into the Football League have mostly remained well-run and successful. They remember the schooling the conference gave them and sometimes use it to move up through the leagues even further.

This match was a full on blood and thunder encounter between two sides desperately fighting for points to get them back to where they felt they belonged: the play-off spots and, beyond that, the promised land. It was a fast paced, crunching, honest match that was captivating to watch.

Everywhere I looked on the pitch there was a story, with players on both sides reflecting the melting pot of experience that is the football conference. For Rovers, there was Neal Trotman at centre back, who played for Southampton against Rovers in that 3-2 match in front of 20,000 supporters a few years ago. Out on the wing they had Andy Monkhouse, who was a constant thorn in the Saints side when he played for Hartlepool against them; four games over two seasons and he was electric in all four, outshining Lallana etc. He had looked to be the one that would go far. But fate, luck, misfortune, or a combination of those, along with Football League clubs' ever shrinking squads due to financial belt tightening, had found them both in the conference on a sunny, blustery October afternoon, hopefully enjoying playing in an entertaining game in front of a crowd of just under 4,000.

In contrast to Monkhouse's experiences, his opposite number in the Aldershot team, Tom Derry, was an example of how clubs at this level had to be very careful in keeping themselves the right side of the financial line. Where Monkhouse had years of Football League experience, Derry didn't even have a contract. The statistics page in the programme had this game down as Derry's 11th of the season and his third start in a row. But next to his name in bold capitals was: NC, and a translation at the foot of the page revealed his non contract status. The fact that he was playing, effectively for free, I imagined, was a testament to his character and his desire to play, as well as to the club's resolve to not spend money that they didn't have.

Derry was lively down the wing in the first half, going in for 50-50 challenges as if he was safe within a decently salaried four year contract. Based on his performance one would hope he would be able to find one somewhere, sooner rather than later, as he was playing a real part in what was breathless stuff.

The game swung back and forth from one end to the other; a weak looking penalty to Aldershot giving them the lead, then a deflected Andy Monkhouse shot looped over the Town keeper in front of the 1,400 travelling gasheads to make things even at half time.

In the second half, an equally weak looking penalty for Rovers gave them the lead, which stirred from the Aldershot bench something completely unexpected but most welcome; no-one had told me that they too had their own wonder-beard!

Mark Molesley, with a resplendent beard of comparable size, girth and power to Sinclair's stepped on to the pitch, replacing young Tom Derry, and began bossing the game. It was one of his (the beard's?) surging runs that provoked a desperate lunge from a Rovers player just outside the box, and from the free kick Jordan Roberts curled a cracking shot into the top left hand corner to equalise, much to the delight of the Town ultras behind that goal.

It was, in truth, a game that neither side deserved to lose. At the final whistle a two all draw seemed fair enough, despite the final ten minutes involving a red card (Roberts of Town), multiple shots against the bar and last-ditch saves. Everything one could hope for.

It had been a great game to watch and as impressive an advertisement for life in the conference as I'd grown accustomed seeing to while watching Salisbury. The only regret I felt as the crowd filed out onto the streets, kids having a kick about in the garden beneath a looming floodlight tower, was that the heavyweight battle between beard Molesley and beard Sinclair didn't materialise, because that would have been something to behold.

The next time I go on Twitter, I am definitely checking to see if Molesley's Beard is on it, giving trash talk to Sinclair's. The rematch is in March and God only knows how much bigger both will have got by then...

9

16 October 2014. Manchester City Women v Arsenal Women Women's Super League Cup Final

I WAS ON the road again with Jen and Tash to further explore the exciting world of women's football and hopefully, hopefully, fulfil that ambition of mine: to finally see Arsenal and England legend Kelly Smith play.

Up until this point I had only ever been to see Women's International matches, so this would be my first experience of club football at the elite level of the women's game. I'd seen Winchester City Flyers play quite a few times in the Hampshire League when my old mate Jamie was coaching them, but, largely due to there being no teams anywhere near Southampton in the current set-up, this would be my first taste of the Women's Super League.

An industrial estate in Wycombe on a wet, blustery night in October might not seem like everyone's idea of a good night out, but in Tash and Jen I recognise that glorious, infectious belief that it is in fact everyone else who is wrong. Adams Park, home of Wycombe Wanderers FC, was most definitely the only place to be, despite the fact that none of us could get off work very early which meant driving through rush hour traffic the entire way.

I spent the days leading up to the WSL Cup final nervously monitoring Twitter posts and bulletins from the Arsenal website, checking that there had been no hamstring tear for Kelly Smith, no niggling injury such as the one that had prevented me from seeing her play on both previous occasions I had tried.

On the evening before the game, a tweet from Kelly announced that the last training session had gone well and she was fit and ready to go, which left me feeling at best cautiously optimistic. *Was it finally going to happen?*

I will argue with anyone over this: Kelly Smith is one of the best players England has ever produced, regardless of gender. Watching her on TV was spellbinding, her vision and movement, her skill is simply at another level to all those around her. Seeing her in action, in person, has been a goal of mine ever since I started watching the women's game a number of years ago, which is why Tash looked at me very strangely as I stopped and stared intently at a TV camera pitch-side as we walked past, having spotted a team sheet taped on it. After a moment or two of squinting at it, my shoulders sagged and I shrugged.

She's wasn't playing.

'She might be on the bench,' Tash offered, trying to comfort me.

Thankfully, she was right. The announcer confirmed as we found our seats that she was indeed one of the substitutes. *That's something, at least.*

In the meantime there was plenty to keep us occupied. We took part in a spot of footballer eye-spy as Faye White (there was no swearing and shouting this time) and Sue Smith, both former England internationals, mingled with any fan who wanted to stop by and say hello. Kim Little, the Scottish international, and England centre forward Ellen White, who was out injured, wandered about with presenter Helen Skelton, chatting to whoever while they waited to start a live feed for BT Sport, who were airing the match. Like a schoolboy proud of getting good marks, I inwardly beamed at every high five I received from Tash for spotting another player. My proudest moment was spotting Fran Kirby, who came on for England against Wales in Cardiff back in September, for which I received a massive high five. Get in!

I've said it before, but it is worth repeating, that this level of interaction, where schoolchildren and fans can talk to their heroines, reminds me of a time when I was a boy, when all of football was more like that, without the vast financial gulf that now separates the players from the terraces. The women's game has got a glorious advantage over the men's at this elite level, in that they have that harmony between fan and player, that genuine feeling of everyone together – no-one being more important than anyone else. There is a wonderful balance and understanding between supporters and players, in that it genuinely feels like they are one and the same.

It is a feeling that has been obliterated at the top levels of the men's game by the excesses of ludicrous wages and the unbelievable sums of money clubs generate and juggle. There is an inevitability, I suppose, that those with and those without, over time, drift apart in their understanding of one another. I have every faith that the women's game won't allow this to happen, even if more money comes into the sport. These links are too important to lose, no matter what. Lower league and non-league clubs in the men's game understand that and the women's game clearly does. Possibly having to cope with the ludicrous stigma that somehow the women's sport is inferior to the male version helps to bind player, supporter and club together.

Amongst all the player spotting and musing on how the women's game had got things just right, I couldn't help but notice a sinister turn of events: there appeared to be some kind of mascot invasion forming.

It was as though they didn't want you to notice all at once, so they wandered about in dribs and drabs. *But I have your number, mascots. I see you.*

First there was Gunnersaurus, the seven foot wobbly headed Arsenal mascot. Fair enough, they were playing, he's allowed. There was also a weird balloon-headed Man City mascot; again, it was their day so that's fine. But then I spotted another mascot; a nondescript one that seemed not to be representing anything in particular. And then, on the far side of the pitch, I saw another TWO mascots looming.

I didn't say anything to Tash and Jen, there was no point in concerning them unduly, after all, but I did check for the nearest exits just in case it ramped up a few gears. I kept an eye on the mascots' whereabouts, promising myself that I would give them a thorough ocular pat-down should they get too close.

Maybe it's just fans dressing up? Yes, let's say it is that, for the time-being.

Thankfully, the distraction of the teams coming out calmed me down a little and the focus shifted to the match that Arsenal dominated from the off, with Jordan Nobbs in midfield completely running the show, setting up attacks and snuffing out any chance Jill Scott and the lively Isobel Christiansen had of moving the ball up to Toni Duggan, who looked very isolated as the lone City striker.

As the pressure built, Danielle Carter had a couple of great opportunities for Arsenal to take the lead; one point-blank save by City's keeper Karen Bardsley defied belief and for the first half hour it looked inevitable – if Arsenal could convert their possession into more goal scoring opportunities then surely the first goal couldn't be that far away.

But slowly, slowly, City started to grow into the game and by half time, though not having created anything significant, they had started to peg Arsenal back. They needed that something special, that creative flair to open up the game.

Kelly Smith? Surely, I thought as the players headed off at the break; Tash and Jen nipping out for tea and Mars bars while I guarded the seats and monitored the mascot situation.

The moment finally arrived, 15 minutes or so into the second half, when Kelly Smith stripped off her track-suit and stepped up to the touchline. Sadly, although my dream of her seeing her play was about to become reality it was, in truth, probably 15 minutes too late.

As she replaced Japanese World Cup winner Shinobu Ohno, the tide of the game had completely changed; City had taken control, despite

Jordan Nobbs' and the impressive Leah Williamson's best efforts they could not halt the growing dominance of the City midfield, with Toni Duggan seeing a lot more of the ball up front. Even so, it was enough to lift my spirits, and my tacit support of Arsenal – given that Jen and Tash supported them, and that Grandad's old mate Cyril Smith used to play for them during the war – stepped up another gear entirely.

Kelly's play wasn't the pure poetry that I had seen on the TV over the years, stifled somewhat by the lack of space and time in midfield, but where I was hoping for fully formed poems, we did at least get the odd moment of brilliance, the odd stanza or rhyming couplet with the ball at her feet. Even with no space to work in, with her first touch she would invariably create some, and look for a pass that so few in the game world can see instinctively. Even these snippets alone were worth the journey; just to see that skill, that motion, right before my eyes. But it wasn't enough to prevent City from taking the lead; Isobel Christiansen scored a great header from a whipped in cross and, with time running out, City looked likely to score again as Steph Houghton hit the bar with a free kick.

The only bright spot for the Arsenal faithful was a whipped Kelly Smith free-kick that nearly crept in and, for me and Tash, the brief departure of Jen's sanity when she started laughing uncontrollably at the score-board that she hadn't noticed in the first half. This scoreboard could only display the first three letters of each team, so it read MAN 1 then beneath it ARS 0.

'MAN ARS,' she kept exclaiming. 'MAN ARS. It says MAN ARS! I'm taking a picture of that!'

That kept her quiet for a time until she proclaimed, still laughing:

'I'm going to get another picture of it, but when it reads 69 seconds on the clock above it. That'll be brilliant!'

Tash and I sat quietly and said nothing, letting it dawn on the chuckling Jen that there is no such thing as the 69th second in a minute, although the eventual realisation did nothing to calm her down.

After four frantic minutes of extra time, where Arsenal threw their goalie forward for a couple of corners, the ref blew his whistle and Manchester City, in their first season in the Women's Super League, had won the League Cup. Very sportingly, Tash and Jen wanted to stay on to watch City lift the trophy, which we duly did before we started to make our way out of the ground.

A few moments earlier, Kelly Smith had disappeared down the tunnel, so it seemed safe to assume that the night was drawing to a close, but as we walked past the tunnel to head out, Kelly virtually bumped into me as she emerged again. We got out of each other's way as respectfully as we could and I turned to look back at Tash and Jen behind me, wide-eyed, open mouthed, Jen repeating:

'Kelly Smith just touched you! She touched you!'

Now that would have been more than enough for me; to see her play, to have my coat brushed by hers, but things didn't end there.

Much to their credit, the Arsenal team had stayed out on the pitch after the trophy ceremony and were talking to fans lined up along the advertising hoardings. And there, at the end of the line, was Kelly Smith.

'Right,' Tash said, virtually dragging me by the arm. 'This is just too good an opportunity. Give me your programme.'

Immediately my mind rushed back over 30 years, to an open day at The Dell, where a ten-year-old me had enjoyed a tour of the ground and a chance to get the player's autographs. But then, as I sat in the lower tier of the west stand looking up at the pitch, it was announced that children could come onto the ground to take part in a training session put on by the club's reserve team coaches.

I froze, absolutely paralysed by fear; the opportunity to play on The Dell pitch too big to comprehend. Looking back, I recognise what an amazing thing that would have been, what an opportunity. But I was just too scared to take it, I think afraid that I would mess up somehow. I just couldn't find a way to stand up and climb those steps. Mum sat patiently by my side for what seemed to me like hours, waiting to see if I'd go up and play. It wasn't until finally, mercifully, the last session had been announced full, that I felt a sense of relief and started to enjoy myself again.

It was at that point, at that young age, that I knew I would never be a professional footballer. I was just too shy, too afraid of doing the one thing I loved doing more than anything else wrong. My quiet, reserved nature, my childhood spent as a wall-flower, stopped me from trying to be what I thought I always wanted to be.

Kelly Smith's career had been beset by insecurities and doubt; from her book I felt a real similarity in temperament between me and her, only she had managed to find solace out on the pitch, in the glare, something I could never have done. But the sympathy and empathy I felt in reading her autobiography had brought me close to tears on numerous occasions.

And now, 30 years on, it felt like my ten-year-old self was being dragged along by my adopted present-day pushy mum in Tash to meet her, something I will always be grateful to her for, because, much like the open day at The Dell, I would never have had the courage to do it on my own.

In truth it wasn't so much meeting, more looking on as she signed my programme, but then Tash asked if we could have a photo together, and as she put her arms around us both for Jen to take the photo I felt a flush of emotion that is almost indescribable; of my child self at the open day all those years ago, with autograph book in hand and awe etched across my face at meeting another football hero, and my adult self at Adams Park, Wycombe, colliding again and existing in a moment, in the present. And with Kelly Smith! The second it was over I meekly thanked her, and she smiled, and moved on to the next set of fans.

I haven't even mentioned what class, what humility that was of the Arsenal players, of Kelly Smith, to stay out and do that for their fans after losing a major cup final. It is a symbol of everything that is right with the women's game.

I tried to appear as cool as I could, not wanting to freak out too much in front of Tash and Jen, but inside I was marvelling in one of the most lovely, pure and honest moments I had ever experienced through football. On the journey home, I kept feeling for the programme in my pocket, just to make sure it was still there. And, like my ten year-old-self would have done, I went to bed with it by my side, but I didn't sleep, just like ten-year-old me would also have done. I just basked in the warm pool of happiness that this simple little sport of ours can sometimes offer us.

And the mascots kept to themselves as well. A perfect day!

10

25 October 2014. Partick Thistle v St Johnstone
Scottish Premier League

IF THIS HAD been any other flight, going to any other destination, for any other reason, then I am certain that Emma would not have gotten on board, given the look of absolute terror on her face. It was clear she was not a happy flyer.

For me, flying is just another means of getting from one place to another. However, this isn't my story, it's Emma's and her ability to overcome – with the help of medication – that fear, illustrates how important this trip to Glasgow was to her. It was so much more than just going to a football match; it was another marker on the long road to a personal recovery and it celebrated all the people, near and far, who have helped her to put herself back together after an indescribable trauma.

Every other chapter in this book has been hand-picked by me, with Emma sometimes tagging along. But this trip is all hers and this chapter details how someone with absolutely no interest in football, through wickedly bitter twists of fate, found it to be a life-line through some of the most appalling moments of her life, moments I really struggle to think about in any detail, even now, more than three years on.

But for this chapter to make any sense then we must tell Emma's story, in order to work out just how we came to find ourselves in what feels like one of the coldest places on earth: Firhill Park, Glasgow, home of Partick Thistle FC. It is a story far stranger than fiction, I think, however all of it is true, no matter how much I wish it weren't.

In early September 2011, Emma, while out celebrating a friend's birthday, fell victim to a horrific opportunistic assault. I still can't really attach the word that describes this assault to her name. It is just too much to bear. But suffice it to say that this chapter is dedicated (along with the work of Southampton police and another person who we shall get to soon) to the wonderful people of an organisation called 'Southampton Rape Crisis', who were her glue in the weeks and months after, as well as before, during and after an equally traumatic court case that resulted in a six year prison sentence for the offender.

Her assault came hours after another awful incident the same evening, at the same venue as Emma and her friend were in. Southampton defender Dan Seaborne, out for a couple of drinks with a friend, was assaulted and left unconscious; with his life, let alone his career, in the balance. It was all over the local news, and Southampton fans prayed for him just to wake up; to hell with the playing football.

In shock, Emma felt unable to talk about what had happened to her that night straight away, but through constantly asking me, whom she knew to be a big Saints fan, about how Dan was doing she very slowly found the courage to tell me what had happened to her the night that Dan's life changed forever, finally confiding in a couple of friends who helped her to contact the police.

From that point on, there was Dan, who was, slowly, and with great dignity, trying to re-piece his life and career back together as well. He was an inspiration, which supported her through harrowing but necessary police interviews with an amazing officer called Anton, through the offender being charged, through the constant and life-saving counselling and support given by an equally amazing woman at Southampton Rape Crisis called Tracey, through the intimidation by colleagues and friends of the offender, then finally leading up to and during the brutally punishing court case itself. Their unwanted connection to that dark day helped inspire Emma to hang on just a bit longer; if Dan could get out of hospital, recover, get back into light training, then maybe she could do something similar with her own life, no matter how impossible that seemed.

Through some cosmic serendipity, after a long, torturous winter and spring, the Saturday before Emma's trial was due to begin in the summer of 2012 just so happened to be Dan's comeback match for Southampton at St Mary's Stadium. I really wasn't sure that a 30,000-seater stadium would be the best place for her, given that she had pretty much become paralysed with fear around people she didn't know, and was almost housebound. She was too scared to be out on her own; an incident in a supermarket one day typifies her nightmarish existence. She was physically sick when a man she didn't know accidentally brushed past her as he moved along the aisle.

But Emma wanted to go; there would be a fun-fair at the match and we were taking my two nephews who could cheer anyone up, or at least take your mind off things with their infectious love of fun and mischief, so, worried though I was, we went.

And there, at St Mary's Stadium, something unexpected began to happen. After months of feeling scared everywhere and of everything, she seemed to relax, to take comfort from the close-knit, friendly atmosphere in the stands; the smell of the boys' hot-dogs; the sounds of the fun-fair outside. It clearly seemed to her like a safe place, where before there had been none. And it must have felt an important place, a significant place, a place for a little hope, when, for the first time since the Saturday before that awful day, Dan Seaborne stepped out in a Saints shirt once more.

If only you could have seen her face, watching him play, a man who could have lost his life that terrible night, back to doing what he was meant to do. I can only imagine the kind of courage and comfort that seeing someone who had been as broken as you finally reclaiming a little of what had been lost could bring to someone about to face the horror of having to relive her ordeal once more in court.

That this had been his first game back, of all days, ahead of the week that was to come, whether it was karma, fate, or just luck, it was very welcome.

From that day on Emma's love for football grew, helped by our dear friend Effie, who had sat waiting for her in a safe room so that she had a friendly face between each of her sessions in court, being a passionate Saints fan as well. We went to as many Saints games as we could, revelling in the happiness and the freedom that Emma seemed to feel whilst at the stadium, even if Dan wasn't making it into the team.

But then, for a League Cup game in late September, word on the street was that he would start. Emma, Effie and I set off early to the ground, where Emma bought a Saints shirt with Dan's name and number on it, and we waited in the car park for the players to arrive. Slowly, one by one, they began to appear, until finally, finally Dan turned up.

With Emma unable to talk, I asked if he could sign her shirt and maybe have a photo with her. Like the legend he is, he did, though he was a little shocked to see a shirt with his name on the back! The whole thing was over in seconds, but she didn't stop smiling for a month. It marked the end of the beginning of her love affair with football.

Dan's positive attitude and his kindness that night; the warmth of the Saints fans; the welcoming atmosphere at St Mary's, these things were something of a life-saver and it really isn't possible to thank them all enough.

However, I did try.

That League Cup match was one of the last times Dan played for Saints; his almost year-long recovery coinciding with the team remaining in the top two of the Championship for the entire season and getting promoted to the Premier League at the first time of asking. Unfortunately Dan, after what had been a great season getting promoted out of League One, then a solid first five matches in that Championship promotion season, found himself a year behind everyone else in a Premier League squad that couldn't afford to wait for him to catch up. The 'what might have been' if that awful day hadn't occurred, and the sad reality that the incident had probably robbed him his chance to prove himself at the highest level, was just one of the many tragedies surrounding it all.

To continue his rehabilitation back to full match fitness, he went out on loan to Charlton, and that Christmas I thought I would write to him, to thank him for being an unknowing inspiration to Emma through their unhappy connection. I wasn't expecting anything from it. It just felt like something that I needed to do.

It had been good therapy to write to the hospital where they had taken Dad after he took his own life, to thank the many nameless doctors and nurses who had tried to help him, then me, my sister and our mum. It didn't matter that it was a good few years later, that all I could remember were sympathetic faces, that I had no idea who or where they were, it just felt good to write to them, and it felt good to write a letter addressed quite vaguely to a big football club for the attention of Dan. It helped Emma too; at least, it cheered her up a little one day when she was feeling particularly down.

I printed her off a copy and gave it to her when she was having a bad day at work, not hearing my phone ringing in my pocket. It was only an hour or so later I noticed I had a voicemail message. I nearly fell off my seat when I heard Dan's voice saying he'd received the letter and asking if he could meet up with us! I had to keep playing the message to Emma over and over again, as she just couldn't seem to believe it. That positive things could still happen, and they could happen to her.

One dark evening in January we met up for a cup of tea and a chat at a local restaurant. From the off it didn't feel like a simple obligation, like a signing session or something like that; he genuinely cared about this connection with Emma and he clearly wanted to make sure she was doing alright. How he could tell if she was is another matter, as she was so awestruck that he had taken an interest in her that she barely said a word! Luckily I was on hand to talk absolute nonsense for the half hour or so that we sat there.

He asked if she was ok and we asked him the same question. He asked if she found counselling helpful, which was maybe a small sign that it was just as hard for a professional footballer to get over great trauma as it is for the rest of us.

Either way, he was playing again, albeit not in the Premier League. By then he was on loan at League One Bournemouth and he told us if we ever wanted to come down for a match he'd sort us out tickets, which he did on the couple of occasions that we could.

Dan and Emma kept in touch via text, checking in with each other every now and then, and when things didn't work out at his next club,

Yeovil, he went out on loan to Coventry and sorted us out tickets there too, seeming to appreciate our support wherever he went just as much as Emma appreciated his concern for her.

So when I told her in the summer that he had moved to Partick Thistle, she nodded and asked where that was...

Glasgow was freezing; chill gale-force winds and a five day long rain storm left over from an Atlantic hurricane meant that this late October weekend felt ten degrees or so colder than home. Torrential horizontal rain stung our faces, and made the fact that Dan had been sent off the weekend before, meaning that he was suspended for the match we had picked out and booked flights for a couple of months ago, smart a little more.

Never mind, though, playing or not it would just be good to say hi again and see how he was doing. Despite being suspended, he would be busy on match day as part of a fan-zone meet and greet, so we arranged to meet him the following morning and settled into Firhill for the match against St Johnstone.

Firhill stadium is perched on one of Glasgow's higher points, which means two things. One, it is a good place to look out on the skyline of menacing Gothic steeples – seeming very much at home among the bruised storm cloud – and cranes from the dockyards. Two, its exposed location means it is quite possibly the coldest, most wind-and-rain-swept place I have ever watched football in.

Partick, in a city dominated by the sectarian rivalry of Celtic and Rangers, are the perennial 'friendly neighbours' and the atmosphere was a relaxed one. (Maybe everyone has been sedated by the cold?) The guy selling half time raffle tickets outside whispered to Emma 'You're a winner,' when we asked if we could have a winning ticket.

While the big city clubs of the old firm can generate crowds around 60,000 on a good day, Partick exists on gates around 4,000; 4,000 who really love their club, forsaking the easy route to success that they could take with the other two. It is a ground full of character, the street-facing stand reminding me of a mini version of the grand facade to Arsenal's old Highbury ground; tall, old art deco doors leading into a reception hidden by great whitewashed walls.

The ground has character, but the game lacked it; the weather pretty much destroying any chance of a decent spectacle. Partick had the better of the possession, St Johnstone the better chance, saved well by Thistle's goalie Scott Fox. Former Scotland international James McFadden toiled in the St Johnstone midfield, while Thistle's exciting Abdul Osman did the same, but ultimately the game was beaten by the storm and it petered

PARTICK THISTLE V ST JOHNSTONE

out 0-0. Regardless, we were both past caring, the cold having gotten the better of us southern softies.

'I don't think I'm ever going to be warm again,' Emma muttered between chattering teeth. I knew what she meant. The last time I had felt this cold was with Effie at a Southampton v Cheltenham FA Cup match four years or so ago, where we were jumping around not at to celebrate a goal, but to try to get some sort of feeling in our feet!

'At least the match was never going to be the big point of the weekend?' I offered and a weak smile spread across her face at the thought of breakfast with Dan.

Montgomery's is an awesome cafe with a wonderful bunch of borderline insanely friendly staff that had Dan smiling from the off.

'That one is proper mental,' he said, nodding at the most eccentric one of the bunch.

I don't know if it will ever stop being a surreal experience, meeting up with a professional footballer, regardless of the reason behind it, and it was hard not to feel like a star-struck ten-year-old again, waiting for autographs from your heroes.

Having said that, I wasn't the person with such an enormous, life changing connection with one, so God only knows how Emma was feeling!

But as I said before, this wasn't just a normal meet and greet; Dan had travelled some distance from where he was staying into Glasgow's West End, to meet us on his day off.

It was a grand gesture in itself, but his genuine warmth and friendship soon had Emma at ease, and they talked about how things were going. He seemed impressed that she was doing a counselling course in order to qualify in that field, and she was relieved when he said he finally felt back to where he had been before that day. That comment from the first time we met up, when he asked her if counselling had helped her, sprang into my mind.

It's easy to appear fine, but far harder actually to be it, and maybe the world of professional football is still not the best place to express your weaknesses and troubles. We can only imagine at how hard his struggles had been behind closed doors. However, on that day, it was good to sit at a table watching two people who had shared the worst day of their lives, both chatting and laughing, both clearly so much better than the first time they had met.

No-one ever gets properly fixed from traumas like those that Emma and Dan experienced. There are always mental scars that stick with you long after any physical ones have faded. When we touched on Dan's time at Southampton, his sadness at having that opportunity of the Premier League taken away was palpable, but it quickly faded when he talked about how much he was enjoying playing for Partick. The prospect of playing at Celtic's imposing Celtic Park on Wednesday in the League Cup quarter final soon had him buzzing.

When we told him that we were heading there in a bit to catch Celtic play Kilmarnock before our flight home, he insisted on giving us a lift. As Dan's Sat Nav took us across the city, the three of us looked on in awe at the enormous Celtic Park looming up out of Glasgow's East End.

That Dan would be playing there, at one of Europe's Cathedrals of football, and that Emma was going there to watch a game was not lost on me and it felt like one final symbolic high five to two people who were back in the vibrant land of the living where they belonged; where there is opportunity rather than fear, hope rather than despair.

We took our seats high up in the top tier and looked out at the awesome sight that is Celtic Park. I couldn't help but think about Anton from Southampton Police, Tracy at Southampton Rape Crisis, Dan, of course, Effie, and Emma's other friends, but also the unknown quantities; the Saints fans who made her feel welcome, and the wonderful Accrington Stanley fans who did the same, home and away; to all the places we have been to, and to football in general for being everything that it is.

It seemed apt that this heartfelt moment of thanks should come at a club that was founded on tolerance and acceptance, built so that those who had been denied entry to others in the city had some place to go. Because there are good people everywhere, despite what you see on the news. And if you are in despair, then reach out. If you can't do that just yet, then just hold on that little bit longer, because, sometimes, good people come looking for you.

The Crown Ground, at Accrington. Run-down but still wonderful. (Photo: Mat Guy)

The teams warm up at the Crown Ground, Accrington (Photo: Mat Guy)

Expectant gasheads at Aldershot (Photo: Mat Guy)

Dan Seaborne and Emma
(Photo: Effie Woods)

Meeting Kelly Smith! (Photo: Jen Hosking)

The Tibetan National Football Team, Zafer Stadium, Guzelyurt, North Cyprus (Photo: Mat Guy)

No man's land outside Zafer Stadium, North Cyprus (Photo: Mat Guy)

A match gets going at Dr Fazil Kucuk Stadium, Magusa (Photo: Mat Guy)

Druk United, Thimphu, Bhutan (Photo: Deborah Guy)

The team that plays the game

Billings' Obsession

By
JAMES DAVIES

RON BILLINGS built his sons a football ground because he was incensed by the bad language he heard at junior matches. "From now on you'll play at home," he told his tearful offspring.

That was 11 years ago, and today the embodiment of Billings's idealism, a sports complex which would shame many a First Division club, stands on a farm lane in Kent, home to the determinedly amateur Corinthians FC.

With its three floodlit pitches, outside and a synthetic one under cover, its Jacuzzi, sauna, squash courts, restaurant and bar, it is the envy of the football world.

Yet, sadly, the ideals which prompted the concept in the first place are now under threat from the success which the team has achieved.

This season has seen Corinthians enter the Southern League, a semi-professional arena which has visited them with the unacceptable trappings of football.

Billings has had to endure vandalism from other clubs' fans, bad language on the pitch, cynical professional fouls and—worst of all—the booking of a Corinthian player.

It is all sadly reminiscent of the plague that has afflicted the senior game, and, for the 82-year-old millionaire builder and farmer, whose players are under instruction not to swear, spit, foul or argue with referees, a bitter challenge to his vision.

Genuine

Moreover, his team which previously played invitation matches only and are genuine amateurs—not even drawing expenses—now weekly come up against men for whom money is a major motivation.

So why go into a league at all? Says Billings : "I was afraid that after I had gone there would be no one to get them their fixtures and the club might have folded.

"I was aware that with this would come gamesmanship and the cheating we see in much of the game nowadays.

Fans and visiting teams at his stadium at Fawkham are treated with consummate hospitality, including sun-beds, a medical centre that would grace a teaching hospital, gymnasium and tiled baths and showers.

His big disappointment that barely a hundred fans a week turn up to watch games.

Billings, whose wife Doreen still washes the first team strip, thinks they could win the League he would rather they were not playing in.

What has this extraordinary obsession with integrity cost him? He refuses to answer. "Money is not important," he answered. "I'm just proud of what we have achieved.

"These were boys who never wanted for anything. Football has brought them into contact with boys who had nothing. Together they have demonstrated that they share the passion, the honesty and the decency that the game is in danger of losing."

'Memo to Matthew from Grandad' (Photo: Mat Guy)

Sam and his dad take in the Crown Ground, Accrington (Photo: Mat Guy)

Winstanley the mascot reading the programme! (Photo: Mat Guy)

Celebration time in Accrington (Photo: Emma Townley)

George living the dream! (Photo: Mat Guy)

'Uncle Mat, can we stand with the ultras?' (Photo: Emma Townley)

Preparing for a New Forest derby (Photo: Mat Guy)

The end of a great season, Accrington (Photo: Mat Guy)

11

21 November 2006. Tibet v North Cyprus
Magusa, North Cyprus

BACK HOME IT was probably cold, wet and dark. But here I was in a disputed state, sat in a swelteringly hot and dusty little ground overlooking to my left the shimmering ocean and Israel, Palestine, and Lebanon beyond it, and to my right a fenced off, desolate, derelict and overgrown no-man's-land of bombed out buildings that constituted a UN monitored buffer zone; a result of numerous wars, invasions and attempted coups between the two peoples either side of it. Amongst all this, as the sun pounded mercilessly down, I was preparing to watch an international football match between two countries which technically don't even exist.

This does, I imagine, elicit a number of questions; 'How?' is a good one. 'Why?' is another. As with all seemingly ludicrous situations, the answer is often based around a series of accidents, chance, stupid questions and, in this case, the love of football and the underdog.

My becoming aware of Tibetan football stemmed from a series of completely unrelated and ultimately misguided thoughts back in 2001 that centred on me thinking that maybe I could re-invent myself as an international footballer with one of the world's worst nations. That maybe some tiny country somewhere might want to snap up an at best poor amateur player to become one of their own!

After realising just how ridiculous a notion that was I still found myself pouring over the alien looking flags and names of little known places right at the foot of the FIFA world rankings, sending vague emails out into the ether to one of them, Bhutan, requesting a little information on a country that had captured my imagination once discovered. Bhutan had kept itself isolated from the rest of the world, partly through its treacherous and distant location, partly by its close control of visitors coming to its borders; only a few thousand tourists were admitted each year to this secretive country. But mostly my imagination had been piqued due to its cultural, religious and geographical proximity to a country that had captivated me from a young age – the troubled land of Tibet.

And one of those chance emails sent innocently requesting some more information on this little known country and its football team resulted in an adventure that, though far removed from my initial ambition, became one of the richest experiences of my life, in this small Himalayan

Kingdom. It is an adventure that is detailed in a later chapter, but it is also an adventure that helped me to reconnect to a country that had always fascinated me. It was an adventure that opened doors into a world that I never dreamt could be possible for me. It opened a door to the mystical land of Tibet.

My interest in the underdog – and there is no greater underdog, politically or sportingly than Tibet – doesn't just apply to football and, as I grew up, it began to translate into art, writing, politics, people and culture, much to my dad's disgust. The tipping point was when I got into being a hunt saboteur, spending countless days trying to prevent posh people from killing foxes. My 'finest' hour was when I was filmed by a local news team (it was aired on the local evening news) pushing a policeman into a dug out badger set during a ruckus. To be fair, I didn't push him, as such. I was pushed from behind by someone else and fell into him, which made him fall into the hole. But as they say, the camera doesn't lie, and Dad didn't speak to me for weeks.

Another of my interests was Tibet, aided by films such as *Kundun* and *Seven Years in Tibet*, which depicted a unique, secretive people and culture, their peaceful Buddhist world hidden away among the highest peaks of the Himalayas; a world decimated by a terrible aggressor, namely the newly risen communist state of the People's Republic of China. Their culture, their religious beliefs, their secretive nature, all fascinated me. And their plight had seemed to a young student to be both tragic and shameful, and stuck with me, though I found no outlet to really express this.

At least not until a moment on a journey that my wife and I took deep into the Himalayas, all as a result of that chance email to Bhutan.

While travelling on the Dochula Pass, a rest point and religious shrine on a twisting road that snuck between towering Himalayan mountains on its way to Bhutan's second town, Punakha, Deb and I got out to stretch our legs, looking in awe at the thousands of prayer flags fluttering on the breeze between tall pine trees. Three Buddhist monks sat among them, all praying in deep, hypnotic, booming voices. We looked out at the magnificent mountains of the high Himalayas in the distance. Our guide got out of the car too and walked alongside us and pointed away to the left, at a stretch of snow topped mountains.

'There,' he said reverentially. 'Tibet.' Then he shook his head and held his hands to his face to pray.

Tibet. There it was. No longer just a concept, or a film. It was really there. We had passed a number of Tibetan refugee camps on our travels, our guide pointing them out in hushed tones. He had explained that they could be found in Bhutan, Nepal and India, camps of varying sizes holding Tibetans who had fled persecution, finding solace in being a little closer to the exiled Dalai Lama who had been given permission by the Indian Government to live in Dharamsala. A pacifist people being tortured and imprisoned, murdered for refusing to give up their culture and religion, for refusing to denounce their spiritual leader, invaded while the rest of the world turned its back; the story of Tibet is a shameful one for humanity.

The first I ever heard of football in Tibet, or rather, in the vast diaspora of refugee camps outside of Tibet, was in 2002, while compiling information for my scrapbooks about Bhutanese football. It was then that I found an article about a match played in 2001 in Denmark between Greenland and Tibet. Organised by a Dane called Michael Nybrandt, the match was a real awakening to the power sport could have in carrying the Tibetan struggle to the outside world, as well as helping to give the exiled Tibetan community a focus and an outlet; a tool to help keep the Tibetan culture and identity alive.

A film was made about the troubles in getting the match on, called *The Forbidden Team*; it is one of the most moving documentaries I have ever seen; a real celebration of a culture struggling to survive, as well as relaying the tragedy of all that had gone before it. That was in 2001, then things went quiet. With no money, no infrastructure and no pitches, Tibetan football fell silent, at least to the outside world.

Until 2006. That year Tibet started cropping up as a potential participant in the inaugural and so far only ELF Cup tournament (Equality, Liberty, Fraternity); a competition entirely funded and hosted by the North Cyprus Football Association.

North Cyprus, like Tibet, doesn't actually exist if you look at it in the terms of the United Nations or FIFA. The only country to recognise it is Turkey, who have funded and backed the disputed state for decades following a coup, invasion, counter invasion and war, leaving it in a position of limbo with its southern Cypriot neighbours, separated by a United Nations controlled buffer zone.

It too has a football team, but as a 'rogue' state that doesn't officially exist to those in power it, like Tibet, cannot take part in FIFA sanctioned international football. This basically means that it can't take part in football full-stop. Like Tibet, North Cyprus has a national football team, but has nobody to play against. This is why the ELF Cup was devised; a big two fingered salute to FIFA and the UN.

The match between Greenland and Tibet caused real political tension between China and Denmark, with China threatening trade sanctions if they allowed the match to go ahead. As Tibet was 'part of China', officially they had no right to play this match as Tibet. To their great credit, the Danish government ignored China and the match went ahead. With North Cyprus there were no such problems. If China or anyone else had kicked off Turkey could say it had nothing to do with them, and as no-one is supposed to acknowledge North Cyprus' existence, it would have been quite hard to threaten sanctions on something that 'wasn't there'.

The tournament's line up was to include the hosts, Tibet, Greenland, Crimea (as a state within the Ukraine, though these days who knows), Gagauzia (similar to Crimea, but a state within Moldova), Zanzibar (part of Tanzania) and representative sides from Tajikistan and Kyrgyzstan. Initially Afghanistan had been due to take part, playing their first matches since the us-led war of 2002. However FIFA, who had provided the Afghan Association with lots of funding to get what was a decimated organisation back on its feet (the football stadium in Kabul had been used by the Taliban as a place of public execution for years), didn't like the idea of a FIFA nation bringing credibility to the tournament and demanded that they pull out, which they did.

As soon as dates, fixtures and so on had been finalised, it became clear to me that this was too good an opportunity to pass up. Cyprus was a popular tourist destination; flights to and from England were cheap. There would never be a better time to watch Tibetan football in person.

It would be easy, right?

Wrong.

As tourists drained away from Larnaka airport, heading to their package holidays along the coast, I picked up my hire car and drove inland to the Capital, Nicosia, where it became quickly apparent that the peace between the north and south was an uneasy one. Banners fluttered on the wind demanding that the 'Turk army and settlers go home'. Across the border 'Happy to be a Turk' flags defiantly refused.

Nicosia was split by the UN buffer zone and it felt disconcerting as night fell; the contrast between driving along streets busy with night-life and then suddenly hitting a roundabout that lead to nowhere, shut off by rolls of barbed wire, imposing walls and UN troops patrolling in jeeps. Beyond, on a hill overlooking the capital on the northern side of the border, a huge North Cyprus flag made up of thousands of bulbs sparkled defiantly. The border is well hidden and isn't signposted, as if the Southern Republic don't want to acknowledge its existence. It took me an age to finally find it and pass through to the North. It felt tense, not surprising, given the semi-recent events of war, coups, invasions, disappearances and murders, all easily within living memory.

Throw in the religious divide that has been created with the mass migrations, voluntary or otherwise, that followed the country's split, leaving the north predominantly Turkish and Muslim, the south Greek Cypriot and Christian, and it becomes easy to see there is no simple way to resolve this stand-off.

As soon as you cross the border you can see the north has been hit economically by United Nations trade sanctions. It is clearly not as affluent as the south, in fact, travelling to the coastal town of Girne (in the south they call it Kyrenia, so that's how it appears on all the maps, but the Turkish north call it Girne, and as I was in the north, Girne it is) feels like travelling to another world, as minarets and mosques appear in the darkness.

It is an old, pretty town that huddles around a picturesque harbour and castle, and the seafront beyond. Tourism is the main source of income, along with Turkish aid, and it is easy to see why people come across to take in the sun (even though I visited in November, it was very hot), despite all the tensions and hostility of the border. It is a beautiful place.

The Northern Cyprus FA had housed all the competing teams in the Dome hotel, and after checking into my own hotel on the outskirts of town and having had a good night's sleep, it seemed the obvious place to go. The Dome is the nicest hotel in Girne and must have cost the North Cyprus FA a small fortune, as they were funding everything, including the travel costs for all the teams.

It was the day before the tournament was due to start and track-suited players from Greenland, Zanzibar and Gagauzia milled about on a terrace that looked out onto the ocean lulling against rocks and the seafront wall. It felt quite surreal, as I sat and sipped a soft drink and watched as the international tournament slowly assembled around me. It was strange to think that in only a day's time I would get to meet the representatives from Tibet; that the moment I had been waiting for was so close at hand.

Guzelyurt is a sleepy, dusty backwater town far from the picturesque tourist hot-spots along the coast. Driving through narrow streets lined with deserted shop fronts, avoiding the odd wandering pedestrian or dog lying in the sun, it was easy to warm to its ramshackle, functional, lazy feel. But even here there were constant reminders of the troubles that cast a shadow over the country; the bridge linking one part of the town to the other carried the warning 'No UN troops beyond this point'.

Zafer Stadium is a lovely, old, run-down ground full of character, tucked away near a Turkish barracks on the outskirts of town. Guards at the gates to the barracks eyed me suspiciously and I wondered if I was in the right place, as the ground seemed as deserted as the town it represented. I felt a little reassured when someone decked out in a tracksuit with the word 'Tajikistan', Tibet's first group B opponents, embossed across the back wandered past.

The man on the gate seemed a little surprised to see me and fumbled about for the tickets he had to sell as if he hadn't actually expected there would be anyone about to buy them. He was very friendly and shocked to find out I was from the UK and had come all the way here on purpose.

'You mean, from England, to see the football?' He shook his head, seeming bemused but proud that football from his country had been the attraction.

Inside, an old crackling PA system piped traditional Turkish-sounding songs around the empty stadium. Flags of the eight competing teams hung limp in the hot, still air; the main stand was a welcome relief to its handful of occupants from the sun beating down on the pitch.

For the match against Greenland in 2001 the sports manufacturer Hummel had produced a kit for Tibet that they also put up for sale on their website, donating a chunk of any proceeds to the Tibetan National Team. Naturally, I'd had to buy one. As the sound of studs began to clatter on the paved surface outside the changing rooms, I draped my Tibet shirt on the fence lining the perimeter and as the players from both sides wandered out to warm up it received a few bemused looks, followed warm smiles and waves from the Tibetan players. I suppose they preferred to see the glass as half full and considered one supporter to be better than none at all.

Tajikistan was represented at this tournament by their national Futsal team. Like Kyrgyzstan in group A, they were affiliated with FIFA and therefore weren't allowed to attend in an official capacity, however their Futsal team could play. Tajikistan is a relatively new country from the hinterland between Europe and Asia, which declared independence after the fall of the Soviet Union in the late '80s/early '90s and, like their former masters', their national anthem is very austere.

Tibet's anthem was a new experience too and it reminded me, unsurprisingly, given their geographical, cultural and religious proximity, of Bhutan's, and the beautiful, lilting traditional music I heard while out there. The old, crackling tannoy didn't do it any favours, but that was more than made up for by the voices of the team, who belted the lyrics out with the kind of fervour you would expect from a people who could be thrown in jail or tortured for singing such a song in their homeland.

The emotion was clear for all to see, and the 30-or-so spectators who had gathered to watch it did so with a respectful reverence and round of applause at its end.

The match was an even affair, with both teams passing well, probing every now and then, with a few long range shots that troubled neither keeper. However in the second half Tajikistan started to apply some pressure and as Tibet began to tire with 30 minutes or so to play, they conceded three quick goals. The final score felt a little harsh on a team who worked very hard for one another. At least their endeavours were appreciated by the spectators, who applauded both teams off after what had been a good spirited and entertaining game.

If it hadn't been surreal enough to be sat in a deserted ground, in a deserted town in North Cyprus watching Tajikistan play a football match with Tibet, things turned even more bizarre when the Tibetan team, rather than heading for the changing rooms, clambered into the stand to come and shake my hand and thank me for my support.

One player, Tenzin Dhondup, apologised for the loss and explained that because of a lack of funds, and because the team were spread around many different refugee camps in India, they only got to meet up for a few weeks every year to train – if they even had a game to train for. His voice was so soft and hushed that it was quite hard to hear him, and at first I thought I'd misunderstood when he said that I should come to the changing rooms with them.

'Here,' he said, 'please,' and beckoned me to sit while they put on their tracksuits to be ready for the coach that would take them back to the Dome Hotel.

The team manager, Kalsang Dhondup, brought out a bag of sandwiches and bottles of water meant for the players, but offered them to me first.

'Please,' he said, 'you must be hungry. There is plenty for everyone.'

'It is important for us to be here,' he began, when I asked what it meant for him and the players to represent Tibet, 'because this region doesn't know too much about Tibet. It is important we are here, to show that Tibet exists, and through our team and football we can try and promote friendship and peace.'

Like Tenzin, his quietly spoken words were dignified and calm; an amazing quality in someone whose past and present was so blighted with loss, injustice and suffering. Indeed, it felt very humbling to sit and listen, and as they headed off for their coach (not before offering me a lift), I sat for a while, trying to take it all in.

Someone once told me that it is always a big risk to meet an idol or hero, in case they don't live up to your vision of them, but as the coach rolled away, a plume of dust trailing behind it, I couldn't have been further from disappointed.

The ELF Cup group stages were held over three consecutive days, as financial constraints prevented the luxury of rest days in between matches. This made it tougher for the players, but was a blessing for the football lover who could catch at least two games a day – or even three, as it turned out, on this opening set of fixtures.

A drive along small, windy roads through dry and arid mountains to the north coast (the journey to Guzelyurt through the flat lands of central Cyprus provided fruit orchards and olive groves as a backdrop) was the quickest way to the next match: Zanzibar's Under 21s v Kyrgyzstan's Futsal team, at the 20 Temmuz Stadium on the western outskirts of Girne.

Here, two competent teams played out a good natured match (Zanzibar's flair, skill and steel saw them edge it 1-0) in a picturesque little ground huddled beneath mountains which began to fade into the gloom as the early evening shadows stretched out toward them. Zanzibar's Under 21 team were really impressive, which suggested that their men's team could surely have done some real damage against some of the African FIFA nations. However, like Greenland, they are unable to do so. This is football's loss.

As it was, this team certainly looked at least good enough for the semi-finals; they were slight and very young looking, but they played with skill and when necessary with a physical edge that was impressive. A crowd of around 100 seemed satisfied with what was on offer, even a vocal following of friendly and good-humoured Kyrgyzstan supporters who, despite the loss, seemed happy enough that their young team had put up a spirited fight.

There was no time to dwell on any of that for too long, as a quick sandwich followed by another drive cross-country through the failing light to the Ataturk Stadium in Lefkosa (the Northern Cypriot, Turkish name for their section of Nicosia) was necessary for the third and final match of the day: North Cyprus v Crimea.

Unlike the grounds at Girne and Guzelyurt, which were very much small, and, in the case of the 20 Temmuz stadium, communal places for people to come and exercise (not long after the Zanzibar match, women began to use the track that encircled the pitch to power walk), the Ataturk Stadium is an imposing 28,000 capacity venue, lit by four huge floodlights on each corner.

An opening ceremony which featured all eight sides parading in front of a crowd of 1,000 or so preceded the finale to the first day's play; a breathless match set at a terrifying tempo with thundering tackles and swift counter-attacks. It was clear that both North Cyprus and Crimea were very good, which was an ominous sign for both Tibet and Tajikistan, who were in the same group. It was clear that a number of players from both sides could, or quite possibly did, play at a professional level. The only real difference between the sides was that North Cyprus took their chances and Crimea didn't.

It was 2-0 at half time and with Crimea becoming frustrated the tackling from both teams became more erratic and aggressive, and it was no surprise when yellow cards started flowing in all directions, soon followed by a red for a bad tackle by a Crimean player. Neither side would back down as the tackles deteriorated. Equality, Liberty and Fraternity it most certainly wasn't, and three late goals as Crimea chased the game saw a 5-0 win for the hosts.

As the night had drawn on the temperature had begun to plummet and it was a relief to get back in the car and turn the heater on for the journey home, which I mostly spent wondering about how the first two matches had featured one yellow card between them, whereas the last had resembled a war zone at times.

It was a far cry from the Tibet match, where they had often found themselves out of position due to stopping to help a Tajik opponent up off the ground after they had both gone in for a tackle. The Tibetan players had played to win and to do the very best they could, throwing themselves into tackles; but it always seemed to be from a position of respect, with spirited play rather than aggression, and when they had committed fouls, they looked to be honest mistakes and their first instinct was not to get back into position to defend, but to check on the fouled player and make sure he was all right.

After the last match of the day, I began to worry a little at the thought of Tibet coming up against the two fast, tough, savvy sides. I felt that their warmth and humility on the pitch could well be abused by such professional and determined teams.

However, it seemed I hadn't counted on what I can only describe as 'The Tibet Influence'.

It was day two of the tournament, and I headed back to Guzelyurt and the wonderful Zafer Stadium for a double header of Tibet v Crimea followed by North Cyprus v Tajikistan. It really was easy, especially for someone who loves out of the way places, to fall for this town; its sleepy charm felt comfortable and safe, while its isolation was quite possibly its great strength. It felt like a town that knew who and what it was, and had no need to advertise its attributes to the world.

The old man on the gate recognised me as one of the few punters from the day before and gave me a warm smile. When I handed him some money he told me that I didn't need to pay again, as yesterday's ticket got me in to all the games –£15 for seven matches, as it turned out. This tournament was getting better and better! He handed me a little four page programme and a team sheet for the first match and ushered me inside. *A programme! A team sheet! For a Tibet match? Better and better!*

Before kick-off, my title of solitary Tibet supporter changed slightly to include unofficial photographer of the Tibetan National Football Team. After having their team photo taken by a couple of journalists, they beckoned me forward to ask if I would take their picture with their personal cameras. Fifteen pictures with 15 different cameras later, I took a quick couple myself. Their smiles of thanks changed to serious expressions as the referee blew his whistle and the two teams assembled for the national anthems, the Tibetan players belting theirs out with just as much passion and pride as before.

Just before the match began, the 30 or 40 spectators were joined by a couple of hundred excited, chattering school children who had been bussed in by the organisers to swell the stands and create a better atmosphere. This didn't seem to be a problem for the children, who were ecstatic to be out of school no matter the reason.

I am prepared to admit that there could have been contributing factors. Crimea must have been tired, having finished their last match at 8.30pm, and kicking this one off at noon the following day. I am also prepared to concede that the loss of their best player, the number six who had got himself sent off against North Cyprus, could have been a significant reason for the different Crimean performance in this one. However I am not prepared to believe that the complete change in attitude by the Crimean team, the absence of crunching tackles and gamesmanship that had blighted the previous evening's fixture, was solely down to those two facts. I am backed up in this by Tajikistan's tougher, more belligerent display against the hosts in the second match. It seemed to have far more to do with this 'Tibet influence' which managed to affect the whole nature of both matches.

From the off the match was very close, although Crimea had the edge, and was played in a great spirit. Tibetans helped Crimean players off the floor when they had been tackled and handed the ball to their opponents when it went out of play. There was no cheating or diving, no cynical fouls, no dissent and no yellow cards; the complete absence of theatrics meant that the game flowed freely, with both teams creating and missing good chances in front of the goal. And when the only goal of the game came, via a penalty conceded by Tibet for a clumsy but honest tackle in the box late in the first half, there was a real humility to the Crimean player's celebrations. I cannot fathom another reason for the 16-hour, Jekyll and Hyde-esque transformation of the Crimean team, other than the spirit of fair play Tibet imposed on the match, enabling Crimea to perform with a simple and uninhibited freedom.

Tibet fought to the end, heads held high, but a second defeat in two days meant they could not qualify for the semi-finals and one of the two objectives they had at this tournament had ended in failure. The second objective, however, seemed to have been a tremendous success, as they appeared to have made a real impression on the spectators in the stands and on their opponents on the pitch.

That isn't to say that the Tibet National Football team had nothing to offer on the pitch. Far from it, they were a decent little team, with some decent players. Their attacking midfielder, Tenzin Rampa, was very good and the whole team passed the ball well – miraculously so, given the dire lack of facilities, training and match practice that they operated under – and that was before taking into account their refugee status and everything else that they had to endure.

The second match ended with a 5-1 victory for North Cyprus, despite Tajikistan putting up a good fight and as the schoolchildren and other assorted spectators began to drift away from the stand I felt both sad and a little nervous: sad because this was my last trip to the Zafer stadium and its welcoming charm, its job as a host venue now complete; nervous because the following day Tibet were to face North Cyprus in the last of their group games. North Cyprus had scored ten goals at a canter, while only conceding one; a side full of professional or ex-professional players with a squad twice the size of the depleted and exhausted 16-man party from Tibet.

Even for countries who technically don't exist and who are excluded from mainstream football competition; with their financial backing, facilities, full-time leagues and home advantage, North Cyprus v Tibet was a complete mismatch. Darkness fell as I drove back to my hotel. The mountains loomed as they fell into shadow around me, which did nothing to help the sense of ominous trepidation that was building.

For my last day of football action I couldn't help stopping off at the 20 Temmuz Stadium to catch half an hour of the Greenland v Kyrgyzstan match before the cross country trip to Magusa and Tibet's date with the hosts. It was easy to find a reason to pause here, as the location beneath the mountains is beautiful. It was also an easy decision because Greenland were one of two teams I hadn't managed to see yet (due to the scheduling I missed Gagauzia completely) and as they had been the team to stand up to China and play against Tibet back in 2001, they were a part of this story that I didn't want to miss.

Greenland, much like Tibet, have a limited amount of playing time in which to improve, though for climatic rather than political reasons. With the country's fierce, long winters, football suffers, and football outdoors can only be contemplated for a couple of months every year. Despite that, and also much like Tibet, they were a decent little team (both sides are an advertisement for what you can achieve, if you really want it), though by this third game in as many days, they seemed very tired. Spurred on by another large band of vociferous supporters (around 500 Kyrgyzstani students come to North Cyprus to study every year), Kyrgyzstan took control of the game, and the lead, although Greenland keep them down to that solitary goal.

It was a shame to leave before half time, because Greenland played with an almost innocent freedom; they were an unlikely but perfect fit for that groundbreaking match in 2001. However, the drive across to Magusa was a relatively long one and I wanted to get there before the match kicked off.

The highway to the east coast is long and dusty, with the occasional turning for a small town and the distant outline of a mosque, its minarets towering above everything else, the only sign of life on the desolate, sun baked road, that leads, finally, to Magusa, a fascinating city that is, like Nicosia/Lefkosa, sliced in two by a UN buffer zone. However unlike the nation's capital Nicosia, Magusa (or Famagusta if you are from the Republic south) has been split in two by a large tract of blocked off city that has stood since 1974 like a ghost town; the buildings left derelict, trees and shrubs reclaiming the deserted streets.

Outside the Dr Fasil Kucuk Stadium, where the match was being held, the roads just stop, cut off by sturdy fences and signs demanding no entry or photography. Beyond them nature has run wild; creepers climbing over and into houses that are almost lost behind overgrown gardens, weeds snaking out into the road, bushes and trees sprouting up through cracks in the tarmac. It stands there, still, eerily silent, like a set for a post-apocalyptic movie, a ghost town, devoid of life.

It isn't visible from the street, but from the stand of the Dr Fasil Kucuk stadium I could see the taller buildings, once hotels and office blocks, peppered with bullet holes and their windows blown out, some even sporting gaping wounds from rocket fire. Alongside them stand half built buildings; the cranes still towering over the site seemed to suggest that those who had lived and worked there must have left in a hurry, scurrying to safety among the fighting, never to return.

It was an unsettling sight; an unorthodox memorial to a battle more than 30 years old. It seemed to encapsulate the Cyprus experience perfectly, this uneasy peace living side-by-side with an attempt at normality; look out to your right from the stand and you see a crumbling, war-torn ghost town, while to your left lies sparkling ocean and beaches; immaculate looking hotels for holiday-makers.

The ground in Magusa is much like that in Girne and Guzelyurt; small and compact, but big enough to hold a decent crowd if necessary. On this occasion, it was not. As I arrived, Crimea and Tajikistan were playing out the last few minutes of their match and as I was taking my seat in the stand Crimea scored to win the game 2-1. Their jubilant celebrations suggested that it meant a lot to them to play and win under the banner of Crimea rather than that of Ukraine. This is something that has become of global significance in recent times, but back in 2006 it meant nothing to me.

It felt hotter here, much hotter, the stadium bleached white, the shimmering ocean beyond stretching out to the middle east and Lebanon, Syria, Israel and Palestine, painful on the eyes.

Among all of this, among the remnants of war, the players of Tibet walked out into the sweltering heat; players who could only train together for a few weeks before a tournament, and who had no training facilities to call their own. Sixteen men, all exiled from their homeland, who had come all this way to play football in the name of peace, and all that stood in their way were North Cyprus, a team packed full of experience and talent, who could do themselves justice on the larger stage of UEFA and FIFA qualifying tournaments if they were only given the opportunity.

It's at moments like this that I wish the Hollywood vision of sporting heroics could come to life and that against all the odds the minnow could come good and claim the prize. But this wasn't a standard football match in a standard football tournament and heroics manifested themselves in a different way: from the passion of the national anthems to the sporting behaviour of helping a fellow human being off the floor when they have fallen, of trying your very best in the face of the absolute certainty that you are going to fail, of never giving up on the thing you love.

Despite all that, at 8-0 by half time one might think that there could be nothing positive to be gleaned from such an experience. However, there were no yellow cards, no bad tackles, and the Tibetan players picked themselves up every time after conceding another goal and set about their opponents as enthusiastically as when it was goalless. I could see a growing admiration from the Cypriot players and spectators, and at the final whistle and a 10-0 victory for the hosts both sets of players embraced each other with a genuine warmth. There were no recriminations after the match, just a few tired smiles from the players as they shook my hand and thanked me for my support before heading for the changing rooms.

Kalsang, the manager, kept apologising to me.

'Our goalie had a bad game,' he said with a shrug. 'Our number one goalie couldn't come; we couldn't get a visa for him.'

He told me about a dire need for sponsorship or help of any kind for the team, as they were basically operating with no discernible resources. He gave me his card and asked me to email him when I got home.

By the time I had finished peering (technically forbidden) into the UN buffer zone ghost town and had made it back to the car, the Tibetan team bus was pulling out of the car park. As usual I was met with warm smiles and waves. The bus pulled away, the sun setting behind them, and with that Tibet's tournament was over. With no resources or funding, who knew when they would get to pull on their national team shirt again; how long would it be before they could offer up their spirit of fair play and respect that had been so infectious to their three opponents here? Not soon enough, that's for sure.

My last day in North Cyprus was a rest day, and after three days driving across the country to watch seven different football matches, a rest day was what I needed. I spent it wandering along narrow cobbled streets in the Girne old town, lingering along the harbour front and exploring Girne castle which overlooks the shimmering ocean, the call to prayer echoing from minarets hidden from view.

That evening, I wandered back down to the Dome Hotel and had a drink in the bar while looking back through the pictures I had taken on my camera. As I was leaving, heading down the hotel's front steps, I noticed someone waving at me from a little veranda to my right, beckoning me over. From my team sheet I recognised Tibet's captain, Lobsang Wangyal, the trainer Jigme Dorjee and their winger, whom I had spoken with after their first game, Tenzin Dhondup.

They asked me if I would like to join them.

'Happily,' I replied.

After a little while of sitting quietly, Lobsang began to speak about how hard it was for the team, as most lived in Tibetan settlement camps across India, where it takes days by bus to get to one another. The team got no help from India or the exiled Tibetan government in Dharamsala and had no facilities at all. He reiterated Tenzin's sadness that the team could only get together for a few weeks before a tournament or match and that these were few and far between.

'If we had our own pitch that would be a start, but we have nothing.

There is nothing for the children, the future players, to play on.'

They had only been able to bring 16 players to Cyprus because two of their best players had been unable to get time off from work, while a third, their best goalie, couldn't get a visa.

'It's very hard to get a visa anywhere on a Refugee Tibetan passport. So even though we could have brought 19 players, we could only find 16 that could get visas. That made it very hard to play three games in three days.'

'North Cyprus had 27 players,' Tenzin said, 'so they could change their team every day to keep fresh. They had a whole new team to play against us. They were very good and fresh, whereas we were tired, and not so good!' He smiled as he spoke.

'It's hard to afford to get to the training camps before tournaments,' Lobsang said. 'We are supposed to be paid 12 rupees (about two pounds) a day while we are there, but very often there is no money, so we don't get anything. That makes it hard for our families, as we are missing work to be there, so there is no money coming from anywhere.

'But we come anyway, for the love of Tibet, and football. We are all Tibetan in here.' He pointed to his chest. 'We love our country, and the Dalai Lama. One player, Tenzin Rampa, came all the way from America where he was studying, because he wanted to play for Tibet. We love our country. Tibet is our home.'

Lobsang went on to talk about his family and their terrible struggles and sacrifices. His father had been in the Tibetan army, which was very small and ill-equipped, and had been quickly overrun by the Chinese in the '50s. He had fled to India to be close to the Dalai Lama, like many others. He spoke about the 30-plus-days trek across the Himalayas they had to endure to escape into India; a trek that could only be done in winter, when there were fewer Chinese guards monitoring the border. One man he knew lost both his feet to frostbite. They had to be amputated once he made it across.

'He puts paper in his shoes now to fill them out.'

Jigme, the coach, spoke of people being shot in Tibet for carrying pictures of 'His Holiness the 14th Dalai Lama' with them. He also mentioned a story I'd recently read about a Tibetan Buddhist nun who had been shot dead by Chinese guards while trying to shepherd a group of very young Tibetan children into India. The incident had been witnessed by a group of European climbers, who had taken pictures and caused an international outcry.

'But for every such incident caught on camera, hundreds and hundreds go unseen.'

Lobsang talked about his cousin, a Buddhist monk, who had been informed that his mother was still alive in Tibet and had trekked back into Tibet to try and find her, but was caught, and forced to work for a year on the construction of the railway line that now connects China and Tibet. The three of them spoke in soft, hushed tones, but the sadness and heartache they felt resonated as strongly as if they had been shouting.

Jigme then offered me his 'Save Tibet' band that he had been wearing on his wrist, 'as a symbol of friendship'. Tenzin pulled four apples out of his bag and shared them out, and for a moment we sat quietly, eating. We were finally disturbed by the sound of a commotion further up the street. The sound of drums and chanting got louder and louder until a group of men dressed in Galatasaray tracksuits and wearing balaclavas marched along the street shouting aggressively. It turned out Galatasaray were playing in the Champions League that night.

'Why do they have those on?' Lobsang asked, and the three of them shook their heads.

We talked a little bit about football around the world. They asked about my team, Southampton. Lobsang said that he played for a team in his settlement.

'But for no money like your team, just for fun.'

Finally, they said that they were tired, and that they were going to bed. Each one shook my hand as they got up. Lobsang took a hand knitted beanie out of his pocket in the colours of the Tibetan flag, with 'Save Tibet' across the front, and handed it to me.

'I would like to give this gift to you, through friendship, and to thank you for your support.'

I was speechless, but somehow managed to tell him that I would treasure it, and wear it with pride. For a people with so little, they were very giving and selfless. It genuinely felt much more than a simple inspiration to have met them.

I felt something similar while working as an intern for the Free Tibet Campaign in London during 2007. We were visited by a Tibetan woman called Ama Ade, whose heartbreaking story of torture and loss (her young son had thrown himself off a bridge due to his anguish when his mother was imprisoned) as relayed by her interpreter was as utterly horrific as her selfless work in Tibetan children's villages in India as a surrogate mother to infants smuggled across to a life of safety and freedom was inspirational. Words do not readily afford enough emotion or import to describe what can be seen looking into the eyes of this woman – whose story, sadly, is commonplace – or the eyes of Tenzin, Lobsang, or Jigme.

Back at my hotel, I sat in the bar and watched the Galatasaray match in a bit of a daze, thinking about what the Tibetans had said. Jigme had asked if I had been at all three Tibet matches, and when I nodded he had thanked me.

'But it's not all about winning and losing for us. It's about letting the world know about our story. We come to these tournaments and people learn about our struggle. They see us, the Tibetan people. We are proud, and want to do well on the football field. But it isn't just about winning or losing, it's about keeping our name, the name of Tibet, alive.'

And against all odds, these 16 players, with Kalsang the manager, and Jigme the coach, quietly, respectfully, did just that.

Postscript

North Cyprus won the tournament, defeating Crimea three one in the final.

Tibet were unanimously awarded the Fair Play Award.

The Tibetan national team returned to Europe to play a few low-key matches in 2008 during the build up to the Beijing Olympics, to highlight the shut-down of Tibet by the Chinese government to prevent journalists getting in, or news of any Tibetan protests about China's repressive regime getting out.

Since 2008 the TNFA have played a few local tournaments in India and Sikkim, but the main focus for Tibetan football has been the annual GCM Cup, where Tibetan clubs to come together from across the refugee camps, and sometimes further afield.

Kalsang is still the manager. Lobsang and Tenzin still attend national team training camps, despite having no tournaments to train for.

I stayed on at Free Tibet Campaign until about September of 2007, at which point it became too much to travel up to London twice a week, hold down a full-time job, and deal with the fall-out of what happened earlier in the year. I did rejoin them a year later, however, to take part in a protest against the Beijing Olympics. This resulted in me being detained and deported from Beijing, and getting frog-marched across the arrivals lounge by armed soldiers. But even then, in a holding cell in a faraway land, football still found a way. One of the young guards, who was clearly very scared of the gruff older soldiers, took advantage of them leaving the room for a moment with my passport to sit next to me and ask: 'Do you know David Beckham?'

12

15 November 2014. Wimbledon v Dagenham & Redbridge
League Two

FINDING MYSELF STUCK in traffic caused by 60,000 plus rugby fans trying to get to Twickenham to watch the egg chasing, and roughly the same number beginning to head toward Wembley for the England men's team's European Qualifier later that evening, I began to wonder whether all this bother was worth it. I was also left doubting whether trying to get to a third, much smaller, sporting event in the capital at the weekend was a very good idea.

Resolutely, I dismissed these thoughts as total nonsense, and I persevered through the gridlock, looking forward to witnessing a number of inspirational stories that had, through fate, found themselves coming together for a League Two London derby between Wimbledon and Dagenham & Redbridge. The fact that I would be joined by a very dear friend who I didn't see enough of was the icing on the cake, and helped me to punch through the clogged roads and carry on to Richmond.

Sarah is a walking, talking encyclopaedia of football knowledge, an avid Ipswich Town fan, and a would-be stalker of 'town legend' Steve Sedgeley, if only she knew where he lived. Sarah lives in London, so she suggested meeting up in Richmond, and taking a long walk through Richmond Park to Kingston and the home of AFC Wimbledon, rather than battle the transport system trying to dodge ever drunker English, South African, and, quite possibly, the odd Slovenian fans.

Richmond Park is enormous, and to someone not from London is a complete surprise and contradicts everything you assume the capital to be. Growing up, I lived right by the New Forest, and would often ride my bike to a little village in the heart of the forest called Brockenhurst to watch some football. However it took a walk through one of the busiest cities in the world for me to tick off the unexpected experience of seeing a stag and other deer grazing as I made my way to a football match. Sarah told me that the Park used to be a royal hunting ground, and there are quite a few deer within its boundaries. Who knew?

What is more widely known is the story of Wimbledon, and their unique journey within football: FA Cup winners in the '80s; Premier League regulars in the '90s; the first club to be allowed (against the wishes of its fans) to be relocated 80 miles away from its roots; then ultimately to have its identity wiped with the club's name change to MK Dons, reflecting the new town of Milton Keynes that they settled in. It is a sorry story in English football that goes against everything that the sport and its clubs are meant to stand for: as beacons and focal points for a community.

Thank God, therefore, for a band of disillusioned supporters who refused to take these FA sanctioned actions, and instead started up AFC Wimbledon, ground-sharing with Kingstonian in a neighbouring borough. With a significant groundswell of support, this 'new' club moved up through the non-league pyramid until it finally gained promotion back into the Football League in 2011. It is a unique story in British football, and let's hope it stays that way.

That wasn't my primary reason for wanting to check out a match between two clubs perilously close to the relegation zone in the Fourth Division. There were also three characters I hoped would be involved in the match that made me pick this one over any other much closer to home; two players from Wimbledon, and one from Dagenham.

In the Wimbledon ranks there was a Salisbury legend called Matt Tubbs, whose goals helped drive what was an average southern league club up through the leagues to the conference and the top table in the non-league pyramid. My grandfather would often tell me about his exploits, reading match reports from the local paper to me about his goal scoring feats, and I think it was the thought of seeing Matt play that took us to the last game of the 2007–08 season to see him and Salisbury beat York City. It turned out to be the last game we went to see together, Grandad already being quite unsteady on his feet, but he had wanted to go and see a player that he admired.

In the following years, we followed his career from Grandad's armchair as he broke into the Football League, and though he never got any higher than League One he was, and continues to be, a valued player for whoever offers him a contract. This season it was Wimbledon. It felt good to be going to see him play again.

The second Wimbledon character that had made me want to take this trip was Tubbs' team-mate Sean Rigg, who had never played for Salisbury, or Southampton, or any club that I have any kind of connection to, but was involved in an incident several years ago that compelled me to write to a professional footballer for the first time in my life (the second and last time being Dan Seaborne).

At the time of the incident Rigg was a young player turning out for his home-town club, Bristol Rovers, in an FA Cup first round match away at non-league Barrow. A Barrow player, completely unprovoked, threw an almighty punch as Rigg jogged past him, breaking his jaw and halting his career in its tracks. The whole thing was caught on camera, and resulted in the Barrow player getting banned from football, and, I believe, spending some time in prison.

It was an awful incident that seemed to come out of nowhere, flooring a young man and his dreams, and possibly his future, and for some reason I felt compelled to send a get well soon card, addressed quite vaguely to Sean Rigg, Bristol Rovers FC. Who knows if it ever reached him? I hope it did.

We will never know whether what happened to Sean prevented him from making it any higher up the leagues, but what we do know is that he finally made it through a long rehabilitation and eventually got back into the Football League, and has been making a living from the game he loves ever since. It may not be the success story he might have hoped his career would be, back when he was a boy, but considering it all it is a career anyone would be proud of, and this season, he was out on the wing for Wimbledon.

The third interest in this match that had Sarah and I pacing through Richmond Park beneath dense rain cloud, was a young Dagenham & Redbridge player in his first season in the professional game called Adeoye Yusuff.

Dagenham, like Wimbledon, operate with a very small playing budget, arguably as small as Accrington's. At the very least, these three clubs are brothers in arms at the foot of the League Two table in terms of wealth and income. Because of this they have to scout extensively around their local non-league teams for any raw talent that they could possibly shape into a first team player, as dipping into the transfer market and actually buying a player is financially a non-starter.

Step up Adeoye Yusuff, a 20-year-old signed in September from Ryman League Division One North side Chatham. That in itself isn't particularly worthy of any note, there are plenty of players given a chance in League Two every season by clubs who can't afford to buy established, proven professionals. What stands Adeoye out from others is his grounded, respectful reaction to being given a shot at his dream to be a professional footballer.

Where others might let it go to their heads, and dream of what flash car they will buy when they hit the big time, Adeoye asked Dagenham if it would be alright to serve his notice at the restaurant where he had worked as a waiter, as well as signing his pro contract. He didn't want to let down those that had helped him while he was a part-time player; he didn't want to leave them short staffed just because he had an immediate opportunity to play in the Football League. So, for the best part of a month, he trained with Dagenham in the day, then while his team-mates rested, he waited tables in the evening. Ever since reading about Adeoye, I had hoped that an opportunity to see him play would come about, and here it was.

In a world where young boys enter academies and are sent through elite training programmes, oblivious to the realities of the working world outside the football bubble, it was a breath of fresh air to learn of a young man from a more connected, by-gone era where the football player and the football fan came from the same street, the same factory; where the game represented those that watched it. In my opinion, Adeoye represents everything that football should be; everything it needs to be.

I love the idea of academies nurturing talent and making each individual into the best possible player they can be, however it is hard to swallow the vast sums of money that some of these players earn at such a young age. How can they ever really represent the fans in the stand when they could earn in a week at the age of 18 what a supporter might earn in six months? It creates two separate worlds, worlds that are forever moving further and further apart.

Thankfully, there are still the lower leagues and the non-leagues that are the foundations of what made football the world's most loved sport, and clubs like Dagenham & Redbridge, Wimbledon, and Accrington Stanley reflect and represent the area they are from and the people of that area. Finding people like Adeoye Yusuff, with their humility and respect, is just another facet of why these clubs at the foot of the Fourth Division are so very important and special, preserving the true soul and spirit of football.

Kingsmeadow is a small, functional, municipal-looking stadium that is arguably too big for its original owners Kingstonian, and a little too small for its bigger tenants, Wimbledon. The first page of the programme detailed plans to move back to a site on Plough Lane, the original home of Wimbledon, with a capacity that would enable them to grow a little.

It is a ground that is easy to warm to, however, looking like a slightly larger, newer Crown Ground (home of Accrington Stanley). Banners hung from the back of the stands behind the goal, reminding the occasional visitor of their recent past. One read 'The original Dons', referring to the annoyance that MK Dons still have the original club's nickname in their title, despite having no connection in any other way. At the other end there was an 'Akinfenwa – franchise slayer' banner, celebrating their man-mountain of a centre forward's recent winning goal over MK Dons in the Johnstone's Paint trophy.

Sarah was sold when she noticed that there were Kit-Kats for sale at the tea hut. For her, the opportunity to buy a Kit-Kat (she prefers chunky, although they only had the four fingered variety which she was happy enough with) is a serious marker as to just how decent a ground she is in.

'They don't sell them at the Emirates,' she told me bitterly, having been taken by a mate to a recent Champions League match that left her unimpressed. She was clearly warming to Kingsmeadow and its position as a bastion of the soul of football.

For her, the only down-side to proceedings was when the team sheets were read out. Whereas I gave myself an inner high five when Tubbs, Rigg, and Yusuff were all announced as starting, Sarah noticeably stiffened and asked to see the team list in the programme when she heard a name she thought she had seen the back of a long time ago.

'Did, did he just say Jamie Cureton?'

Indeed he had; on the bench for Dagenham was the veteran Norwich legend, and apparent enemy of any self-respecting Ipswich fan, Jamie Cureton.

When he started warming up just in front of us, I feared the worst, and asked her to text me the name of the police station they took her to when the inevitable barrier leap and barrage of abuse took place. She assured me that she was fine, but the glare on her face told me otherwise, and I checked the perimeters for potential escape routes just in case.

The match was a good, honest contest between two sides struggling for form and consistency, and it was clear from the off that Wimbledon had the cutting edge. Man-mountain Ade Akinfenwa and Matt Tubbs worked well together up front, while Sean Rigg and George Francomb probed down the wings. For Dagenham, Ade Yusuff cut an isolated figure in attack; with the rare opportunities he received he looked a threat, with a decent touch, real potential for the future. For this game, however, there just weren't enough of those moments for Dagenham to be dangerous, and when Wimbledon's right back Barry Fuller stabbed home from close range it was a fair reflection of the first half. With the wind in their sails, Wimbledon looked to add a second, but couldn't, even with the support whipped up behind the goal by a pogoing mascot (naturally a Womble) that really looked like he'd had too much coffee or Red Bull.

The second half was notable for two things: Firstly, the barrage of abuse one Wimbledon fan gave Dagenham player George Porter, who was playing on the wing nearest us. This fan behind us really didn't like George, and harangued him constantly. It turned out that Porter had played on loan at Wimbledon for a part of last season, and clearly had done something that this particular fan had taken real exception to. I could maybe understand a whole stand booing an ex-player if they left under a cloud, or had been poor in their team's shirt. But this seemed personal, which is probably why it eventually got to Porter, much more I guess than the usual sledging players endure at every ground they play at, and which would normally be water off a duck's back to them. The constant stream of insults clearly affected Porter, who reacted by mouthing a few words that no-one heard back in the general direction of his abuser, often looking across into the gloom of the stand.

It was a first to see a player react to such abuse. Normally they just have to take it on the chin. He seemed a decent player, a real trier, and I wouldn't have picked him out as the weakest link on the pitch by a long way. His reaction was new, as was the reaction from a another fan a few paces further along the terrace, who started to defend George by shouting that it was a disgrace to be yelling obscenities at someone who was just doing their job.

It was a fair point, but one I didn't expect to hear from a fan of the team Porter was playing against. It did need saying however, and I'm glad someone did, as it really was unacceptable, regardless of which side of the terrace divide you stood on. Either way, the abuse stopped after some sarcastic shouts of 'you're not very good George! Boo George! Is that alright?' aimed at Porter's terrace defender.

That abuse would, I suspect, have paled into insignificance to what Sarah wanted to say when, with Dagenham still losing, and with 20 minutes or so to play, arch nemesis Jamie Cureton, now pushing 40, stepped on to the pitch to replace Ade Yusuff. He had shown flashes of real promise, but this just wasn't going to be his day. Somehow, Sarah held back when Cureton came on, and continued to resist when he contrived to nearly equalise twice in the space of a few minutes. Even in his advanced years, he had the knack for bothering defenders, creating opportunities where there really shouldn't have been any. If Yusuff was going to learn the trade, he couldn't hope for a better teacher than Cureton.

As the game drew on, Dagenham huffed and puffed, but just couldn't find a way through. The crowd erupted on the final whistle, Sarah especially loudly, as she looked at the beaten Cureton, shoulders drooping as the Wimbledon fans and players celebrated three points that had them looking up into mid-table, and leaving Dagenham peering nervously at the bottom two beneath them.

The man on the tannoy announced that that was goal scorer Barry Fuller's first goal in eight years.

'And we look forward to welcoming you back for his next one which we expect sometime around 2022!'

'I really enjoyed that,' Sarah said. 'So much more than the Emirates.' She is a purveyor of real football, and this hidden fixture among a sporting calendar in the capital involving high profile international matches was the real thing, and had everything that makes football such a captivating experience the world over.

The floodlights burned up into the cloud choked night as we walked away from the ground to tackle the ever increasing numbers of by now very drunk rugby fans throttling the London transport network. Sarah had a mini epiphany.

'I'm coming here again,' she said. 'I've really missed this. This is what it's all about.'

Wimbledon v Dagenham didn't create many ripples in the media afterwards, but Sarah was right. This is what it is all about, and despite being hidden in the papers behind pages and pages on Wayne Rooney's one hundredth Cap for England, his penalty that set up a home win, and an away win for South Africa in the rugby, there in the small print was the score, attended by nearly four thousand souls; that was our match of the day.

As for the three characters that made me want brave the deer infested wilds of London; Matt Tubbs and Sean Rigg both looked to be enjoying their time at Wimbledon, celebrating their ever lengthening careers with a real freedom of play. Both had tried out at a higher level, and both now seemed content with their lot in what was a very good standard of football.

Adeoye Yusuff, who cut one of many forlorn figures in the Dagenham team as they huddled on the pitch for an immediate debrief as the fans drained away around them, well, I was very happy to have seen him play. Everything about his attitude on the pitch: his touch on the ball, his tireless efforts for the team, led me to believe that he has a bright future in the game. For his attitude, both on and off the pitch, I really hope that he does make it, because football needs more honest, grounded role models like him.

13

23 November 2014. England Women v Germany Women
Women's International Friendly

THIS, THANKS ONCE again to Jen and Tash, was a third and final opportunity for me to explore the women's game this year. And despite only being a friendly, it was by far and away the most important occasion of the three.

The symbolism of an England Women's international fixture finally being played at the 'home of the national game' was huge. It is true that a low-key friendly against Sweden was played at the old Wembley back in the '80s, but this match, to be played out in front of a crowd of 50,000 (that number would have been more had the FA not capped it at that due to public transport disruptions around the stadium), is altogether on a different scale, and is an enormous message that women's football is thriving.

It's not a message for those who made the trip to the national stadium, or to the many who were unable to make it and watched at home; it's a message to the football-loving public in general, to the FA, to local and national government that fund sporting initiatives, to anyone that will listen; that women's football is here, now, and is very, very good indeed. Not just the national team, but the elite teams of the Super League, and the countless teams and junior sides beneath them that make up the football pyramid, right the way down to the grass roots.

It's a message that had me feeling excited on the way up to Wembley, and, like with so many other moments in this book, there was a kind of serendipity in that this latest visit to the national stadium was to see the same country that were the opponents for my first ever trip to the then twin towers of Wembley. When I mentioned this to my passenger Jamie, an old friend who also happened to have been on that school trip way back in the day to watch a schoolboy international, we started remembering things from that original visit: buying a rosette; the sound of rattles rasping as their owners flung them about above their heads maniacally; the clatter of turnstiles.

The turnstiles, though computerised these days, gave off the same reassuring sounds that had echoed around Wembley way back then, but rosettes, and rattles! You don't see those much these days.

'Jesus! How long ago was that?'

'Well,' I reasoned, 'Germany was still West Germany...' With a terrifying sudden Sherlock Holmes-esque burst of memory, I visualised the front cover of the programme – an advert for Dentyne chewing Gum, a drawing of some schoolboy trophy, and the date – June 1981.

'But that was over 33 years ago!'

The car descended into stunned silence, as two excited ten-year-old schoolboys, playing at being married, with mortgages, and in their 40s, began to realise the full extent of their schizophrenic existence. I don't think any football fan ever grows older than about ten, or whenever their first significant footballing experience happens. Whenever I see a Southampton player walking about in town I immediately turn into that shy, blushing boy hiding behind his autograph book, wondering if he will have the courage to ask for a signature. That boyhood state seems just as real and immediate as the reason I was walking about town in my 42-year-old shell: going to the bank to talk about mortgages; taking the car for an MOT; buying paint to touch up the bathroom.

Football, and the romantic notion of how you saw it as a little boy or girl, no matter the bitterness and cynicism you may pick up through modern living, always seems to persevere somehow, deep down. This match, in 2014, had all the romance and excitement that I remembered feeling on my way to the old Wembley all those years ago. This was an important occasion, for many different reasons, and on many different levels. At the most basic level it was a celebration of all that women's football is.

I've already discussed the glorious integrity of the women's game, and the bond between club, player, and fan that is reminiscent of how it felt to support Southampton and Salisbury back in the '80s. Because of this bond that has been created between club, player, fan, the women's game works with an idealistic honesty and integrity that was once the founding blocks for every club everywhere; basic ideals of belonging and community that many feel have been lost with the advent of the big business that the Men's Premier League has become.

This match at Wembley Stadium was a celebration of the women's game doing things right, both on and off the pitch, and it is fantastic to know that the players that make up the national team will get to live out a childhood dream of playing at this famous ground. Each and every one of them deserves it, even though, for me, this enormous and rather impersonal venue doesn't really represent the basic truths about the women's game.

For example, at every women's match I have been to, either an international or a super league game, the players have milled about with the supporters afterwards. It is a given that there is that level of closeness and affinity; however Wembley, with the seats way back from the pitch and separated by a barrier, does not allow for this. It is a basic disconnect that doesn't sit well with my understanding of the life-force between fan and player that flows through the women's game.

However, for this showpiece statement I could let that slide, as this England team deserved their day in the sun – or torrential rain, as it turned out. So did the fans, the future Lianne Sandersons and Jill Scotts who would see their idols out on that famous pitch and start to dream of their own futures; the Tashes and Jens who had supported the national team and Arsenal Ladies for years, whose passion, along with countless others, have helped build the game into what it now is: a thriving sport chasing hard on the heels of countries who have years and years of professionalism, development, and funding behind them.

It was an exciting time, and as we parked up and watched young boys and girls waving flags and blowing horns – the 21st century rattle, it would appear – it was hard not to get caught up in it all; this history in the making. It was difficult not to get excited for some of the characters we were here to see. Players whom I had seen play in front of just a few thousand fans in Bournemouth, Cardiff, and Wycombe were now warming up in front of such a large crowd that was almost exclusively willing them on. Characters like that almost certainly couldn't have thrived in the Men's game.

I've already mentioned my joy at finally getting to see Kelly Smith play, one of the greatest players ever to wear the England shirt, male or female. She was absent from today's squad, however there were other players with careers packed with humble dedication whose stories deserve to be told as well.

One such person, who deserves special mention on an occasion like this, is Liverpool's Fara Williams, playing her 133rd match for her nation. This fact alone stands her out as an exceptional athlete, but the person behind the stats is just as inspirational as her dedication on the pitch.

After a very difficult childhood, Fara endured six years in her late teens and early 20s of homelessness, jumping from hostel to hostel to keep a roof over her head. Where some people on the streets turn to alcohol or drugs to cope, Fara had football, and a dream to play for her country one day that fuelled and inspired her to keep on going even when, I imagine, there were plenty of moments when it felt impossible.

To come from such a terrible start, and make it to World Cups and European Championships, to winning the Women's Super League Two years running with Liverpool, and now, 133 appearances on from the fulfilment of her dream, leading her country out at Wembley Stadium to play in front of the largest ever crowd for a home England Women's match, well, sometimes words like inspirational don't really grasp the enormity of it all. It would be an honour to watch it all unfold for her.

Another person, who, like Kelly Smith, was absent from the team, but deserves a mention here as she is a large part of what makes the women's game so unique, is Casey Stoney. Casey was the captain of the national team for the first women's international match I saw back in September 2013, and with 116 caps to her name she is another legend in the England squad. As with Fara, this feat alone should be enough, but her courage in coming out as gay earlier this year signals another reason why Casey, Fara, Kelly, and the women's game as a whole is a very special entity that this country should cherish.

At a time when it still remains unthinkable for a male player to come out publicly, and the men's game seems stuck in a cycle of institutional racism, bigotry and homophobia, her choice to come out was met with universal acceptance and celebration by all within the women's game. I think this shows us that, despite being so far behind the men's sport in terms of finance and profile, women's football is light years ahead of it in a great many things far more important than money and fame: tolerance, acceptance, and respect of all race, colour, gender, and sexual orientation. Throw into the mix the undoubted quality, passion and intricate skill within the women's game and you have the complete package for any supporter that has had enough of the big business of the Premier League and the backward state of the sport's governing body.

Casey's actions, Fara's actions, and the actions of players and fans at every match up and down the country are a beacon of light for the men's game and the many disillusioned fans fed up with the current state of it, and shows what can be achieved if you demand that tolerance and respect become the norm.

There was so much to celebrate as we met up with Jen and Tash and their entourage inside the stadium. The only nagging doubt I had, among all this positivity, was England's opponents: Germany. Like their male counterparts, the German women's team are terrifyingly good, and right at the top of their respective FIFA world rankings. For such a historic match it was fitting to host the world's best, but the risk of losing was very real. As it turned out, neither Tash, nor Jen, nor it would appear the entirety of the Wembley crowd would let even the possibility of an absolute thrashing dampen their spirits. This match was never going to be about the result, but more the journey it had taken to get there, and all the possibilities for the future.

Picking the best team in the world was a brave decision, but a brilliant one six months out from the 2015 World Cup in Canada. Why test yourself against anything less than the very best? What value would a routine win against an average side offer? It is admirable to want to face the best, then appreciate what is needed to succeed at the World Cup, to see the work ahead, to see the level needed. And Germany definitely are another level.

Rousing national anthems done, and with England hitting the bar after only 20 seconds, Germany began to exert their excellent passing onto the game. Just like their male counterparts, Germany pass for fun, never losing the ball, looking for the killer pass. They were amazing to watch, and it was no real surprise when they took the lead after only a couple of minutes through sharper, faster reactions at a corner kick. Within a few minutes it was 2-0 when a slip in defence allowed them back in, Celia Sasic putting away the chance with ease.

Despite things not looking great, the England team took to a huddle before they kicked-off again, and the crowd roared its support. All apart from Jen, who was still giggling after the announcer read out the name of the German goal-scorer. I looked at her to try to fathom what was so funny.

'Sasic,' she laughed. 'It sounds like sausage.'

Jesus. A few seats further on, Tash sighed and looked up to the heavens.

The third German goal on the half hour was a work of art; incisive passing, an excellent cross, and Sasic headed the ball back across the goal and into the far corner. We steeled ourselves for the rest of the match, and the imminent sniggers from Jen when the announcer had to read Sasic's name out again. 3-0 was no real surprise from a squad long used to professional football and some of the best coaching in the world, but I prayed for no more goals. England's endeavour and passionate play did not deserve that.

Flicking through the programme at the break, I stumbled across a statistic that confounded me, and had the cynic in me wondering whether it was an omission. The facts and fixtures page had the line-ups for the national team going back to October 2012. Each England match had the goal scorers and substitutes noted, a capital P if the match ended in penalties. Along with the explanations for these icons at the foot of the page there was also a yellow square and a red square, denoting which player received a yellow or red card.

Only there weren't any. Not one yellow card across over two years of matches.

If I hadn't seen a number of women's matches by this point I would definitely have considered it to be a printing error, but the absence of cynical and 'professional fouls', diving and all the rest at each and every one of the matches I'd been to suggested that it was entirely possible that a team could go 28 games without a single yellow card. It was yet another cold, undeniable statistic highlighting the refreshing disposition of women's football.

In the second half, England began to exert themselves more. The introductions of Fran Kirby and Jill Scott solidified the midfield and allowed Toni Duggan to move up front with the tireless Lianne Sanderson who threw herself into every attack and challenge, and all of a sudden England started to have more of an edge. The change of tactics pushed Germany back, though they were still very dangerous; passing their way out of trouble and on to the counter-attack in a flash.

It was an engrossing match, even though the result was long gone before half time, and at the final whistle England could feel satisfied that they had given their all, and had learned a lot about what they would need to do in order to defeat the world's best next summer. The crowd's standing ovation at the end certainly suggested that the fans had seen enough to feel positive about progress next year, and, after all, that is what it is all about. The fans, the players, everyone applauded what had been a historic match; a celebration of the fact that between them, those in the stands, and those on the pitch, the future of the women's game in England was in very good hands. It was a reassuring feeling as we filtered out of the stands and into the cold night.

Bring on the summer and Canada 2015, I thought, cowering beneath the driving rain as we tried to locate the car. A whole tournament of football played out in the way Germany and England just had. I for one cannot wait.

14

13 December 2014. Portsmouth v Accrington Stanley League Two

IT WAS A long time coming – nearly three months in fact – but we were, at last, back, stood on the terraces with the Stanley faithful waiting eagerly for our next instalment of Accrington magic. Ever since the demise of Salisbury, this book has been a means of coping with that loss; replacing that connection to the wonderful world of the lower and non-leagues that Salisbury used to represent. And if this book is an attempt to reconnect with everything that made going to watch them with my grandfather all those years ago so special, then Accrington Stanley – the club, the players, and most importantly their fans – are the beating heart of it.

It was never my intention to replace Salisbury with another club, to find another 'second team' to redress the imbalance created when the Southampton/Salisbury partnership failed. This book was always supposed to be a simple testimony to experiences of the past and present in the hope that others may give the world outside the Premier League a look. However, the friendship and kindness bestowed on Emma and me by the Accrington Stanley fans and backroom staff during our first few visits only added to the unique nature of the club that is there for all to see on any given Saturday down at the Crown Ground. It was virtually impossible not to fall in love with it all.

This is a love that stretches far and deep enough for two Southampton fans to make the 20 mile trip to a place as inhospitable and hate filled toward the red and white half of Hampshire as any on earth. A hate so venomous that you feel certain that, despite walking around Fratton Park to the ticket office in an Accrington shirt, the throngs of Pompey fans around you somehow know that you are a lifelong Saints supporter. The hate, from both sides, was ludicrous in my eyes, and as we nodded at the few smiling Pompey faces who acknowledged the fact that Accrington fans had made it all the way down to the south coast, I nodded back and wondered what they would had done if I had been walking around in a Southampton shirt. It wouldn't have ended well for me, I am sure.

And that, to me, is the point. We are all just people, following different football teams, so why does wearing an Accrington shirt get me benevolent smiles, and a Saints one get me hospitalised – if I'm lucky?

Sporting rivalry is great, it helps make the drama on view that bit more special. But when did it turn into full on hate? When did it become so dangerous to go and watch your local team take on their local rivals that you can only attend by getting a voucher for a seat on a coach, and are only get your ticket for the match once you are safely on board and being transported directly to the away turnstile? When did it get so bad that it is deemed too dangerous to simply drive 20 miles, park your car, and walk to the ground? The last two Saints v Pompey matches were run with this military precision, and sadly no-one seemed to bat an eyelid, probably due to the two derby matches that came before them ending in near riots.

I just don't get it. I understand the need to do better than your local rivals. I get and feel the passionate support for your team during a local clash, and the need for bragging rights from a derby win. I get the satisfaction from being above your rivals in the league system. But hate?

My wife's grandfather grew up during the Second World War, and remembers that before the war broke out Pompey paraded the FA Cup they had won around The Dell to warm applause. He often tells me about how after the war, when Portsmouth were winning Division One and Saints were drifting between Divisions Two and Three, Saints fans would regularly go to Fratton Park when they were playing away to see a higher standard of football; to see international players and the big clubs of the day. They would stand together on the same terrace; Pompey and Saints, with not a hint of aggression from anywhere. I guess after the horrors of the Second World War there was a general sense of perspective on things as genuinely inconsequential in the greater scheme of things as football, and who supported who.

With the advent of hooliganism in the '60s and '70s, and with the realities of the war fading from memory, urban legends grew as to why Pompey and Saints should hate each other. Broken picket lines during a dock strike that no historian on either side of the Hampshire divide can find any evidence for suddenly grew into fact and became one of the justifications for decades of animosity and pure venom.

To me it is really sad, and unnecessary, for this rivalry to have turned into something that now seems to be uncontrollable; a juggernaut of violence and hate that makes me fear the FA Cup and League Cup draws, praying that Pompey get knocked out before we enter to prevent it all from exploding once more. I can't help but think about Hannis and Jacob from the Faroe Islands, and their consternation at the animosity between local teams that never made it to their country, and is unthinkable to them.

'If you live close by you should be more friendly, not less?' Hannis had said when I mentioned trouble at local derbies, 'people would have more in common?'

As for me, for the past few seasons I've tried to recreate, in some very small way, the environment in which my wife's grandfather first went to Fratton Park, as a Saints fan wanting to watch some football when they were playing away. I've gone once a season for the last three seasons, this Accrington trip being the third, but because of the fear I've always gone in the away end, just in case someone somehow fathomed who I was.

The irony was not lost on me when both Accrington and Pompey players came together on the pitch for a photo to commemorate the 100th anniversary of the Christmas Day truce and football match on no-man's land during World War One. Beneath the header 'Football Remembers', teams across the country were coming together to pause and consider the horrors of The Great War, the heroic and moving actions of those soldiers among the killing fields, and maybe, just maybe, the insanity of all the hate that is now based around a simple sporting activity, maybe finding a little of that perspective that once allowed Pompey and Saints fans to share the same terrace. Perhaps one day we can have a 'Football Forgets', and shed the poison, but keep the passion, as a fan run initiative called for during the Christmas 2014 Tyne v Wear derby. Maybe. One day.

For the time being, Emma and I were trying our own version of a Christmas football truce by inviting a Pompey fan, who hates all the animosity as much as I do, to sit with us in the Accrington end, along with a complete neutral who had never been to see a football match before. I hoped they both felt as welcome as we did among the Stanley faithful, numbering no more than 80 or so. Warm handshakes and waves greeted us from those we had met at Northampton back in September, and a few new friends came to talk to us about the writing on the blog and how things were going. The Stanley fans truly are a caring and special lot.

As the ground began to fill, and the tiny band of away support became dwarfed by the home fans swelling stands that had hosted Premier League football only a few short years ago, we tried to describe to the neutral, and football novice, Rich, the mismatch, that we were about to witness.

'In simple economic terms the gap between the clubs is huge,' I explained. 'Accrington average around 1,400 fans for a home game, most paying about £20. This, along with sponsorship and advertising determines what sort of playing budget they can afford.'

Rich typed the figures into the calculator on his phone and nodded.

'Portsmouth on the other hand average around 14,000 fans, all paying around £20.'

Rich did the maths and whistled.

'Jesus, that doesn't seem fair?'

'I know. But that's what they are up against, to varying degrees, every single week.'

Rich sat up a little in his seat, his interest piqued, as the players broke from the group photo and got ready. Emma showed him the league table, revealing that both teams were level on points in mid-table. He shook his head.

'How can that happen?'

Then the referee blew his whistle and, yet again, like every other time we had been to see them play, the players on the pitch and the Stanley supporters in the stand begin to show Rich exactly how that could happen.

It was an entertaining match, made even better when Stanley raced into a two goal lead. First Rob Atkinson volleyed home from a set piece, and then minutes later Sean Maguire, who caused Pompey all sorts of problems all day, fed John O'Sullivan, who fired home from outside the box, sending the tiny band of Accrington fans into delirium. It was at this point that Kieran, our Pompey friend who didn't understand why, in a civilised society there needed to be segregation at football matches at all, wished he was sat in the home stands, with his fellow miserable Portsmouth fans numbering an excess of 14,000.

Even the most benign and tolerant fan needs to be left to suffer with like-minded people when their team is getting trounced, because it hurts like hell, no matter how open-minded you may be. Kieran certainly didn't need Emma smiling like a Cheshire cat, nor did he need the playful taunts from a fan behind us, reminding the Pompey fans nearest us that while they were watching Portsmouth in the Premier League ten years ago, Stanley had been playing the likes of Frickley in the Northern League!

It was sobering stuff, which only got a little better when Portsmouth scored two themselves to level things up, however it still didn't sit right; Portsmouth only drawing with Accrington in the Fourth Division as half time approached. Indeed, a poster in the programme of players celebrating a goal against AC Milan in the UEFA Cup only five years earlier hinted mournfully at a time where such fixtures would have seemed impossible, except maybe for a cup match. A time that the editor of the programme at least couldn't quite consign to distant memory in the face of the realities of Fourth Division life.

In truth, they were a little lucky to still be drawing at half time, as Stanley missed a penalty, which led neutral football novice Rich to go over the maths again as he warmed himself up with a cup of tea. No matter how many times he looked at the numbers however, two all just didn't seem to be a plausible outcome.

As it turned out, he was right. It didn't finish two all.

After surviving a Pompey onslaught in the first five minutes of the second half, where young loan keeper Jack Rose made a number of wonderful saves, the game went a little flat. Portsmouth seemed to be running out of ideas, and for 20 minutes or so the match descended into a sparring contest, until Accrington took the initiative and started pushing forward again. The sleek passing from the first half returned and they probed down the wings, switching play with excellent long range passes from centre back Tom Aldred. Substitute Shay McCartan went close, firing narrowly over, and Sean Maguire again threatened to let loose.

But finally, with an almost fairy tale inevitability, and with ten minutes remaining, winger Piero Mingoia cut inside and fired another long range shot into the far corner to make it 3-2. The team ran to celebrate in front of the away fans behind the goal. Kieran slumped quietly in his seat while Rich tried to fathom the unfathomable: how could a team with so little not only compete, but thrive among those with far more resources than them?

It doesn't make sense. In the cold light of day, things like this just shouldn't happen. There will always be the odd freak FA Cup shock here and there, but time and time again throughout the season? It just doesn't seem possible, until you begin to consider an unknown quantity, the x in the equation; the spirit of a group of players and fans that belong to a 'club that wouldn't die', who make up for what they don't have in material terms with blood, sweat, tears, time, and endless dedication. Accrington Stanley are proof that money can't buy you everything, and that togetherness, belief, and hard work can take you a lot further than you ever dreamed possible.

Unlike most Accrington matches we had seen, there was no need for heroics, no need for players to throw their bodies on the line to protect their lead. Instead they kept the ball with neat, intelligent passing, and even created a chance for a fourth goal, although it ultimately came to nothing. At the final whistle there was elation in the away end and a chorus of boos from the home stands, and as the Stanley fans filed out, hands red raw from applauding the players who came over to salute them, I paused to think about the crazy statistic that was quite possibly unique to Emma and I: were we the only fans in the world never to have seen the team we support lose? Four games in and four wins, 24 goals, 14 of which were scored by Stanley. I know it was only four games, but all four were against clubs much better off than Accrington, and two of them were away from the Crown Ground; for me that is much more than a small victory.

Would I exchange all that for a win in Stanley's next match however? Well, that is for another chapter. For now, it is nice to bask in the warmth of another piece of Accrington magic, where they out-passed and out-fought a club with ten times the support and potential playing budget, where the guile and passion the players displayed out on the pitch was matched by the tiny band of Stanley supporters tucked away in one corner of the 20,000 seat Fratton Park.

Bask yes, gloat no. Among all this was poor old Kieran, despondent at another low point in his club's recent history, and this was no time for gloating. We have all felt that crushing pain when our team gets battered at some point, or possibly worse still, when they slowly fall apart without even a whimper. We all know what that despair feels like, and we all know the routine, so as the Stanley fans filtered out into the mass of blue and white scarves we kept our delight to ourselves out of respect. Likewise, a couple of Pompey fans nodded and said, 'Well played, safe journey home,' as they walked past us.

Such magnanimous behaviour should be the norm, and in my experience it is, derby matches excluded. I felt no need to mock my friend, who looked broken and lost as we said our goodbyes outside. The phrase 'I wouldn't wish that on my worst enemy' applies to pretty much every walk of life except football, where Pompey and Saints fans, Newcastle and Sunderland, Celtic and Rangers supporters, routinely do exactly that. Maybe one day a little bit of that perspective brought into sharp relief after both horrific World Wars might return, a little bit of respect and empathy, because fundamentally we are all part of the same tribe; a tribe in love with football.

At least for Kieran, as we watched him fade away into the crowd, and indeed all of us, there was always the next match, and that chance at redemption, which could just possibly save his Christmas.

Portsmouth v Accrington Stanley definitely wasn't the same as matches of old, where Saints and Pompey could stand shoulder to shoulder on the terraces to watch a football match. After all, Kieran, Emma, and I were incognito, albeit the latter wearing our Stanley colours with pride. But in our own little universe it felt good that we could do this as friends, not divided by a pointless hatred, enjoying a simple game of footie.

In the car on the way home it felt good to talk about the symbolism of commemorating the Christmas day truce with our own tiny, insignificant display of friendship through football. It went quiet for a second or two, and then Emma spoke up.

'When was it?'

'What, the truce?'

'Yeah.'

'A hundred years ago.'

'Yeah, but when?'

'What, the Christmas Day truce?'

'Yeah, when was it?'

'You want to know when the Christmas Day truce was?'

'Yes.'

'Emma. Christmas Day!'

'Oh,' she said. There was a pause, then: 'OH!'

When she had stopped laughing, she looked at me.

'Jesus, you're not going to put that in the book, are you?'

I smiled, and her shoulders drooped a little, just as Kieran's had, and she looked out the window.

'Crap, he's going to put it in the book.'

15

16 December 2014. Yeovil Town v Accrington Stanley
FA Cup Second Round

BACK ON 16 AUGUST, Cowes Sports beat Team Solent in the extra-preliminary qualifying round of the FA Cup. The next round, the preliminary qualifying round, Emma and I saw them lose to Yate Town, who in turn lost to Dorchester Town. Dorchester went on to beat Abingdon and Hendon before coming unstuck to Bristol Rovers at the final qualifying stage. Rovers then lost to Tranmere in the first round 'proper' of the Cup, then Tranmere drew their second round tie with Oxford United. This was the replay to determine who got a day in the sun against Premier League Swansea City, along with a number of other replays.

So surely, for continuity's sake, we were up at Prenton Park, Tranmere, to see this chain of events that began back on a warm August afternoon on the Isle of Wight through to its conclusion? To see it through to the promised land of the third round of the competition, where all the top clubs join in?

We were not. We were in Yeovil, Somerset, unable to pass up the opportunity to see the potential romance and magic of the FA Cup in action, but also unable to pass up seeing Accrington Stanley play once more, less than a two hour drive from home.

An FA Cup second round replay in Somerset on a cold, wet, Tuesday night in December may not sound like the natural breeding ground for the notion of romance and magic. However, for both sides – one languishing near the foot of League One, the other battling on with the lowest playing budget in League Two – this match represented why football is so special, and why, fundamentally, the FA Cup is a unique and wonderful competition unlike any other played throughout world football.

When I was still playing, I strove to better myself in order to make it for a local side that would feature in the earliest rounds of the competition. The thought of being able to say 'I played in the FA Cup' was a wonderful one. It would have been an amazing achievement, though unfortunately ability put paid to that.

At the Cowes game back in August you could feel the atmosphere charged with that excitement that it was the FA Cup. It binds the football pyramid together, connects it with just the thinnest thread of hope that maybe, this year, it could be your team hosting global giants such as Manchester United in the third round. For either Yeovil or Accrington, this is the carrot dangling tantalisingly in the shadows just beyond the floodlights. A home tie against Manchester United, live on television, could define their season both on the pitch and at the bank. For the Chairmen of these clubs, a match against United is the thing that dreams are made of. Enormous gate receipts, television money, and advertising and sponsorship revenue could set the club on a footing that would keep them in the black for years.

The match programme pointed out that to a club the size of Accrington, an FA Cup dream tie against such an enormous institution boggled the mind with potential consequences. The programme also contained an interview with Stanley boss John Coleman, who spelled out how important it was to receive the £18,000 prize money for getting through the first round, and explained that a further £27,000 for winning through round two would be fantastic for the club, let alone anything else. These sums of money that mean so much to clubs like Accrington are nothing to the players waiting for them in round three, where the time it takes for Wayne Rooney to sneeze probably earns him more than the prize fund on offer for this match.

For everyone milling around Huish Park before kick-off, the importance of this match's result was well recognised, and had people daring to dream. The ticket office was doing amazing business; expecting a crowd up to twice as big as an average league game.

The away end was busy too; a supporter's coach supplementing the convoy of cars that had made the torturous trip from Lancashire to deepest, darkest Somerset. The Stanley faithful looked to number over two hundred; an amazing display of loyalty and hope, so far from home on a cold winter's night. That's what the FA Cup does. It ignites passion and hope, it makes you dare to dream, and for me at least the competition is all about these sorts of nights; the early rounds, the qualifying rounds. This was the FA Cup I grew up on.

Sadly, due to the lure of Premier League riches, the third round can also herald the end of the magic for another season. Lots of clubs choose to field weakened sides, keeping their best 11 back for league games that might help to ensure they remain in the top flight to reap the millions of pounds of television revenue. Meanwhile, Championship clubs sacrifice the cup in order to keep themselves fresh for a promotion push toward the big time.

But for this night, at least, the magic was alive and well.

With time to kill, we wandered round Huish Park and stumbled across something that took me back, once again, to Victoria Park and my grandfather. It wasn't quite the little shed that Grandad and I held in awe next to the pavilion at Victoria Park, but Yeovil's programme shop was everything that little ramshackle hut had been; rows upon rows of programmes from all over the world, every club, thousands upon thousands of them! From what looked like every Yeovil programme from the last 40 years, to obscure foreign clubs, to boxes of random league and non-league programmes, this place was a little piece of heaven right out of the warmest memories of my childhood. It was made even better for Emma when I found her a copy of a Yeovil programme from the early part of last season featuring an interview with Dan Seaborne. He had spent the first half of last season here before heading out on loan to Coventry. She was made up, and that was before the football had even started. This shop was a great find, and if I'd had a spare fortnight I would have settled down for some serious browsing. As it was, we had a match to watch.

Night matches are always special; floodlights burning into the night making the pitch seem to come alive, a vivid, shimmering green. Ever since my first experience of a night game at The Dell as a young boy, watching Saints play Hull in a League Cup match, I find myself looking forward to them more than anything else; the floodlights in the distance drawing you through the streets toward them, the thrill of stepping out into a stand, the pitch lit up taking me back all those years to that first special moment.

As we settled into the ever-filling away end, I noticed a blast from the past warming up for Yeovil. A large chunk of the programme was dedicated to the Yeovil striker James Hayter's achievement of amassing 700 professional appearances, which was reached up at Accrington in the initial cup tie that ended in a draw. Grandad and I had watched a young Hayter, only eight games into this amazing milestone, when he went out on loan to Salisbury. It was obvious that he was much better than the Southern League standard Salisbury played in at the time, and we followed his rise up into the Football League with interest, and some satisfaction, glad that our little club had helped him on his way.

Six hundred and ninety-three games later, he was trying to knock the team that had replaced Salisbury in my affections out of the cup, and try he and his team-mates did. Yeovil pressed hard and stifled Stanley's passing game in a tense, nervous first half, and they often looked more likely to score, but the enormity of the prize on offer had them snatching at chances which came to nothing.

The tension had clearly got to the home support as well, who were pretty quiet, suffering with the weight of expectation; something the boisterous, and often very funny Accrington fans pointed out gleefully.

'It's quieter than Accy library!'

A couple of them followed with:

'Where the f**k is Accy library?'

To which the response was:

'There's no books in Accy library!'

In football, it's always best to mock yourselves before the opposition can.

At half time there was a collective exhale from all sides of the ground; everyone relieved at a break in the tension. Amongst the crowd I thought I spotted someone we had met back in September at Northampton; a friendly face who had spoken about visiting our neck of the woods and The Dell back in the '60s.

'When Stanley went bust and folded in 1962 I didn't know what to do with myself. Eventually I went with a friend to watch Blackburn, it being better than nothing, and we came down to The Dell a couple of times,' he had told me.

I wondered how he was doing tonight, having been through the trauma of losing your club for the best part of eight years, then watching it slowly come back, all the way from the Lancashire Combination League to the brink of playing one of the biggest teams in the world, in the oldest and biggest club competition in the world, with a potential global audience watching on television? If I felt nervous as a novice of only five games, I could only wonder how he was holding up.

In the second half Stanley began to take control, once again belying their inferior playing budget and league position. They seemed to settle into the game, and started to get their playing style going beneath an ever intensifying rain storm. Piero Mingoia again looked a threat on the wing, and Shay McCartan began to get the size of the Yeovil defence, driving at them time and again.

The home fans started to get nervous as Stanley continued to improve, especially when second half substitute Lee Molyneux started to cause problems in a match that was becoming a real blood and thunder affair. Tom Aldred, Luke Joyce and Rob Atkinson pulled off some amazing last ditch tackles to thwart Hayter and co. and set Accrington off on another attack, and as the clock ticked on toward 80 minutes every single player was putting it all-out on the line, throwing themselves into tackles, getting up and looking for decisive passes, dying out on the pitch for the cause.

It was one such pass, created through heroic tackling and quick thinking that set Shay McCartan off on another mazy run, which took him to just outside the Yeovil penalty area. The away fans gasped as he let fly with a screamer that smashed against the bar and bounced down, Matt Crooks throwing himself at the rebound that dribbled agonizingly wide. It was a close escape for Yeovil.

The away fans kept singing, the Stanley players kept fighting for another chance, but sickeningly fate had turned its back on Accrington as, from a corner, Jack Rose punched clear only for the ball to fall to the only Yeovil player in a position to take a shot. Ex-Saint Simon Gillett did exactly that, and after 84 minutes of tireless graft and heroics Stanley conceded a cruel and crushing goal. As the Yeovil players and fans celebrated, Accrington bodies slumped to the floor, exhausted both physically and mentally from their efforts.

With only a few minutes to go, Stanley fans and players tried to compose themselves, to go again one last time, but with time running out and energy drained Yeovil killed the game off with a sublime header from Kieffer Moore, and the dream was over. It would be Yeovil who would have the chance to emulate the giant-killing sides of their past, and good luck to them. They had battled hard as well. It was genuinely heartbreaking to see the Stanley players sink to their knees at the final whistle, some in tears, as their efforts really had deserved better, had deserved the chance to line up alongside Manchester United.

As they applauded the travelling support that sang on in honour of their crestfallen heroes, I appreciated the sadness at missing out. But, as we started to file out into the wet night, the over-riding emotion was one of hope. This didn't feel like the end of something, but more like the start of the rest of the season.

Accrington had proven over two games that they could match a League One side comfortably. They had proven that among their small band they had the quality, dedication, belief and passion to really go for promotion.

Hopefully such an amazing display, which ranked right up there with anything I'd seen of Stanley in the past for me, might inspire a few more people to come out and support them up at the Crown Ground. One thing is for sure, the pride and passion both on the pitch and in the stands most definitely deserves it.

16

27 December 2014. Lymington Town v Brockenhurst
Wessex League Premier Division

THE BUSY CHRISTMAS football schedule is always a special time. Fixtures come so thick and fast that it feels like, well, Christmas, to football fans across the land who get to enjoy their team and many others in action up to four times between Boxing Day and New Year's Day.

It is a tradition that has withstood time and the advent of big business and the Premier League. It is seemingly one of football's few basic, pure elements that does appear to be untouchable; the Christmas calendar is so special to so many that the annual complaints from the odd Premier League manager over their hectic schedule are universally ignored.

It is a special time, whether old or young, Premier League fan or non-league supporter; it always has been, and hopefully it always will. As a child I would sit in front of the television watching the vidiprinter scroll through, waiting excitedly for scores for Southampton and sometimes even Salisbury to pop up, before heading out into the freezing cold to play out how I imagined the games had gone. Often I was in my brand new football kit that would be worshipped like it was the Turin shroud, running around in the snow in the failing light. I would commentate as I went while my arms and legs became red raw, the eerie pallid glow of the snow as darkness fell illuminating play until either someone called me back into the house (whilst questioning my sanity), or I finally lost the feeling in my feet to carry on. That, to me, is the magic of football at Christmas. Also, with games coming so thick and fast even a defeat doesn't feel so bad, as within 48 hours there is another opportunity to put things right.

My grandparents used to stay with us over Christmas, and I would often cut out the local fixtures from the paper so that I could appear to be mentioning in passing to Grandad, clearly unable to hide my excitement, when Salisbury, or Andover, Lymington, Brockenhurst, or his Achilles heel Wellworthy Athletic were playing. A few calls later, to check if matches were still on, we'd find ourselves at one of them, Grandad apparently unable to turn down the opportunity of sitting in the freezing cold in the middle of nowhere in the New Forest with a few other hardy souls, pouring over a programme to see if we recognised any of the players on show.

The whole Christmas week felt like some wonderful bone-chilling carnival, where you had maybe a day's rest before the vidiprinter would crank up again and you would find yourself either wrapped up somewhere obscure waiting eagerly for a match to start, or cross-legged in your new kit, staring expectantly at the television to play out in lines of primitive text all of the day's action, itching to get out into the gloom of the back garden to add meat to those basic statistical bones. The magic doesn't seem to fade even when you grow up, or at least it hasn't for me, despite people less in the know hinting that possibly it should have.

From my playing days I can remember details about matches over the Christmas period far more clearly than any other. I can recall moments of an obscure reserve team match between Winchester City and Alton Town, a decent tackle, or a neat pass. I can recall a game for Wellow at Durley, another decent tackle and pass to set up an attack. I can remember the excitement of actually being a part of this ritual, actually playing a part. It set those games up on a pedestal while other matches around them faded and disappeared into time.

The same can be said for watching matches. I remember as if it were yesterday the excitement of children and families, and groups of friends as they took their seats at The Dell on Boxing Day 1998 to watch Southampton play Chelsea. It was a game we lost, but I can remember everything about it, because it was one of those wonderful Boxing Day experiences. It stands out where no other game that season seems to have done.

It is this coming together of friends and family over Christmas, those few short days to relax and take stock, which quite possibly makes the Christmas football schedule so special. Like the Christmas Day Truce 100 years ago, the football calendar, and the whole holiday, is a time to stop, to breathe out, and to just be for a while.

For me, that 'being' manifests itself as a little boy kicking a ball around in the dark and the snow, or sitting in the stand at Lymington Town with some of my favourite football companions. Now that Grandad has passed, this includes Nick, my old friend and brother in law, and my two nephews Sam and George, flicking through our programmes and looking forward to the New Forest derby between Lymington and Brockenhurst.

Barely five miles separates the two clubs, both nestled deep within the forest, and for anything other than these footballing derbies the two places are basically one; nice places for tourists to visit in the summer, and nice places to have a pint or two in front of a roaring fire during the winter. Flipping through the player profiles in the programme proves the point, as ten of the Lymington players had also turned out for Brockenhurst in the past; a similar number of the Brock squad having spent time with Town.

Happily stocked up with all the essentials required for a local derby: for 11 and eight-year-olds respectively comprising Fruit Shoots, Lucozade Sport and a bag of Haribo, for the 'grownups' £5 to get in (the kids are free), a mug of tea, and a programme, we settled down in the small stand to watch a full-on blood and thunder match.

Both sets of fans, numbering no more than 100, milled about with each other chatting and laughing as neighbours and work colleagues do; handshakes between opposing players as they warmed up proving the point that this was, outside of the 90 minutes on the pitch at least, a friendly derby.

When the whistle blew, friendships on and off the pitch were put on hold as the game became a fast paced, very tough tackling encounter. The supporters, friends and colleagues outside of football, decamped to different parts of the stand and began to chide each other when an opposing player fell over, misplaced a pass, or anything else that could be used to playfully wind them up.

As tackles flew in which would no doubt have resulted in red cards in the Premier League and an eight-a-side match by half time, I couldn't help but appreciate the honesty of the match; it wasn't a dirty game at all. It was just a good, tough, full-blooded contest where fouls were mostly mistimed tackles, albeit strong ones, rather than cynical 'professional' fouls. If a player got scythed down there was none of the rolling about or histrionics that has become the norm at the top end of the game. Only genuinely injured players stayed down for any length of time, and even then they tried to get up to carry on. No-one tried to get an opponent sent off, dived or feigned injury; everyone tried to play as decent a game of football as they could on a bobbling pitch that at times made it almost impossible. Despite the footing, there was some decent skill out on show that managed to bypass the hard and uneven surface.

It was a match that soldiers returning from the horrors of the killing fields in France and Belgium in 1914 and the Christmas Day truce (which was commemorated in the match programme) would have recognised as a good old game of football. The question of whether or not they would recognise a Premier League match would probably speak volumes about the disconnect that is growing between fans and the financial behemoth at the top end of the game.

One player was outstanding despite the bobbling surface; the wonderfully named Brockenhurst winger Will Tickle caused Lymington trouble all match long. His skill and trickery set up decent chance after decent chance for the visitors, and marked him out for some special tackling from the home side; often as a result of him just being too fast for the Lymington defence, sometimes as a little bit of revenge for jinking past them once too often.

Sam and George giggled at my suggestion that Will could use his name for mischief at things like his wedding, when at the altar he could pronounce 'I Will Tickle', and then tickle the vicar or his bride to be, or possibly maraud through the church congregation tickling all in his path like some despotic tickling robot. Funny name or not, Tickle is a class apart, and like many a player Grandad and I picked out on our Christmas match travels over the years, I will look forward to watching his progress, which should be significant.

After a goalless but entertaining first half, everyone decamped to the clubhouse for a cup of tea or a pint; the factions in the stand who had spent most of the half ribbing one another joining back up as friends and work mates to have a drink as if nothing had happened, just as it should be.

It was at half time, before the match restarted, that I was really reminded of the labour of love that clubs at Lymington and Brockenhurst's level are. At the half time whistle I saw a couple of people jogging back to the clubhouse to prepare drinks and the tea urn for the 'rush'. They, like the old-timer who sat on a bar stool by the entrance to the ground taking gate money before kick-off and selling programmes, are volunteers, and they do it because they love their club. For many who help out with the pitch, collect the corner flags after the match, take down the nets, sweep up the stand, sell raffle tickets, serve cups of tea, sell club badges, and much more besides, they do it simply because the club is a massive part of their lives.

Volunteering for a club can, especially for the numerous old-timers carrying out these tasks, be a valuable source of friendship and human interaction. These clubs could not survive without them, these mainstays of the tiny communities that they represent having little in the way of money to pay anybody. Without the volunteers' selfless love, clubs like these would wither and fail. It is the love of belonging, of feeling a part of it all, which keeps these little institutions going. They truly are fuelled by friendship and community, and this makes them just as vital, if not more so, as Manchester United or Chelsea.

These clubs are for the people, by the people, which is why my youngest nephew George could borrow a ball and have a kick about in the goals with a couple of other kids he met during half time without any fear of being told off. Watching him play out what he had just seen on the pitch took me right back to those Christmases of old, playing out scores from the vidiprinter in failing light in my new kit in the back garden. The experience was made all the more poignant as Sam had been quietly doing a commentary of the match to himself during the first half, programme open on his lap so that he could find the name that went with each shirt number.

Between the two of them, they played it out exactly as I did all those years ago, recreating what the Christmas schedule meant to me when I was their age, the excitement and possibility of it all, the seemingly never ending carnival of football laid out before me.

The second half carried on where the first had left off, with both teams trying to play the right way, passing the ball around before trying to pick out a defence splitting pass. Brockenhurst had the edge, with Tickle pulling the strings and getting in behind the Town defence all too often. But the goal wouldn't come for them, and almost inevitably Lymington managed to score on a breakaway.

Tickle set about Lymington once more, drawing foul on foul from the desperate Town defence with inevitable consequences for the home side's centre back, who picked up another yellow to go with the one he received in the first half, earning him an early bath. As all this played out, we watched George continue his kick-about with his new found friends behind the goal. (Sometimes they tried playing other games, such as 'let's climb behind the clubhouse to see what is back there', which had Nick rushing out of the stand to retrieve them.) Meanwhile, Brock huffed and puffed but couldn't break the hosts down, and as darkness and the temperature both fell, the skies draining from a pastel blue to a pale red, Lymington held on for a derby win, their celebrations from within their dressing room in the clubhouse afterwards echoing across the fast deserted ground.

It may have 'only' been a Wessex League match on a cold, dark Christmas holiday Saturday, but a derby win is a derby win, and that match which only cost five pounds to watch was as captivating a contest as anything that would appear on Match of the Day.

It's all about context really. If you expect a five pound match to be rubbish, it probably will be. If you think that the Wessex League is beneath you, then it will be. But if you simply hand over your fiver, and watch, really watch, then Lymington v Brockenhurst is just as enthralling, as full of incident and chances, of incisive passing, of drama and passion, as anything you might see higher up the football pyramid.

Is the skill as great as the Premier League? Of course it isn't. But is the passion, the drama, the intensity as great? Possibly more so, I'd say, because it is football without the corruption of vast wealth and corporations. It is football of the heart, football for a community, by the community.

As we left, Sam, clutching his programme (good lad!), asked his dad when they could next go to watch their local non-league team, AFC Totton.

'Whenever you like, Sam,' was the answer. 'Shall we look when the next match is when we get home? George, do you want to come?'

George, who had been air-kicking footballs as he wandered on ahead of us, smiled and nodded enthusiastically.

They may even get to see Salisbury play again in the not too distant future, as word is that a group has taken over what is left of the club, though there is no indication what league they might play in next season, or what ground they might play at. There is every chance this newly formed Salisbury may end up in the same league at Lymington and Brockenhurst.

Unable to use the name Salisbury City anymore, an online poll determined that the new name of the club would be Salisbury FC, the name Grandad and I knew them as before they added 'City' in the '90s. While it is good to know there will be a club for people to support, I am struggling with the concept. It won't be the club that Grandad and I went to watch. It will be a new version, and because of that, right now I just don't feel any connection to it.

It will be a club Grandad never knew, had no part of, and now never will. Maybe things will change with time, but right now it feels like these adventures for this book will continue to fill the void left by mine and Grandad's club folding, for the foreseeable future. It still feels like they hold the connection between the past and the present, not the possibility of this new club. Regardless of this new incarnation appearing it still feels like the club we knew and loved is gone, and gone for good.

Would I be able to resist a Christmas match in the New Forest between Lymington and this new club? Who knows? Whatever the future holds at least the happiness of memories of old, made vivid through this book, are alive and well, happily mingling with the present, and, in Sam and George, the future.

And that makes me smile.

Happy Christmas everyone, and a Happy New Year.

17

10 January 2015. Downton v Amesbury Town
Wessex League Division One

FOOTBALL PROGRAMMES HAVE always been an integral part of my football experience, from the very first trip to The Dell with a family friend when I was ten. I was too shy to stop Colin and ask him if I could buy one that first time, but I was completely captivated by the one the programme seller held up as he called out to the crowd to come and buy it, and the many others in the box at his feet.

They had a bright red cover with an action shot and the word 'Saints' across the top in a font that the team had used for a number of years, which reminded me of the yearbook I had received at Christmas. The possibilities of this programme fascinated me, just as the yearbook had, packed full of interviews, pictures of players, statistics, league tables, fixtures, and results. I used to pour over that yearbook, and pretty much knew it by heart. And now here I was, discovering that they did a mini version for every match!

Shyness got the better of me that first game, but not the second, when I tugged at Colin's coat and asked if we could stop and get one with the correct money already in my hand. It didn't disappoint with its player features and photos of recent matches, with its bulletins on reserve and 'A' team matches, a team photo of the opposition (Aston Villa), fixtures and scores, lists of players and games played.

For a kid crazy about football and living decades before the internet, where all this information is now just a click of a button away, the match programme was a fortnightly bible for all that it offered on my favourite team, and I treated each of them as such, storing them safely away in my room for future reference.

After that first programme, well, a match without one almost felt like half a match. Why would anyone want to deny themselves this fount of knowledge, this ever growing library about your favourite team and their opponents? Whenever I stopped Colin to get one, watching many in the throng carry on past unmoved, I couldn't help feel a little bit sorry for them, because they wouldn't be able to hoard all this amazing information forever.

Though my football-going experience at the time was limited to the wonderfully atmospheric ground that was The Dell, home of Southampton, my love of football programmes wasn't restricted solely to one team.

Having seen me spending hours and hours quietly, reverentially studying the ever increasing pile of programmes by my bed, Grandad put the word out at Wellworthy's, the factory he worked in, that his Grandson was football and programme crazy. He requested that anyone who went to a match should try to bring back a programme for him. So every now and then a brown envelope addressed to me would drop through the letterbox, sometimes containing a programme from Swindon Town, sometimes from the latest England home match, allowing me to study the Romanian team squad, marvelling at the exotic sounding names of the clubs they represented back home. Even an FA Cup final programme or two found their way to me via a factory in Salisbury.

But of all the programmes that Grandad's work friends generously provided, it was the one that was nearly discarded due to its condition, and was offered up with embarrassment when finally found in an old work coat that captivated me the most.

It was folded into quarters, its back cover smudged with grime transferred from over a year's worth of grubby hands from the factory floor being stuffed in those pockets on the walk back to the lockers after a long shift. Bobby Andrews offered it almost apologetically once he had discovered it, as did Grandad when he handed it over to me, having tried to flatten it out as best he could.

Maybe it was because it looked like it had lived a life, maybe it was the simple but attractive cover with the club crest on it, maybe it was the endearingly haphazardly typed pages inside, maybe it was that it had actually been given to me by a player named in the team line ups in the centre pages that made this programme the best one I had ever received. I don't know for sure. It certainly couldn't have hurt that Downton played in the same league as Southampton's third, or 'A' team, nor could it have hurt that it was such an obscure programme. No other 11-year-old at school could boast a Downton programme in their collection, which made it extra-special. That it came from Grandad just sealed the deal. If there had been a fire, it would have been one of the first things I would have looked to save as a boy, and this remains the case over 30 years later.

From that first programme, I was able to follow Bobby's career through the other programmes he passed on, probably bemused when Grandad told him that I had absolutely loved the first one, but definitely more careful to keep any others that he picked up in a better condition. Grandad and I read about his last hurrah in the semi-professional ranks with RS Southampton of the Southern League, before he dropped back down into the Hampshire League with Romsey via programmes from

Wimborne and Taunton. Though they weren't as professional as the Saints' ones, the programmes were still lovingly and painstakingly put together, each and every hand typed page created by a volunteer editor on their nights off, and they still contained information, vital football information for a young boy to absorb, and that made them precious historical documents about the most amazing game in the world. Maybe they didn't contain as much as the Saints' programmes, and weren't as detailed, but they held more than enough for a young boy to be getting on with.

When Grandad started taking me to see Salisbury play the first thing we did, after paying to get in and chatting for a minute or two to Cyril Smith, was safely stow our Salisbury programmes for reading later at home. Then we would make a beeline for the old programme hut next to the clubhouse to marvel at all the programmes for sale. It seemed cruel to have to choose a few out of the what seemed like thousands on display, as they would all have been fascinating to a young boy's desire for knowledge, but pocket money only stretched so far, so often it would be a case of the most attractive cover winning out.

Unlike these days, where some non-league programmes are knocked up on a computer at home and printed out or photocopied, the vast majority of them back in the '80s had at the very least a professionally printed cover which helped to make them look the part. It is hard to get excited about some programmes today when you know you could have done the same on your laptop. But back then the likes of Sheppey, Addlestone and Basingstoke all came alive through their painstakingly compiled and printed 'Match Day Magazine'.

And out of all of the programmes that had been crammed into that old hut in Victoria Park and found their way home with me, that Downton programme, and the Salisbury ones during my first seasons watching them with Grandad (the cover of the first season ironically displaying a couple of action shots from a pre-season friendly between Salisbury and Downton and featuring Bobby Andrews) stood out as the best, or at least by association meant the most, and still do to this day.

While it was easy, or at least possible, via two buses and about a two hour journey, to get from home to Salisbury to meet up with Grandad and head down to Victoria Park, Downton wasn't on any bus route that I could get to. However that Bobby Andrews programme meant I always kept an eye out for them, and as an adult I found myself making the occasional pilgrimage there to catch a game. I even lived out a childhood dream by playing for, and, as it turned out, finishing my playing days with Downton Reserves; a wonderful but short lived experience as the reserve side were disbanded a few weeks after I joined.

It didn't really matter that I didn't know anyone there. They were, are, and always will be a very friendly and welcoming bunch. More important than the welcome was the overwhelming feeling that I belonged in that shirt, the badge that meant so much to me seemed so familiar after decades of looking at it on the cover of that old programme, and I never felt so at home playing football as I did at Downton. The connection with Grandad, Bobby Andrews, and that battered old programme made non-descript reserve team fixtures mean the world. So from time to time after my knees gave up, I continued to find myself popping along for an afternoon of happy memories, which is why Emma and I headed in Downton on a cold day in January.

With Salisbury's demise, Downton v Amesbury Town in the Wessex League Division One has become one of the biggest games in the area; the south of the city against the north, though even the prospect of a local derby could only attract less than 100 hardy souls.

But for Downton and other clubs at this level, it isn't necessarily all about numbers through turnstiles. It is about far more. It had been about six years since I last played for the team, and yet I recognised the man on the gate taking the money and selling programmes, and the old-timer in the tea hut who joyously tried to flog half price Mars Bars to anyone nearby.

'They're going out of date tomorrow, but they are perfectly fine, just so long as you eat them today!'

As I scanned some old black and white photographs of teams long gone in the clubhouse, I noticed the same tea hut old-timer, maybe 30 or 40 years younger, wearing a tracksuit and beaming in a line up. It was clear from the photo that even back then his playing days were over. He appeared much older than the players, and it looked like he was the team's trainer or physio. The pictures seemed to be from the '60s or '70s. Just how old was this man who had flogged us soon to be dodgy chocolate?

Had there been a more photographs hanging on the walls it would be easy to imagine that you might be able to trace this man's entire life with the club. He'd go from a youngster in the first team in the oldest, more faded pictures, to regular on the team sheet, to veteran in the reserves, to trainer or maybe manager, possibly to secretary, and finally via god knows how many other roles, to tea hut attendant.

Like a more benign version of the final scene of *The Shining*, where images of Jack Nicholson appear in old pictures from The Overlook Hotel, these old team photos expose one small community's history and the people that made it; the man handing out tea and chocolate one small but vibrant part of that, and, unlike Jack Nicholson's character, fully aware of where he has always been.

Having felt so at home here myself I always feel a tinge of sadness that my Downton playing days were so short lived. I often wish that the reserve side could have kept going, just for a few more months, enabling me to possibly have become a tiny part of that history displayed across the clubhouse walls.

In the programme for this Salisbury derby there was an advert for Gary Tanner, Painter and Decorator. In the one Bobby Andrews gave Grandad was an advert for RE Tanner, Painter and Decorator. The same RE Tanner advert had appeared in the programme the last time I had been to see Downton play, back in 2008, 25 years after. RE Tanner also appeared in the list of officials back in 1984 as chairman. By 1989 he had become Vice-President, and an S Tanner was appearing on the team-sheet for Downton. It's entirely possible that three generations of the Tanner family appear in the odd couple of programmes that I have for Downton between 1982 and the present day. Who knows how much further back in the history of this club the name of Tanner appears? To those in the know there may be further clues in the pictures in the clubhouse. Either way it is clear that our friendly tea hut custodian isn't alone in his life-long association with the club, and looking at the other supporters milling about before kick-off, chatting away with their buddies, I couldn't help but wonder how many more carried such impressive records of dedication.

It had been a tough season for Downton, though a string of three victories in December had at least got them off the foot of the table and given them a little breathing space. Amesbury, on the other hand, were pushing for promotion, and they began the game with a confidence that a lofty league position gives a team.

They were in control from the off, despite some neat play by Downton on a very rough surface, and it was no real surprise to anyone when Amesbury took the lead. To make matters worse, Downton were forced into two substitutions before the half hour; players carrying knocks from previous matches found themselves unable to continue, and as Town pushed forward again and again I couldn't help but wonder how many more walking wounded were out there, knowing that they would have to struggle on to the almost inevitable bitter end, since the Downton bench was now empty.

The ominous signs didn't dampen the mood of the club officials congregated in front of the clubhouse, leaning against the barrier that lines the pitch. The old-timer from the tea hut shrugged his shoulders, and the group laughed as someone offered up some words of wisdom.

Humility and perspective are a necessity when supporting teams at this level.

When a club means far more to someone than a simple result in the back pages of the local paper, one defeat among decades of friendship and camaraderie doesn't really amount to much, which was just as well, as Amesbury were a very good team, and dismantled Downton at will. They were clearly going places, and promotion would be well deserved if it arrived come May.

By half time the match was effectively over, and the old-timer scampered back into his hut to sort out those that chose to stay outside rather than head back into the clubhouse.

To warm up, Emma and I wandered round the perimeter of the pitch, pausing to retrieve a ball that sailed beyond the far post of the goal we had just passed – an errant shot by an Amesbury substitute that became lodged among the trees behind it. As I kicked it back the sub waved and said: 'Thanks. Sorry. That's why I'm on the bench.'

His humour and humility took me by surprise and I laughed out loud. In fact, I was still chuckling as the second half got under way, still appreciating such a refreshing bout of warm and playful self-depreciation.

With the match won, the game ticked along, Amesbury adding a couple more well worked goals, but I sat up when the funny sub came on with 15 minutes to go.

Go on, I urged. *Score that screamer you tried at half time. Live that dream!*

He didn't, although he did put in a decent shift protecting his back four as the match petered out.

6-0 seemed like an absolute thrashing, but the match itself didn't feel that way. To their credit, the Downton players kept going till the final whistle, respecting the spectators who had paid a fiver to watch, aware that at this level, with players turning out for nothing but a cup of tea afterwards, sometimes injury, unavailability and suspension conspires to leave you facing the certainty of an afternoon of damage limitation before you've even left the changing room.

As the players trudged off, the old-timer shutting up shop ready for another match, floodlights stretching shadows out toward the clubhouse where old friends sat and laughed and drank, the perspective of one result became apparent.

Win, lose, or draw, the real point of teams like Downton was clear as we walked past and looked in at people huddled round tables, enjoying being a welcome part of something, and unwittingly adding to the history hanging on the walls. It was a nice feeling to watch it all, and to know that once, a long time ago, that battered old programme I hold so dear was probably a part of a similar scene of laughter, beer, and friendship, albeit stuffed in Bobby Andrews' coat pocket.

Another reason to make sure it stays safe.

18

31 January 2015. Corinthian v Beckenham Town
Southern Counties East Football League

WHEN SALISBURY'S FIXTURES for the upcoming season came out in his local paper in the summer of 1985, Grandad carefully cut them out and posted them to me so as I could study them as intensely as anyone could study a thin strip of The Salisbury Journal. Among all the familiar names of teams faced the season before were two strange and, to a 12-year-old boy, exotic ones, which would be Salisbury's first two visitors to Victoria Park.

The question of just where and who on earth Ruislip and Corinthian were had Grandad and I rummaging through his old road map. Ruislip turned out to be from just west of London, but Corinthian didn't seem to be a place that could be found on any map.

It turned out that Corinthian was a spirit, a moral code rather than a physical destination, but neither Grandad nor I knew that until a little while after we saw them play and lose 4-2 at the park. It had been an entertaining match, and at least they had done better than Ruislip, who lost 5-1 on the opening day of the season.

It was some weeks after the match that I received another letter containing a couple of paper cuttings about Corinthian with 'memo to Matthew from Grandad' written across the top of the largest one, just above the headline: 'The team that plays the game'. The article explained that Corinthian were formed by Ron Billings, who in 1985 was an 82-year-old millionaire builder and farmer who had been so upset by the foul language and behaviour he witnessed while watching his sons play in junior matches in the early '70s that he pulled them out of their team and decided to form his own, where respect, tolerance, and sportsmanship were not optional.

Like Kevin Costner in the film *Field Of Dreams* Billings transformed a field on his farm in Kent into a pitch complete with floodlights, a small stand, and a training complex containing indoor and outdoor pitches and a clubhouse. All were encouraged to join his sons in this new team, as long as they honoured the Corinthian code of fair play and sportsmanship; there would be no swearing, no spitting, no arguing with referees, and no intentional fouls. Corinthian would play hard, but always fair, and defeat would be met with a warm handshake rather than recriminations. Thirteen years on, the team had progressed up into the semi-professional Southern League, though still fully amateur, and still upholding their founder's ethos.

Corinthian were, as the size of the article suggested, a small-time and small-scale victory for honesty, integrity, and fair play. Although they held their own in the Southern league for a few seasons they didn't progress any higher, and dropped back down into the Kent League to continue Ron Billings' dream quietly and respectfully. But while their profile may have slipped from its modest high water mark back in 1985, their attitude and spirit endured, at the very least in me, an impressionable 12-year-old boy.

Living in a pre-internet age where the only information you could find about non-league football came via the Salisbury programme or an excellent little non-league magazine called *Pyramid*, it was no surprise that Corinthian, to all intents and purposes, fell off the face of the earth to a boy that didn't live anywhere near Kent once they had dropped out of the Southern League.

Despite all that, however, that small paper cutting Grandad had sent me survived, tucked away inside the cover of the Salisbury v Corinthian programme. I knew that it was important and deserved to be kept, that what Corinthian were trying to do was valuable whatever the scale.

And there it stayed for nearly 30 years, until one evening in late 2014. I'd just written an article on the Tibetan National Football Team, and their fight to be heard and seen, both politically and sportingly. The Tibetan culture is the living embodiment of the Corinthian sporting values, but encompassing all aspects of life. It is an overwhelmingly beautiful vision of the world, in which tolerance and respect are seen as more valuable than oil and gold.

Having watched the Tibetan team play back in 2006 I felt sad that, one, they were prevented from playing the game they loved because of politics and money, and two that the world and I were denied the joyously refreshing experience of watching Buddhist footballers creating a beautiful vision of what football can be, without intentional fouls, dissent, play acting, swearing or intimidation of the referee. A simple joyous expression of playing football for the sheer love of it, just as we all once did as young children. The thought of never getting to see that again made me feel very sad indeed. If only there were more people like them in the world, more people with the same philosophy. If only.

And there it was, from somewhere in the back of my mind, that old and faded article Grandad sent me. *What about Corinthian? They couldn't still be going, all these years later, could they?*

It seemed unlikely. But unlikely things often happen, if you look hard enough, and where there is a will sometimes good things can persevere. This is why, on a very cold January Saturday under the threat of snow, I found myself driving into the back roads of rural Kent looking for my own personal field of dreams that would, weather permitting, be hosting a Southern Counties East Football League match between Corinthian and Beckenham Town.

It's easy to believe that not much has changed at Gay Dawn Farm since the ground was built; an old set of disused dugouts on the far side of the pitch made obsolete by newer, larger ones nearer the changing rooms the only obvious sign of recent improvement. But then, if isn't broken... and Corinthian's home is most definitely not broken.

Leaning up against the old dugouts watching snow slowly tumble out of ashen skies, I could imagine the Salisbury team of nearly 30 years ago plying their trade here; distant echoes of a match long gone between players I used to idolise at Victoria Park, a ground, like the club it used to be home to, now consigned to history along with the result. It was exciting to be here, at the home of Ron Billings' dream, but also sad. With Salisbury gone, driving two hours into deepest Kent was the only way to reconnect (flicking through old programmes aside) with those memories of Victoria Park and time shared with Grandad.

Before this season, only 40 minutes would have stood in the way of an afternoon at the Raymond McEnhill Stadium, Salisbury, where you could have looked at the plaque in the foyer with names (Grandad's among them) of fans who bought a brick of the new home of Salisbury. There it was easy to find a path back to those happy times at Victoria Park with Grandad; the familiar badge, familiar faces manning the turnstiles and dotted among the crowd, helped the echoes of the past and Grandad to step out once more. It was easy.

But if a drive out to a remote farm standing at the end of an ever narrowing warren of twisting roads was all that was left, then so be it.

Given its remote nature it's hardly surprising that attendances at Corinthian matches aren't what other clubs in the league might attract. Indeed, dotted about the corners of the ground are a couple of seemingly abandoned turnstiles losing their personal battle with ivy that made me think of *Field Of Dreams* even more; helped by the barn behind the changing rooms and tea bar that house large farming machinery and a lazy ginger cat looking on from a bale of hay. This is, after all, a ground built with love for a set of sons by a man with a vision of sportsmanship and respect. It was not built as the foremost destination to watch football in the county.

Attendance is encouraged, but isn't the point of this particular club. If people want to come and join in with Ron Billings' dream then they are made most welcome, but it would appear it will continue, while there is a will, regardless. As if to cement the point, in the tea hut there is a small framed obituary from November 1991 on Mr Billings under the headline 'Ronald Billings (Corinthian) – A Remarkable Man.' A picture of him looking out on proceedings is the only indicator to the unique nature of this little club. The ethos of the club is already ingrained in every fibre of its being, so a grand gesture like a Ron Billings Stand would be totally unnecessary.

The only nagging worry as I kept warm wandering around the pitch was: *could one man's dream survive more than 23 years after his passing?* It would be heartbreaking to dip back into that bank of happier Victoria Park times to find that another of those institutions had fallen.

It was a comfort to read in the programme that the club were still very much under the control of the Billings family; there were a number of different Billingses, as secretary, chairman, director, child safety officer and programme editor. There was also one Billings on the team sheet and another listed as having played earlier in the season.

Were they the second, or possibly third generation of Billingses to have played for Corinthian since 1972? I'm not sure. Were they Ron's grandchildren or great grandchildren? Did any of the family listed as directors or any of these other roles play in that match against Salisbury at the beginning of the 1985-86 season? Either way, their presence was an impressive show of solidarity to one man's vision, and had me hoping for the best.

Corinthian v Beckenham Town, who the programme informed me had travelled 19.8 miles to attend, were third and fourth in the table respectively, and with Corinthian having applied for promotion this season there was a lot at stake. Both teams needed the points to narrow the gap on the top two teams, Phoenix Sports and Erith & Belvedere who, along with Canterbury City lower down the table, were another blast from the Victoria Park past.

Beckenham, whose past club presidents include former Prime Minister Harold Macmillan, were described in the programme as having undisputedly the best pitch in the league, and even on a heavy, bobbled surface like the one at Gay Dawn Farm, they clearly had some of the best players too. Their passing and movement in the opening few minutes had Corinthian on the ropes, and I couldn't help but wonder what sort of a display they could manage on a surface that wasn't cutting up so terribly, fast beginning to resemble the ploughed field that it had quite possibly been pre-Corinthian days.

It took Corinthian a while to find their feet, but finally they did, and still against the run of play they managed to take the lead, with the majority of the 40-strong crowd cheering from the wooden stand behind the goal.

It was a captivating game between two good teams desperate to do well and climb the table, but as well as enjoying the drama on the pitch, I found myself looking at the match in a slightly different way: the Ron Billings way.

From Beckenham, you could hear the standard amount of swearing that one would expect at any adult match across the land, however now that I was looking for it, it seemed to stand out more, especially as almost none seemed to come from Corinthian. During the course of the whole game I counted three Corinthian 'F' bombs, mostly dropped in the minutes leading up to and after a brilliantly worked equaliser from Beckenham at the beginning of the second half, when it looked like they could possibly run riot. Corinthian also picked up two yellow cards, however the first one looked to be a simple mis-timed tackle rather than anything malicious, and for the second booking the referee fell for a cheeky dive from the Beckenham left back, reaching solemnly for his pocket while the Corinthian player rightly protested his innocence.

It may not have been the immaculate display that Mr Billings senior had hoped for, and not the idealised one that I had imagined, but in the heat of an entertaining and tense top-of-the-table clash it still came across as refreshingly free from the wholesale abuse that sometimes blights whole matches. Indeed, the last time I had seen anything similar was from the Tibetan National Team in 2006, which went three matches without picking up a yellow card or using dissent or professional fouls.

It really did seem, 42 years on, that one man's vision of creating a little oasis of sporting integrity on his farm in Kent was still alive and well, even long after his passing. And for that, for the solidifying of one of those Victoria Park dreams into present day fact, well, I am truly grateful.

Beneath failing light and what looked like snow-choked cloud, the game swung to and fro like all good games do, and when the Corinthian captain converted a well worked move to make it 2-1 with a few minutes remaining it seemed the perfect end to a good day, though I couldn't help but feel sorry for Beckenham at the final whistle, who deserved more from such a decent display. As both teams shook hands and trudged off the pitch exhausted, I was sure that their day would come, and they were destined, sooner rather than later, for bigger things than the Southern Counties East Football League.

As for Corinthian, as the floodlights illuminating their pitch flickered and cut out, it was clear their fiercely amateur sporting principles still persist, and as they look to move back up through the leagues, back toward those heady days of the Southern League in the '80s, I can't help but wish them luck, even though I know they probably don't need it.

Because if it ever comes down to professionalism over principal, then I know perfectly well which way they will go. And more power to them for doing so.

19

14 February 2015. Eastleigh v Torquay United
Conference Premier

THE LAST TIME I was at the Silverlake Stadium in Eastleigh, it wasn't called that; rather it was called Ten Acres, and instead of getting ready to host not far off 2,000 spectators for a match in non-leagues' elite division, it was preparing to welcome three men and a dog for a pre-season friendly between Wessex Combination League Eastleigh reserves and Hampshire Combination League Winchester City reserves.

A lot has changed in the years since that hot summer's day in 1997. For one, I no longer play (that 97–98 season playing for Winchester reserves was an enjoyable experience despite the club being in the doldrums), two, Eastleigh's home ground is pretty much unrecognisable as the one that I played in. The line of tall conifers that hid the pitch and a small stand from the road back then looks over a ground fit for the Football League these days, with a brand new 2,500 seater stand behind one goal complimenting the main stand on one side, and covered terracing on the other. The trees are the only reminder of bygone days, that and the clubhouse that once contained the changing rooms, whose roof could just about be seen behind another swathe of terracing behind the far goal. Three, and just as importantly, the upsurge in facilities demonstrates that Eastleigh are no longer a side making up the numbers in the Wessex League in the fifth tier of non-league football. Instead, in 2015 they were serious contenders for promotion into League Two at the close of play in May.

Just how a club can be transformed in such a relatively short space of time is a quirk of non-league football up and down the country. Eastleigh is by no means the first club to come from virtually no-where to upset the applecart. Rushden & Diamonds rose up through the non-league pyramid and into the Football League, resplendent in a state of the art ground the envy of many, before going bust a couple of years ago and slipping into history.

Modern day success stories such as Crawley and Fleetwood, both of whom now play in League One, having risen up through provincial football and into the third tier of the professional game with the help of wealthy benefactors, are about as common as stories of failure. Teams like Histon, Lewes, and Droylsden all rocketed up into the Conference, but once they had made it they couldn't sustain it, and drifted away again into relative obscurity almost as quickly as they came.

Eastleigh is not new in that respect, and will certainly not be the last. AFC Fylde in the Conference North has come from nowhere in recent times, and stand on the brink of another promotion to the pinnacle of non-league football. The Conference is a melting pot of teams on the up, teams reeling from dropping out of the Football League, and teams that have found their level and go about their business. For Eastleigh the journey hasn't been easy, and has been littered with bumps along the way. They sailed close to financial meltdown on a couple of occasions when playing budgets hadn't been set correctly, or benefactors/sponsors hadn't been forthcoming. But they were, at non-league's top table.

The momentum of winning the Conference South, backed up by some serious recruitment of some serious players in the close season, had propelled Eastleigh to just outside the play-off spots in the Conference, and with only a few months remaining, they were being seen as real contenders to muscle in on the promotion act into the promised land.

That they were doing this within a couple of miles of Southampton, a Premier League team, makes it on first glance an even greater achievement. How can you attract crowds large enough to sustain a club in the Conference Premier, playing Alfreton and Dartford as well as some more renowned former Football League teams, when you have a close neighbour entertaining some of the world's biggest clubs, and playing excellent football right at the top of the biggest league in the world? The fact that Eastleigh crowds averaged around 1,400 this season, which saw them sit right in the middle of the Conference attendance league table, suggests that they were doing something right.

Attendances had risen sharply since promotion to the Conference Premier, which is a clear indication of the respect the division holds within the football community. It is a standard of football on a par with League Two, and at £12 for an adult ticket and four for a child it presents an affordable option to families becoming squeezed out of St Mary's just up the road and other Premier League grounds up and down the country.

No matter how much my brother in law loves watching Southampton, the cheapest tickets for the lowest category match he could buy for himself and his two young sons this season would come to £60. That figures rises to £70 if they wanted to see one of the top teams play. When you add on a couple of programmes (four pounds each), a couple of drinks, maybe a couple of portions of chips, his day out at the football with his boys could conceivably cost close to £90.

Southampton's success has created a vacuum in which an ever growing number of fans see a trip to see their team play as a treat rather than the norm, myself included. Within that environment a club a couple of miles down the road playing good football in a respected league, where a parent and two children can get in for £20, have a wonderful opportunity to increase their league gates. And this is what Eastleigh had done.

It's not even that Southampton tickets are the most expensive in the Premier League, because they are not, not by a long way. But for some people the financial elastic can only stretch so far, no matter how much they enjoy seeing the Saints. For me, having to pay close to £800 for a season ticket that covered 19 league games was my breaking point, despite having bought one every year since the League One days.

Do I miss going? Yes, I do. But have all the experiences through this book as a consequence of being priced out of St Mary's more than made up for that? Absolutely. I will always love Southampton. But because football at the top table is defined by money, which is something I don't have enough of, my trips to St Mary's have to be tactical and limited.

As an aside, the cost of the tickets for the matches visited in this book so far, with Eastleigh being the 18th, comes to just shy of £200; only a quarter of an average St Mary's season ticket.

If you have the money then that is fine, but if you don't then Eastleigh and clubs like it can be a lifeline, and inside the ground it is refreshing to see so many children bustling about excitedly, rattling a set of 'clackers' – three small plastic hands attached to the end of a small stick, which clap like castanets when you wiggle them. Depending on your outlook it doesn't help when Nick, my brother in law, leans across to tell me and Sam his 11-year-old son that in Australia clackers is slang for bum-hole! Cue endless jokes about finding a clacker in my pocket, or pointing out that some child has left his clacker on his seat. There are an infinite number of jokes to be made, and we did our best to tell as many as we could.

Offering children, who are after all the future of football, four pound tickets to become a part of what they are doing at Eastleigh, offering them a great standard of football in a great league, is inspired. Largely by luck and circumstance, partly by design, Eastleigh has found a potential football fan-base of the future right on their doorstep that they can tap into to hopefully help sustain them and then enable them to grow further, as it is clear that a simple consolidation in the top tier of the non-league pyramid is not the height of their ambition.

One place outside the play-offs and with games in hand, The Spitfires, as they are nick-named (the planes were made just down the road during World War Two) were looking for back-to-back promotions into the

Football League; something that would not look out of place in such an impressive ground.

With that in mind, the Eastleigh team sheet in the programme was littered with recognisable names; the club having spent big in the summer, and again in January, to help the cause. Up front was Deon Burton, who played in the Premier League with Derby County and at the World Cup finals with Jamaica. In midfield was Brian Howard, who played at Championship level for most of his career, and Harry Pell, who I saw play for Bristol Rovers against Southampton at a packed St Mary's during the Saints' League One promotion campaign. On the bench were Jack Midson and James Constable, both of whom had been banging in the goals in League Two the season before, for Wimbledon and Oxford United respectively.

These relatively big names for non-league circles help to cement the notion that the Conference is a very good standard of football and that it can pay well enough for this calibre of player to play in it. In turn this captivates and inspires fans who could be the future of the club for years to come to drag their parents or children out on a cold February afternoon to see these names in action; the circle of footballing life.

By contrast, the Torquay squad, though playing for a club with decades of Football League history, was more modest. As a club so isolated in the West Country, and newly relegated into the non-league, they were clearly not the most attractive proposition for some. Only the name of Angus Macdonald jumped out at me. He had played for Salisbury last season and was a stark reminder to me of why I was here, and not somewhere else.

Torquay had taken time to adjust to life in the Conference, and it was getting close to now or never if they were going to string some results together to get them up toward the play-offs. As Nick, Sam, and I settled down behind the goal in Eastleigh's enormous new stand both teams set at each other with a hunger that suggested neither could really afford to lose this one.

It was frantic, end-to-end stuff, with decent attacking and counter-attacking play keeping everyone's clackers busy. Deon Burton's tap in after Joe Partington had headed back across goal from a corner sent them chattering manically around the ground. But as neither team could dominate, it seemed fair enough when Ollivier Guéguen equalised just before half time.

The best thing about non-league football, even at some Conference grounds, is the absence of segregation between sets of fans, enabling you to wander around at your leisure. Sat not far from us was a Torquay fan in his 60s, kitted out beneath his coat in an old Torquay strip, shorts and all, which was brave purely because of the weather rather than being surrounded by home supporters. The Torquay fans had a section of terracing allocated to them, which in the main they stuck too, but they could easily have wandered elsewhere, just as we did at half time, mingling with them as we battled round to the clubhouse and the shop for Sam to buy a badge.

I pointed out an Eastleigh fridge magnet and showed it to Sam, wondering if I should buy it for my wife, seeing as it was Valentine's Day. He giggled and said he thought it best if I didn't, seeing as she hates football. But it's the thought that counts, right?

During the second half, we stood by the corner flag near the Torquay support in the sun, basking in wonder at the yellow thing in the sky that had seemed absent from our lives for so long. We had to shield our eyes to watch Torquay's second goal: a Ryan Bowman strike from outside the box crashing back off the crossbar, Louis Briscoe controlling the ball and steering it home to send the away stand delirious.

Cue Jack Midson and James Constable from the bench to try and salvage something. And as the sun began to set behind the main stand and those ever present conifers, Eastleigh began their onslaught of the Torquay goal. That's when I heard it, coming from a small but vociferous number behind the goal Eastleigh were attacking: chants about Salisbury and their demise.

Having played all but the current season in regional leagues rather than the national set-up that begins at Conference Premier level, Eastleigh had a lot of local rivals. They had had Basingstoke, Havant & Waterlooville, and Salisbury in and around them for a number of years, enabling a few feuds to arise over poached players and managers, feisty games and bad decisions by referees. The higher these clubs rose, the deeper these rivalries grew, and with Salisbury being the first to make that ultimate step up into the top flight of the non-league world, it makes sense that they became the focus for everyone else.

Even so, it was really sad to hear rival fans revelling in their misery, especially as Eastleigh's trajectory and Salisbury's when they first went up was remarkably similar. Rather than a cause for celebration, Salisbury's fate should be a warning to Eastleigh, and to anyone else; a vision of what can happen if you don't quite reach where you want to get to.

Salisbury, like Eastleigh, went up with momentum on their side and hit the ground running in their first season in the big league, pushing for a play-off spot at the first time of asking. Crowds at Salisbury, like Eastleigh, were way up on the previous season, the novelty of big name visitors week in week out were a major draw. However once the novelty of it all wore off, and a season or two of mid-table finishes followed, crowds began to drop as the cost of travelling the length and breadth of the country caught up with them.

I really hope Eastleigh are a better run club than Salisbury were. I have no way of knowing from the outside looking in, but there have been precedents of Eastleigh over-stretching themselves, and the higher you rise, the more money you need, and the harder the fall if it isn't there. The quality throughout this current Eastleigh squad can't come cheap. What happened to Salisbury is an extreme example, but it should be seen as an example none the less; a forewarning of things to come if you don't keep your feet on the ground and a level head on your shoulders.

I genuinely hope that Eastleigh can do that, as it is great to have successful local teams to visit. But as has been seen at Salisbury, a couple of great seasons on the pitch can only really be seen as such if they are as equally successful off it.

I hope that deep down, those Eastleigh supporters who take pleasure in Salisbury's fate (a tiny minority I have to say), appreciate their chastening story; better to believe in 'there for the grace of God go I' rather than fall blindly to the same fate, because without the grace of God, Saturday afternoons can be a very lonely place

At the final whistle that, despite Eastleigh's late onslaught, confirmed a Torquay win, we filed out, clackers safely stowed away. I genuinely hope that Eastleigh remain a success story. For their fans, for the area that needs an outlet of good quality, affordable football for all the families that could otherwise be priced out of it altogether, for those three men from back in 1997 (I didn't see a dog anywhere) who I hoped were still stood somewhere around the place that had been there to see the Hampshire League and Wessex League times, and the odd awful reserve team friendly (sorry about that), I really hope Eastleigh go from strength to strength. They most definitely deserve it.

20

28 February 2015. Plymouth Argyle v Bury
League Two

THIS IS IT, the furthest extremity of the Football League.

Beyond Home Park, Plymouth, professional football ends. The town looks out on Cornwall, which starts just across the River Tamar; a county littered with small, picturesque towns and villages, with small and picturesque football clubs all playing in the likes of The South West Peninsula League. Only Truro bucks that trend, playing in the semi-professional ranks of the Southern League.

Plymouth Argyle really does represent the end of the Football League world. Drive on into Saltash and all you will find are pretty harbour villages on a rugged coastline that today, like most days during winter, looked out nervously, waiting for the impending storm that had been forecast to hit from off the Atlantic. Strong winds and swirling rain had built up over the Godless wilds of The Grand Banks way out to sea. Plymouth, like those small Cornish dwellings, was waiting too, warily peering into the ever deepening gloom that was building up around us.

Whether today was the best day to visit England's most southerly and westerly Football League team is a thought that was really beginning to gain momentum. It was going to be a drive against the elements to try and beat the storm home again. Early August seems a more rational time to visit Home Park, or maybe in the dying embers of the season in early May, but like the fans of Bury, we don't have that option. For them and for us, for this season, it's now or never, imminent winter storm or not.

Plymouth, like their brothers in arms Carlisle and Hartlepool from the most northerly extremities of the League, have to live life out on a limb. Isolated geographically from the majority, and plying their trade down in the Fourth Division, they have to work hard to attract players, to persuade them that a spell way out here doesn't signal the end of a career. Getting the right calibre of player to uproot their family, to take them a long way from home, indeed a long way from anywhere, for League Two wages must be a harder job than for those clubs in and around larger cities.

Home grown talent can't do it all; these journeymen players willing to head out into the extremities to fight for the cause are vital, and getting the right ones will determine which end of the table you'll be working at. For Carlisle and Hartlepool this season it was the wrong end, while Plymouth were still chasing the dream, tucked in the play-off places at the start of the day.

Being at the business end of the league must help to make those endless, arduous away trips from the end of the football world all around the country, cramped up in a coach for hours on end, just that little bit more bearable. It must make it feel more worthwhile an endeavour.

For Carlisle and Hartlepool, however, fighting for their Football League lives, hour upon hour sat in a coach peering through the condensation on the windows, contemplating the struggles that lay ahead and their fears, both for the game ahead and for their futures, must be a stressful, joyless experience. But at least they are getting paid to do it, unlike the real life blood of these clubs from way out in the middle of nowhere: the fans.

The simple mathematics of being a Plymouth, Carlisle, or Hartlepool fan is mind blowing. A page in the Plymouth programme brought the dedication of a supporter that travels home and away to follow Argyle into terrifying proportion.

Travelling from Argyle to Plymouth for every away trip this season would amount to 11,596.6 miles. The furthest trips, to Carlisle and Hartlepool, are 778.8 and 775.8 miles respectively; a potential round trip of some 14 hours by car or coach. Even the local derby against Exeter is a 92 mile round trip, the next shortest to Newport is 277.4 miles (a little under what it took us to get from Southampton to Plymouth, a three hour journey each way along tedious A roads past Broadchurch country and the Jurassic coast. Motorways are a luxury Plymouth fans don't get to use when visiting south coast clubs like Portsmouth). The average away trip for an Argyle fan clocks in at around 500 or so miles, and the best part of ten hours travelling time.

The numbers are just horrific, or inspirational, depending on which way you look at it, because you can be sure that stood all round Home Park for this match were fans that have gone, and will go, to every single away fixture this season, last season, and next.

That 264 people gave up so much of their time to travel to Hartlepool one Saturday in January, that possibly more will go to Carlisle at the end of April, especially if they are in with a shout of promotion, that the rough average Argyle away support this season was around the 500 mark, all for football in the lowest tier of the Football League, says much for what a football club actually means to those who support it.

We are living in austere times. Money is tight for almost everyone, and with so much live top end football on television, attendances at the lower end of the spectrum have inevitably dropped. But there are still those that cram themselves and their buddies into their car, pool resources to fill up the tank, and head off on stupendous round trips in awful weather, all to see the team they love.

We have witnessed already this with Accrington Stanley, where the four away games we have been at, dotted all over the country, and all contained a handful of familiar faces looking out hopefully from the terraces. I have no doubt they are at them all, or at least a vast majority of away games, as suggested by a wonderful few seconds of *The Football League Show*. When Piero Mingoia scored a winner for Accrington, a familiar bomber jacketed Stanley fan with a '50s rocker hairstyle ran frantically out from the shadow of the away stand that had been hiding the 30 or so people who had made the trip and the cameras captured his joy as he jumped up and down in front of the advertising hoardings. It was clear that for him, that single moment had most definitely made the day's travel worthwhile. It is these glorious, relatively small moments that get you up at the crack of dawn on a cold winter's day, and steel you for the long days travel ahead.

And with the memory of aching legs and a sore back from the journey still fresh as Emma and I pulled up outside Home Park, stretching it off before wandering bleary eyed about the place, I couldn't help but think of people like our bomber jacket Stanley friend, and salute the 67 Hartlepool, 65 Dagenham & Redbridge, 66 Morecambe, and 56 Accrington Stanley fans that went before us down to Plymouth this season, driving a hell of a lot further than we did in the process.

Some people ask: why? Why do people feel the need to use their free time and money they probably don't really have to travel the country to support their team? Why have 100 or so Bury fans made a ten hour round trip to come down for today's game? Why did the same number of Morecambe fans take the same amount of time to head down to Newport County last Saturday to watch a match my brother in law Nick, his two boys and I went to see?

Even if you take these trips, the answer may still not be an easy one to give; 'because I love my team' often doesn't cut it with those that don't. After all, you can love your team, but go to the odd home match rather than every single game, home and away.

It's certainly not for the glory, as away trips can often end up in defeat, and for every Southend moment of joy, there are also the Wimbledon away trips, where nothing went right for Stanley and they came up way short with barely a whimper. As we left that day, our '50s rocker friend stood slumped against a terrace barrier shaking his head, contemplating the horror show on the pitch as well as the horror show of trying to get out of London, let alone the rest of the journey home.

To me these trips to the furthest-flung places are an act of devotion; a modern day pilgrimage of suffering and discomfort, with a real emphasis on the suffering and discomfort, to truly express to yourself and others the extent of your love.

Long, insufferable journeys in a cramped car or coach, maybe train, though fully air conditioned and rammed full of electrical devices to take your mind off the motorway, and peppered with service station breaks offering food, drink and anything else you might need, could almost be the very tame modern day equivalent of the medieval Christian devotees risking bandits, illness and possibly even death to travel to Jerusalem; the Muslims travelling to Mecca; the Buddhists prostrating themselves on the floor every step they take on a trip to Mount Kailash and other sacred places. Though instead of dodging life threatening situations, all the modern day pilgrim need worry about is avoiding charity collectors rattling buckets and the odd car insurance salesman! Taking your place on a blustery terrace far from home, forgoing all comfort in the process, is a way of expressing, to others and yourself, just how much your team means to you, and how big a role it plays in your life.

Like religious pilgrimages, the more discomfort you experience, the greater your experience is. I can bore people stupid about trips up to Newcastle on a Sunday in February, in the snow, to watch a match that was on television, only to see my team go 4-0 down after 20 minutes, and Newcastle miss a penalty. Or a trip to Carlisle where the sole of my shoe fell off at a service station and it was freezing cold, and we lost 3-2. Or a trip to Hartlepool on a Tuesday night in February to see a goalless draw, not getting home until five in the morning, and starting work at nine.

On a devotional scale, however, my efforts are insignificant compared to those that turn up week in week out, home and away. Even in our League One days, when tickets were affordable, I'd go to maybe five Southampton away trips a season. The time and dedication required to get to 23 away League games, and however many cup matches on top, is unfathomable. It's impressive to say the least.

Like religion, your team is a crutch, a family, a constant on your journey. Becoming a part of a faceless huddle of bodies lost in shadow behind some goal miles from home is a way of reaching a state of devotion and belonging to something that most, who have never undertaken such an act, can't understand. And in return for this act of devotion, rather than the spiritual enlightenment of Jerusalem, Mecca, or Mount Kailash, there is a decent, honest performance from your team, and for them to come and applaud you at the end of the game, win, lose or draw. It seems a fair trade.

To her credit, my wife, who does not like football, has actually been on a few of these pilgrimages, although all they did was help convince her that it wasn't for her. The second date I took my wife on way back in the day was a trip up to Shrewsbury to watch my mate's team play a Fourth Division match (lucky woman!).

That she went, even though she didn't like football, that she came to see Southampton play at Watford one Christmas, shows a different kind of devotion. (One that I suspect would soon have faded had she been pressed to go to too many more!) That she lets me go on these damn foolish trips shows that she understands the importance and significance of them to me, culturally, emotionally, spiritually, even if she doesn't wish to crawl on her hands and knees towards some sacred Himalayan mountain again. Once is enough! That she did actually come with me to Bhutan, all in the name of football, is another story (see the next chapter), as well as a constant reminder that the odd act of devotion in her direction is most definitely in order.

Home Park is wonderful in the way it straddles modernity and the past. Three quarters of the stadium which, Fratton Park aside, is the largest in League Two, has been modernised and looks like a green version of St Mary's stadium back home in Southampton.

However, running along the far side of the pitch is an old grandstand that looks like it hasn't been touched since it was first opened. This grandstand, which appeared from our point of view in the stand opposite to house rows of old wooden seats slipping away into shadow, looks out on a deep and steep stretch of terracing beneath it that helps you to imagine what Home Park would have looked and felt like in eras long gone; one section of the terracing that stretched on beyond the stand and toward the corner flag stood hopelessly exposed to the elements. It's not hard to imagine the kind of experience supporters of generations past would have received stood on it on a winter's day. Indeed we'd seen hardy souls battered by rain on a similarly exposed terrace at Newport the weekend before.

Roped off and deserted now, this stretch of terracing beneath such a grand old stand is a tangible monument to the past, and it felt good to have that connection, like the old Victorian-style entrance and turnstiles that offer entry into this section of Home Park's living history.

It was sad that the terracing wasn't in use, but even to a terrace romantic like me it did look very steep, and pretty dangerous if ever there were a significant number of supporters on it at any one time. With no barriers compartmentalising it I could easily see how a big crowd could cause a crush, or worse. Some aspects of the modernisation of football have been for the better, and though it looks like a wonderful icon of the past, I can imagine it may not have been the most fun to stand on.

Of all the things I had been expecting of this journey: checking out a new ground I'd not visited before, marvelling at the good-humoured Bury fans that had made their long way down from greater Manchester, one thing I hadn't expected to see was a classic Barcelona-like pass and play, pass and play style of football from Bury. It's not the first thing you would expect from a Fourth Division match, but it is exactly what we got.

I settled down with a pasty (obviously) to watch. Most of Bury's play was spellbinding; keeping the ball with composure, passing it round with an assurance that was great to see. If they played like that every week the long trips of devotion must have been that little bit easier for their hardy fans huddled behind the goal.

Argyle could play too, and when they got the ball they tried to exert a bit of pressure of their own in what was a very entertaining match. So entertaining, in fact, that pretty much everyone in the ground missed the darkening skies above us as that Atlantic storm loomed ever closer, finally reaching the country's most south-westerly club as the second half started; rain and wind swirling in the floodlights.

But even that couldn't dampen the match. Plymouth had a goal disallowed for offside, then hit the bar, and all the while Bury passed and probed before deservedly taking the lead after the impressive Nicky Adams set up former Exeter striker Danny Nardiello to head home, making an already unpopular figure with the locals even more so.

As the weather worsened, Plymouth went all-out in trying to find an equaliser, leaving themselves open to counter-attacks, one of which resulted in Bury sealing the win in the dying moments of the game when sub Danny Rose finished things off, sending the band of Bury brothers and sisters behind that goal into delirium, and leaving the vast majority of the 7,000 plus crowd nervously checking the league table in the programme as results from around the country confirmed that while Bury had cemented their place in it, Argyle had slipped out of the play-off spots.

Tucked up inside the stands, the Bury fans, like Emma and I and the rest of the crowd, had been sheltered from worst of the wind and rain driving in from off the ocean. As we all left the sanctuary of Home Park, however, it didn't take more than a few moments before we were all drenched, skittering frantically across the car park, coats flailing above heads like washing on a line as we tried to take them off before getting into our cars.

In conditions like this it was going to be a long drive home for us on dark, narrow coastal roads, rain and fog bringing visibility to virtually zero as we crawled on toward Bridport, back past Broadchurch country and home.

But no matter how tough it might be for us, at least we knew we would get back by eight o'clock. For those happy few from Bury, the not so happy few from Wimbledon who saw their team lose up at Hartlepool, and the desperate Carlisle fans down at Southend who not only saw their team lose, but also saw them drop back into the relegation zone with their neighbours in isolation Hartlepool, the second half of their day was only just beginning. Their homeward journey probably got them in, for Carlisle and Wimbledon most definitely, long past midnight.

And as we and the Bury fans slowly filed out and away, the stands and floodlights of Home Park fading into the darkness, a long and tortuous road ahead, we, just like those Argyle fans that would make the 517 mile round trip to Stevenage the following Tuesday night, well, we wouldn't have it any other way.

21

12 March 2015. Sri Lanka v Bhutan
World Cup Qualifier, Round One

EVEN THE SMALLEST of pebbles thrown in the largest lake creates ripples. Often too small for the vast majority to notice, these ripples continue to radiate out long after the pebble has sunk to the lake bed and been forgotten by most. But continue they do, and every now and then they wash up, sometimes years later (supposing it was a very big lake) at the feet of those that helped to set that one little pebble in motion.

It is a miracle that, despite the amount of time passed and the myriad consequences of life, they manage to find their way to shore, to reach home, these tiniest of ripples. Find their way they do, however, resurrecting experiences long since consigned to history, making them as fresh as the day that little pebbled was tossed, and explaining why an anonymous international football match between Sri Lanka and Bhutan had my complete attention.

Traditionally, a pre-qualifying match for a tournament that wouldn't happen for another three years and three months, and between a country ranked 209th (last in the FIFA world rankings) and a side 36 places above it, makes precious few headlines among the world's football press.

However this World Cup qualifier, taking place only eight months after Germany won the last edition in Brazil, had my full focus. It represented a glorious full stop in an adventure of football and friendship that began more than 13 years ago and culminated in a moment of awe that, until now, I had thought could never be topped: standing on the top of the Dochula Pass, surrounded by great pine trees littered with prayer flags, listening to the deep rhythmic boom of Buddhist monks sat to one side reciting ancient texts – one crashing a small set of cymbals together, another blowing into a great horn. Deep in meditation they, like my wife and I, looked out on the vast, distant mountains of the Himalayas; beyond them and their awe-inspiring peaks, the mystical and troubled land of Tibet.

It was a moment that remains as clear in the mind as any more recent; a moment that compelled me to think of everything that got me to that point, to the training session we had witnessed the day before, where young boys played football excitedly on a scrap of ground usually reserved for archery contests with infectious enthusiasm and joy.

That was not long after the pebble had been set in motion. And now, all these years later those ripples had come back and had me rushing home to my computer to check on the score-line from Bhutan's first ever World Cup qualifying match. But why, and how, did a match sandwiched between equally modest fixtures featuring East Timor and Mongolia, Cambodia and Macau come to be the biggest match of my year?

I have already explained how, in late 2001, I came up with the ludicrous notion that maybe there could be a nation right at the foot of the FIFA world rankings, a team so bad that they might consider the offer of a poor amateur player like me. I was briefly prepared to switch nationalities all for the chance of a football adventure, and maybe a few minutes of international football.

The realisation of just how unrealistic, stupid, and just plain patronising that notion was dawned on me within minutes, but by then I had already started trawling through the nations at the very foot of the rankings. As I looked through the names and flags of countries I had never even heard of before, I became lost in their strangeness, marvelling, as I still do while flicking through old copies of *National Geographic* magazines in flea markets, at all that there is out there in the world that I have no idea about.

There was one name, one flag that stood out somehow: a flag halved diagonally and coloured red and yellow, a beautifully designed dragon emblazoned across the front, and next to the flag, the name of Bhutan. It was a name that meant nothing to me, and I had no idea where in the world it might be. I could have shrugged and moved on to something else. I could have checked my emails, or the BBC football website, but thankfully my inquisitive side couldn't leave it there and I clicked on Bhutan's nation profile on the FIFA site.

A small, isolated Buddhist kingdom high up in the Himalayas, Bhutan had only entered the world football community in the late '90s, and had left their first taste of international football, an Asian Cup qualifying tournament, with a 3-0 loss against Nepal, then a 20-0 defeat at the hands, or feet, of Kuwait. 11-2 and 8-0 defeats in their remaining games constituted a real success by comparison to that baptism of fire.

But it wasn't the results that had captivated me; it was the fact that this football crazy, but very poor country had remained completely unknown to me, and indeed to the vast majority of the planet, my entire life, despite being culturally, religiously, and geographically very close to a country that the whole world has heard of, a country that I had been fascinated by for a very long time: Tibet.

By sticking to its Buddhist culture, and adhering to the Dalai Lama's teaching of non-violence, Tibet was helpless when invaded by China. That the world did nothing to protect such a unique and wonderful culture is a tragedy of modern times.

This country had fascinated me since my childhood. And now here I was, looking at a country that, from an outsider's clumsy view, is virtually identical in spirit, religion, and culture to its more celebrated neighbour to the north. And on top of that, is has a football team.

A few random emails sent out to the online version of Bhutan's only newspaper, *Kuensel*, asking for a little more information on the national team and football in Bhutan resulted in a lovely reply from a man named Karma Dorji, steeped in warmth and Buddhist humility that I would grow to love even more than I already did. He explained that Bhutan loved football dearly, and that they had a national league that plays a few months of the year, but there weren't many teams, as Bhutan is a very poor country, and there isn't money for football equipment or any kind of development.

The more I read about Bhutan, the more similarities I found it had with Tibet; it was what Tibet should have been in the 21st century, had it not been invaded. The humility, the peace-loving outlook on life, the emphasis on respect and tolerance that permeated Bhutanese culture, and all these Buddhist mantras that helped to create an intoxicating ideal for a society. In Bhutan I had found a living, breathing, and most importantly, free manifestation of what made me fascinated by Tibet.

And, after a few more emails with Karma, I had also found a purpose. I could combine my love of the Himalayas with my love for football.

It became quickly apparent that, to a country with virtually nothing, a little could make a real difference. Between Karma and I we decided that maybe we could start a new football team in Bhutan?

I would try and raise some money in the UK in order to buy some kit, boots, balls and everything else needed to start a football team, while Karma would see how easy it would be to sign a new team up for the national league. Due to the isolated geographical nature of the country, where there are no trains or internal air flights, and the roads are small and winding as they thread their way across mountain pass after mountain pass, the national league actually consisted purely of teams based in the capital, Thimphu. It is said that in all of Bhutan's road infrastructure there is only one stretch of genuinely straight road, which heads across the Paro valley and lasts for no more than a minute or two. This goes some way to explaining the excitement our driver showed when he used it to drive us an ancient, but derelict monument. (If you get car sick, Bhutan is not for you!)

Karma already knew of a few boys who would love the chance to play for a team, he put the word out to see if there were any more. Two days later he sent me a picture of roughly 100 children who had turned up to the first ever meeting/training session of this potential new team. As Karma had said, they were passionate about football, and desperate for the opportunity to play.

With that picture I knew we couldn't let them down. We needed to raise some money. And by 'we' I meant my friend Mike and me. Back at the turn of the century, sending emails was about the limit of my technological expertise, whereas Mike could design websites and could also post items on eBay that had been donated to the cause. So, while Mike started to raise the profile of what we wanted to do online, I wrote to as many football clubs as I could explaining the situation in Bhutan, in the hope that one or two might donate something we could raffle off to make a bit of money. That's when things started to get out of hand.

From Premier League giants to teams at the foot of League Two, things started turning up in the post: signed balls, pennants, programmes, and photographs, as well as a signed shirt from Leeds United and a pair of complimentary tickets from Halifax. All told, thanks to Mike, we raised nearly £700. It was more than enough to buy some kit, balls and decent boots (most of the children only had very cheap knock off ones from India that fell apart after a couple of weeks, but were kept together lovingly by whatever means at their disposal – goodwill, mostly).

Before long, after numerous visits to sports shops with shopping lists for boots (the sizes provided by Karma), I got used to the strange looks of the assistants when asking if they had a certain make in stock, and if they did, did they have nine pairs in size five, and four in size seven! If those looks were strange, the people behind the counter at the post office were even more bemused when I would turn up with another parcel ready for dispatch.

'Bhutan?' they would say, then pull out a large and mostly unused book for obscure countries, to work out the postage, 'where's that near?'

'India?' I would offer in return, 'does that help?' The consternation on their faces suggested that it didn't.

Somehow all the parcels made their long, long journey high up into the Himalayas safely, and within days of their arrival pictures would come back of the young players decked out in their kit, with new boots and big smiles, kicking about pristine footballs. It was a real thrill to see, and even more of a thrill to see just how much they appreciated this chance; some of the children walking for miles after school to attend practice sessions.

With the aid of Chokey Nima, the new team's coach and captain of the national team in that inaugural tournament that culminated in their 20-0 defeat, Karma whittled down the players that would actually take part in matches to the most dedicated 40 or so, separating them into two squads: an under-19 and an under-14 squad. And it was from those players that the country's newest team, Druk United (Druk-Yul being the ancient name for Bhutan) was chosen. They stepped out in their bright red shirts, the club name emblazoned on them, for their first ever match in the National B division against Thimphu Ravens on the 20 August 2002.

In our age of mass communication, it is a strange feeling to be sitting patiently by a computer, waiting for an email from a far-flung land like news outlets once did; sitting by the phone waiting for scores to be rung through from distant grounds before they could be put up on the vidiprinter. But that's what I did that morning, waiting impatiently and excitedly for any news, any pictures of this team that had miraculously materialised out of multiple emails and goodwill.

I had had no expectations, no plans for Druk United beyond the simple gratification in knowing that kids would be able to play the game they loved. I hadn't anticipated anything more, and certainly not report after report of this team of kids winning match after match, topping the Group B table, and scoring 17 goals in five matches.

I hadn't reckoned on just how much it meant to these kids, this chance to play, in a proper team, with a proper kit and a proper coach. I hadn't reckoned on their dedication and passion, which got them promoted into the National A division at the first time of asking, where they would be playing players from the national team; a modest challenge by world football standards, but for a team of children, in a country of few sporting opportunities, it was a big deal.

We continued to raise money, by any means possible, to help keep this momentum going, trying to keep up with the enthusiasm of the team and the board members that ran it with Karma. Instead of the team going into hibernation once the short football season had ended like most teams in Bhutan do, the Druk United players kept on training, three or four times a week, with more and more children coming along to take part. And the passion, dedication, and pure enjoyment that Karma and the team possessed didn't go un-noticed.

The Bhutan Football federation declared Druk United to be the most progressive club in the country, five of the national team enquired about joining for the following season. The ever growing numbers of youngsters desperate for the opportunity to play resulted in a third team being formed, pushing the Druk United family close to 80 in number, ranging from adult to the ages of ten and 11.

Fundraising in the UK tried to keep up with the enthusiasm within the team, with more parcels of boots and kit winging its way over the distant peaks of the Himalayas as soon as they had been made up. The whole experience boiled down to a very simple equation: relatively minimal effort in the UK provided basic equipment that gave young children the chance to show just how dedicated and motivated they were for football, and their club.

It was an overwhelming experience to see young people, given such a small opportunity in a pair of football boots, or a new ball, some organised coaching, take it far beyond anyone's wildest dreams. They reached the summit of Bhutanese football in less than a year, and they weren't finished there. To help our fundraising efforts in the UK, Karma and the team decided to organise a couple of concerts in Thimphu, to raise both profile and money. And they wanted my wife and me to come over for them!

Bhutan is far, far away, and allows only 3,000 people in on very expensive tourist visas each year. I told Karma that we would love to, but we just couldn't afford flights and the $200 a day for the visa. Undeterred, Karma contacted the Bhutan Football Federation and explained the situation, and they in turn authorised a couple of Visas on the grounds of a cultural and sporting benefit to the country. If we could get there, the rest would be fine.

Paro airport, Bhutan's only airport, is not for the faint hearted. Only a select few pilots are qualified to guide the small Drukair planes among the mountains of the Himalayas, before descending steeply through ominous tree covered ravines to the small runway on the Paro valley floor. While my wife was looking at yet another spectacular view through the right hand window, the Valium from the connecting flight from London to Calcutta fast wearing off, I was watching the left hand wing tip getting perilously close to the tree line. We came so close that I could make out fir cones among their branches, and colourful patches of chillies drying on rooftops of the occasional small dwelling that clung to the steep rock face. I prayed that she wouldn't look round, not knowing what kind of reaction our bare knuckle ride would provide. Thankfully she didn't. As we taxied up to the small airport terminal, the Bhutanese passenger sat by the window next to me smiled, and pretended to wipe his brow.

The next five days were a blur. A long hike up to see the Tiger's lair, a beautiful monastery perched high up on a mountainside not far from Paro. The rarefied air of the capital Thimphu that stands so high above sea level that walking any distance was tiring. Watching Buddhist monks praying in the summer Capital of Punakha. Shooing monkeys out of the road on our way to Wangdue, another stunning monastery seemingly defying gravity atop a steep drop. From the breathtaking views from the Dochula Pass; to the wonderful music at the fundraising concert, we never wanted the days to end. Sleep seemed trivial when confronted by such beautiful architecture, people and culture, and with so little time to explore and immerse ourselves in it all.

The concert was surreal. The day after we went, the entire board of the Bhutan Football Federation, as well as the entire squad of the national team, came along to show their support. While we were there, the cameras of the Bhutan Broadcasting Service turned up, wanting to interview me, to try and understand how and why an Englishman had found his way all the way out here, all in the name of football. It wasn't just the hypnotic blend of Indian, Nepali, and traditional Bhutanese music that made the cold night feel so dreamlike. The music, the geography, the culture, combined with the knowledge that we were so very far from home in one of the most isolated spots on earth, having found our way here due to a few random emails and a lot of faith and goodwill, made it hard to not walk around saucer-eyed with bewilderment.

Oh yeah, and we went to the King's birthday party too! A huge celebration at Changlimithang Stadium, the only full sized football pitch in Thimphu at the time, it included dancing, singing, traditional wrestling in ancient costumes, food and drink. It was a dizzying experience, but still by no means the most dizzying of the trip. That honour was reserved for the training session we got to witness before we left.

It is hard to fully comprehend through photographs, even if they are accompanied by emails expressing just how happy and proud those in the pictures are, what something as small as a £15 pound pair of football boots could possibly mean to someone. But standing next to coach Chokey Nima at the touchline, watching the young children of Druk United training on a hard and uneven pitch that was used most days as an archery ground, that was something else. Laughing and smiling, they tried to dribble balls round cones on a ground littered with stones and pot-holes the size of small craters, the studs of their boots skittering and scratching at the hard earth, took shots at the goalkeeper in a goal made up of Chokey's tracksuit top and his bag, cheering if they scored, laughing if they missed, running off to retrieve their ball before starting again. Actually seeing them in action, high up on the side of the steep Thimphu valley, the capital beneath them, dogs barking, the smell of wood fires drifting up into the clear mountain air and the town falling into shadow as the sun began to set behind the breathtaking peaks of the eastern Himalayas; well that feeling, of seeing their unrefined joy unfolding right in front of us, there just aren't any words to express it. How much a simple thing as a ball, a pair of boots, a shirt, can make people soar, if only within themselves, is truly a priceless thing to see. It was a very humbling experience.

That moment, standing next to Karma as the passers-by that had wandered up from the town after work slowed, then stopped to watch the boys train, was, to me, priceless. Dressed in the traditional national dress of Bhutan (known as a Gho for men, Kira for women, and resembling the kimono of Japan) these spectators clapped and smiled as the odd shot flew high and wide and into some trees beyond.

Karma smiled and shrugged as another ball ballooned away.

'The pitch is a little uneven,' he said, laughing, 'but we have to use the archery ground when Changlimithang stadium is too busy. They don't care where they play, as long as they can.'

At the end of the session we all came together for a photograph. If I had the choice, and could remain suspended in time, trapped in the thoughts and feelings of one single moment in my life, then I think that photograph would be the moment I would pick. Every time I look at it, even more than 12 years on, I get that same feeling looking out on those happy, peaceful faces, a feeling of great warmth and comfort in being able to say: 'I know them'. The little boy sat cross-legged in the bottom left hand corner of the picture sums it all up: an innocent smile, looking up lovingly at his friends in football, waving warmly at the camera. It was a moment to be savoured.

That moment, just like the rest of the five days spent mingling with Buddhist monks, footballers and TV camera crews, enjoying the hospitality of a farmer and his family in Punakha, wandering the sacred halls of monasteries, was experienced in a state of awe. But before I knew it, it was gone, the five days were up, and Bhutan, and its lovely people, were just a glorious memory.

In five days I could only get a taste of a country that gauges wealth spiritually rather than financially; to my knowledge, Bhutan is the only country in the world that openly strives to improve and promote the official policy of 'gross national happiness' over the more globally traditional mantra of gross national profit. Five days is not long enough to be among such respectful, humble, peaceful souls as the Bhutanese. Maybe five years wouldn't be either.

Year two of the Druk United revolution remained as upbeat and dedicated as the first. With three teams to support, we continued to raise money and send out parcels through post office assistants who no longer needed a dusty book to work out the price of postage to the Himalayas. The young Druk United played well in the top division, though often losing out by the odd goal to more experienced teams with players with international experience, albeit limited. However the Bhutan Football Federation deemed Druk United important to football in Bhutan and informed Karma that they would remain in the top division. Not only that, but 11 of our players were selected to represent the country at under-19 and under-17 level.

All the efforts of Karma, Chokey, the board, and the players had paid off, far beyond mine or their wildest expectations. Just a few pieces of kit had enabled passions to soar to new heights. It was an amazing thing they had achieved. Amazing.

Finally, with Karma, the driving force behind it all, starting a young family that needed a lot of attention, the club wound down, passing on kit and expertise to other clubs. The children, now grown up, joined other teams, and carried on the amazing work they started with Druk United, playing and enjoying the game they loved.

And so the wonderful journey that had begun with a few cursory emails came to an end, barring a few messages a year between Karma and I, talking about all that had been achieved. Or, at least, so I thought.

Carefully stored scrapbooks full of emails, pictures, articles, and receipts began to gather dust, a Bhutanese flag and shirt folded neatly on top of them, a semi-deflated Druk United football next door; and a photo album which found its way on to my lap every now and then, featuring page after page of stunning scenery and smiling faces. Every now and then the scrapbooks would be added to with news of the national team playing a rare match, but by and large life moved on, and our Bhutan adventure sat proudly, but quietly in the past.

Until nearly 12-and-a-half years after it first began.

Wednesday 11 March 2015 started off like any other Wednesday, but ended with those old sensations I had felt while at the height of our Druk United days coursing through my veins. Bhutan, being a very poor country, had never had the finances to enable its national football team to take part in the qualifying process for the FIFA World Cup before. For a poor country, with a team ranked 209 and last in the world rankings, it had not been a priority.

Bhutan's rare adventures into international football usually comprised of regional tournaments such as the South Asia Games, where a team would play three games in a qualifying tournament in quick succession, and all at one venue; a decent return for the money spent. However the first qualifying rounds of the World Cup were a simple home and away leg against one opponent, and the finances needed to potentially travel anywhere within Asia for just one game had been prohibitive to the Bhutanese.

But now, as a small news article on the BBC Sports website explained, Bhutan were in Colombo, Sri Lanka, preparing for their first ever World Cup match the following day against a side ranked 36 places higher than them. It was only newsworthy because Bhutan propped up the rest of the football world in the FIFA rankings; 209th out of 209 nations, and the British love an underdog.

For a qualifying match taking place over three years before the main event in Russia, in a country more renowned for its cricket than football, Bhutan v Sri Lanka wouldn't make many waves the world over. Or so I thought, as I sat down by my computer to try and find updates on the score on the morning of the 12th, finally finding a staccato Twitter feed from the Bhutan Football Federation that began to relay a close match.

Goal for Bhutan! Tshering Dorji put them in front, and from there they stayed in front, keeping Sri Lanka at bay to record an historic win that made the sports news the world over: 'World's worst team wins first ever World Cup match.'

The result, the display, though really heart-warming (I could only imagine how excited Karma and everyone must have been) wasn't the reason I felt the need to write this story down. That motivation came in the 71st minute of the match, when I was hit by a double whammy, when this game suddenly became quite possibly the most important of my entire life.

In the 71st minute Bhutan's number nine, Ugyen Dorji, was replaced by number 23, Karun Gurung; a relatively obscure substitution in a Preliminary round of World Cup qualifying that would be long forgotten before the finals in Russia in 2018 by pretty much the entire world football community, but not by me. I read the name again, then again. I recognised it. I had seen it before, all those years ago, because Karun had been one of the first intake of players for the very first Druk United team.

It couldn't possibly be the same person, could it?

Not long after the match, I found Karun on a social media site and sent him a message. His response made my day, my year – my decade. It was indeed him, he had played for Druk United right from the start, he had received a pair of new boots from our fundraising, he had been there at the training session my wife and I attended, he had been in the photo that I cherished so much. That a player who had played for the team we created had just represented his nation in a World Cup match is something that will never stop seeming surreal to me.

Karun went on to explain that he wasn't the first ex-Druk United player to have played for the senior Bhutan side. A number had gone before him, but it was he who had been lucky enough to play in a World Cup match, and also, did I know that Chokey Nima, coach of Druk United, was now coach of the national team?!

It may never sink in, that the smallest of gestures in providing a pair of £15 boots and a team to play in, to a young boy in a faraway country had a part, no matter how small and insignificant, in that boy going on to play for his nation in the World Cup. I know it was only a pre-qualifying tie in the grand scheme of things, but Karun got to live the dream that every football-loving boy and girl around the world dreams of.

That he is part of World Cup history, that he is part of his country's sporting history is undeniable; it may be just a tiny ripple on a very large lake, but it was profoundly moving and significant to me, and a glorious full stop to the fantastic journey that was Druk United. A full stop I thought had been put in place a decade earlier.

And who knows, it may not quite be a full stop yet.

Bhutan took that 1-0 lead into the return leg at the Changlimithang stadium on Tuesday 17 March and finished off the job with a 2-1 victory thanks to two goals by Chencho Gyeltshen, the Ronaldo of Bhutan, which took them into the main qualifying stage of the tournament. Next up visiting this wonderful country could be Japan, South Korea, Australia, or any of the other Asian football powers. Who knows when and if this wonderful journey will ever end?

Maybe in Russia in 2018?

It seems unlikely, but then, it also seemed unlikely that a young boy, having such fun playing football with his friends on a rough piece of land that doubled as an archery ground, could end up playing for his nation at a World Cup match. Even if they don't make it, victory over Sri Lanka probably went a long way to significantly raising the level of the country's 'gross national happiness'.

And at the end of the day, that is what it has always been about.

22

21 March 2015. Accrington Stanley v York City
League Two

FOOTBALL MEANS A great many things to a great many people, such is the passion that the game can evoke.

It can be all encompassing; it can be the only thing that gets you out of bed in the morning, it can be the perfect antidote to all the problems in your life, such is the feeling of belonging that a fan has with his or her club. Stood on a terrace in the lower leagues with fellow hardy souls you feel a part of something, you are an important cog in the preservation and upkeep of your team. Your support, emotional and financial, keeps the club alive, and in return its existence and your devotion to it gives you a focus. You are valued, almost as much as you value your club.

Your club is a wonderful escape from the realities of the rest of life; from the drudgery of an unfulfilling job, or no job, to relationship problems, or loneliness, money problems, the list is potentially endless. Football, and more importantly your team, is an escape from all that, for a few hours on a Saturday afternoon or a Tuesday evening it can take a back seat.

Football is, unwittingly and to so many people, a therapy for life. It always has been, and let's hope it always will. As long as you have your team, and next Saturday, then other things don't seem quite so bad. I'd never seen football as therapy until my father took his own life. As a child football was just so vibrant and exciting, colourful, intoxicating. Every fan strives to keep those feelings they felt on their first visit for the rest of their lives. It's the blueprint for happiness, for adventure, aspiration, hope, that stays with you well into adulthood, hopefully forever. It's also the blueprint for coping when things aren't going so well; a formula to try and return to a familiar and warm environment to help try and shelter you for a while.

Football is a place you can retreat to when everything else is going horribly, horribly wrong. After Dad killed himself (eight years and six days before our trip up to Accrington to see them play York), football was one of the only things that made sense, along with my wife, sister, mum, and brother in law. It was one of the few things that held together a world that had been thrown into complete disarray, turned upside down and back again, together.

A quiet non-league match, as close as I could ever get to the long since departed Victoria Park, Salisbury, and the comforts that that would have brought, helped provide some quiet, stability, familiarity, and a little respite from the chaos in my head and all around me. It was a Godsend, as was the kindness of friends at the last Southampton game of that season, six weeks after Dad died.

I met Nick, my brother in law, and his dad, and a few other friends before that match, the first I'd been to since his passing, against Southend. It's the little things that make you realise just how sacred these friendships, and the institution of football itself, really are.

I remember clear as day that it was an early kick-off, and that probably we were a little pushed for time. We had met up outside a pub, and possibly should have gone straight to the ground. Nick's dad, John, asked if anyone wanted a drink, everyone else said no, thinking about the time, but I heard myself say that I could do with a pint.

I had been a little nervous about the big crowd expected at the match so soon after a packed funeral service at the crematorium for Dad. I had found myself getting very claustrophobic around people after that.

It's the small things that make a big difference, and I'll never forget the warmth and kindness in John's words when he said: 'If you want a pint, you can have a pint,' holding the pub door open for me. To hell with the time.

It became apparent in the years that followed just how much of a therapy football, and all it brings with it, can be. With the inspirational story of Dan Seaborne and Emma's recovery from her own traumatic, life changing experience, it really brought home how our simple game can help to rebuild lives, and then help to keep those lives together.

That we found ourselves back up at the wonderful Crown Ground, home of Accrington Stanley, with the warmth and friendship that builds life-long allegiances like the kind forged at Victoria Park all those years ago, so soon after the anniversary of Dad's passing, suggested that a little therapy of the very special Stanley family kind was most definitely in order. But we had also found ourselves up here, compelled almost, by the need to witness another football rehabilitation in its infancy, as one of Accrington's players continued on their own personal journey of recovery after tragedy.

Accrington Stanley is such a unique club, surviving and thriving on the dedication and passion of its players, management, board, and supporters in equal measure. Like a fading banner that flutters at the back of the Clayton End stand at the Crown Ground and reads: 'Pride not pounds', it is real football, where both club and fan are respected in equal measure, neither able to exist without the other. What I hadn't expected of Stanley however, was for it to provide another case of football helping someone in trouble. I hadn't expected to find another reason to respect Accrington, to find another bond with it, in helping a lost soul, much like football had helped both Emma and I.

In October 2014 Stanley winger Kal Naismith's girlfriend of eight years, Ashley, suddenly passed away from an epileptic fit. The 23-year-old, obviously devastated, went home to Scotland to be with her, her family, and his family, spending a month away from football, trying to come to terms with something as unfathomable as his childhood sweetheart leaving him before their life together had really begun.

With the encouragement of both sets of family, Kal finally came back to Accrington to, as he said in an interview: 'get back to some kind of normality, even though things would never be normal again.' He went on to explain his housemate and fellow Stanley player Shay McCartan helped him tremendously, keeping him busy, keeping him company; small things that friends do that make a massive difference, without them really even realising it.

The first time we saw him play after the loss of his girlfriend was a dour match in January against Wimbledon. Kal seemed a shadow of the effervescent player we had seen driving at defences, tricking them with neat pieces of skill against Wimbledon on the last day of last season, and against Tranmere and Northampton in September.

Maybe that game in London wasn't a fair reflection on Kal as an individual, as the whole team didn't click that day and lost at a canter. If he was struggling, it certainly didn't seem to affect his effort and work rate even though Stanley were fighting a losing battle, and I couldn't help but marvel at that.

It's something I couldn't have quantified before Dad's sudden death; the physical toll it takes, as well as the mental, trying to come to terms with something that just can't be quantified. For months, years after I felt like I was living life at three quarter pace, just getting by at work, socially, at anything. And just getting by was exhausting.

As each season wound down to the anniversary of Dad's death I felt the enthusiasm in what is usually the most exciting part of the season, relegation and play-off scraps, begin to drain away. The energy required to cope with all the myriad questions you have in trying to understand something that can't be fully understood, all the emotions, often contradictory, swimming about in your head making it hard to really care about anything else as fully as before, even something that was so ingrained and important in my life.

So seeing Kal playing professional football, an intensely pressured situation, even in League Two, in front of thousands of people, was nothing short of inspirational to me, no matter how well he was playing. It was a feat of courage that I couldn't have considered after Dad died, and indeed I really struggled to play in front of a few people in Hampshire League games for Wellow the season after, so much of a shadow of my former self I felt.

I know football is his job, but it is like no other job on earth. You don't get thousands of people screaming at you if you forget to send an email, or drop a wrench, lay a brick upside down. Playing professional football is not a job in which you can hide, or just drift through come match day. For all those people who have paid their hard earned money to stand on the terraces you have to be giving your all, and that is where my respect for Kal, for all that he has done, and is doing, stems from.

Ever since Kal returned I have found myself checking the Stanley line ups to see if he is playing, hoping from afar that he has a good game. Because his bravery in getting back to work, and not only that but getting back into such shape as the manager picks him to play, to someone who has spent time in the same dark hole as Kal has, and possibly still is spending a lot of time, is nothing short of miraculous, courageous, and heartbreakingly brave.

A week after the anniversary of Dad's passing there was only ever one game that I wanted to have my little moment of therapy at: Kal Naismith and Accrington Stanley v York. It would be important, symbolic, and empowering to see him play so soon after a date that had so nearly destroyed me. It would be great to see another person fighting that same fight, and doing the only thing any of us really can, not give up.

The Crown Ground, after only three visits, really did feel like a home from home, nestled behind The Crown pub in a dell, the red stanchions of the main stand peeping through the trees really lifted the spirit and levels of excitement, because it's a Stanley game day. The guys working in the club shop gave us a warm welcome, obviously recognising Emma from the pictures on the blog.

'Safe journey up?' they asked. There it was, straight away, that unity and togetherness that that is far more valuable than money,

Should Stanley stay up this season, they would be celebrating ten straight seasons back in the Football League whilst much larger clubs have fallen into non-league. This says an awful lot, but especially that money isn't more powerful than passion, and indeed pride is more important than pounds.

No trip to see Stanley would be complete without a pint of Pride of

Pendle in The Crown, and sitting in the sun in the beer garden felt very similar to our first trip up on the last day of last season, looking on excitedly at the top of the Clayton End stand just popping up above the fence. We didn't stay too long, however, as we wanted to get into the ground early to soak up the atmosphere.

As it was only our third trip up, standing in the sun looking out at the ground that was slowly getting busier, trying to take in everything that has made Accrington a special place for us to visit didn't get boring: the banners and flags draped across the back of the Clayton End Stand, the rows of red seats in the main stand slowly filling up with old-timers chatting to one another, children playing football excitedly behind the Clayton End terrace, the drums that would lead the Stanley Ultras in song tucked neatly away waiting for their owners.

Since the club and ground is small in scale compared to others, just standing and watching, listening, gives up a lot about the character of the place, and the good people that populate it. You can see and hear things that probably get swallowed up at larger stadiums by booming speakers, and being further from the pitch. From the smiles and laughter of old friends meeting up on their usual spot behind the goal, to the volunteers on the turnstiles stepping out to sun themselves and have a chat while admissions were slow, to the eight-year-old mascot Lottie Heys kicking her disability into touch, slowly dribbling a football around the outside of the pitch, asking the club official with her if she was doing well with a heart-melting innocence and excitement, red and white ribbons in her hair fluttering in the wind.

'You're doing brilliantly, Lottie,' the official said, no doubt as choked up as I felt at her wonderful spirit shining out on her big day.

She paused right in front of me, hand over her mouth in excitement as the chaperone, who was absolutely fantastic and a credit to the club, knelt down. She pointed out at the players, as they began their warm up, and at Luke Joyce, the captain, with whom Lottie would walk out onto the pitch before the match.

As Lottie carried on around the pitch, assistant manager Jimmy Bell put the players through their paces, geeing them up by reminding them of newspaper articles by the York manager on how they planned to win, and drag Stanley back into the relegation fight.

'You were better than them on Boxing Day, and you'll be better again today. Focus. Three points, and lets push on up the table.'

The players, Kal Naismith included, nodded seriously, deep in the zone, ready to go. This was Accrington after all, the club that wouldn't die; one newspaper article wouldn't put the frighteners up them.

We made our way from our spot in the sun by the side of the pitch round to behind the goal, where we had stood the previous two visits. We were just in time to see Lottie wheel away, arms raised, having just scored a goal, the chaperone punching the air and clapping, her relatives taking pictures and jumping up and down at the front of the main stand. Brilliant!

The match was unsurprisingly fast and furious; with games starting to run out York found themselves at the start of the day out of the relegation zone only on goal difference. Where there had once been plenty of time to turn things around, it was getting very close to now or never for the teams fighting to stay in the league.

Eight points clear of the bottom two, Stanley tried to pass and play, but kept coming up against a team who were desperate to get the ball, but were perhaps trying too hard to make anything of it when they did.

It felt like a match in which the first goal, for either side, would light the touch paper, and after a stalemate in the first half that's exactly what happened. York broke away after a Stanley attack, hit a pot-shot that took a wicked deflection off a Stanley defender and completely wrong footed Scott Davies in goal. 1-0.

Stanley, with Jimmy Bell's pre match talk ringing in their ears, went at York looking for an equaliser. Piero Mingoia and Kal Naismith pushed down the wings, trying to create something. The impressive Matt Crooks in midfield drove forward to try and link up with Terry Gornell, but it was Sean Maguire who fired home a deserved equaliser after mounting pressure, sweeping home the ball after York tried to clear. One all, and relief all round among the Stanley ultras. Stanley went on the attack for a winner, but got done on the counter-attack by some neat passing, leaving Jake Hyde the simple task of tapping home what started to look, as the clock wound down like a vital winner. 2-1.

But then somehow, like their motto says, like a team that wouldn't die, in the final seconds of the match the ever reliable Josh Windass ran at the defence, took a tumble over a defender's outstretched leg, picked himself up and fired in the resulting free kick via another wicked deflection to level the scores. The York players sank to their knees, fearing the worst from results elsewhere around the country. Two all.

At the final whistle it was the Stanley players and fans celebrating a decent point and a battling performance which suggested that they had no intention of allowing themselves to get drawn any closer to the bottom end of the table.

Results elsewhere also suggested that it was a good point for York as well; with two teams losing beneath them they had taken a point lead in what would be a close-run thing to the very last day. As for Accrington, now nine points clear, they knew that a couple more wins would enable them to start looking toward next season, a tenth year in the Football League, and all the hopes and aspirations that a fresh set of fixtures in August might bring.

Throughout the match I had kept a close eye on Kal, who seemed a little isolated out on the left wing, the team seeming to feel more natural in always sweeping the ball toward the right. But whenever he did get it he tried to run at defences like of old, and tricked them a few times with some neat footwork to get a cross in. All things considered he had a decent game, and more importantly, for me at least, he was out there, doing what he loved to do, in memory of, and for, his girlfriend.

Seeing that, seeing his courage in carrying on, that for me was worth the four-and-a-half hour drive on its own, never mind all the other great experiences that going to an Accrington match can offer. It's stupid, as I've never met the man, but you have no idea how much I was willing for him to score, for something good to happen to him.

I wish he could have seen little Lottie Heys' adventure on the pitch before the match, which showed that there still could be wonderful, unbridled joy in what can seem like a very cruel world. Just as Kal's actions have been an inspiration for me, then Lottie's clearly infectious love for life can be an inspiration for both Kal and me, and anyone else that needs it. Another little piece of Stanley magic from the Accrington family.

The guys from the shop and a few other mates, one of whom we recognised as the steward at the entrance to the terrace behind the goal, came over to say hello. Keil, who was in charge of the shop, told me how funny it had been when he read in the blog that his mate had discounted the coat Emma had bought back at the Tranmere match without him knowing. His mate just shrugged while playing on the fruit machine.

'Look, I'm all about making the sales, me.'

Keil, it turned out, had pretty much done everything behind the scenes at Accrington, from helping out with the kit at away matches, where he cowered by the door in the changing room while boss John Coleman gave the team the hair dryer treatment at an away match at Southport in their non-league days, to stewarding, to working at the ticket office. Anything and everything that needed doing for his beloved Stanley. His other mate, the steward, turned out to be one of the funniest men on the planet.

'Show them your impersonations,' Keil said. 'Do the old bloke from *Family Guy*.'

This he did to perfection, along with Goldmember, the Dutch villain from the third Austin Powers film, and the Joker from *Batman*.

Keil and all his mates were so friendly, so happy to share their love of Accrington with us as we drank and shared stories of our football travels. We were having such a nice time we almost didn't notice the old man sat at the table next to us, leaning around a few bodies to get a view of the rugby on the TV. The table had been reserved, with a small note saying it was for Bill. In a break from the rugby, he asked if we'd been to the match. We said we had. He hadn't gone, as he thought it was a little too cold for him.

Bill, it turned out, used to play for Accrington in 1954, before going on to play for Derby County and Mansfield. He had also played for Motherwell in his home country, Scotland. When I asked him if he enjoyed his time playing for Stanley he gave a wistful smile and nodded.

'Very much, that's why I moved here to retire rather than anywhere else.' It seems that special Accrington magic has been at work a long time.

Before we left with warm handshakes and questions as to when we would next be up, Bill told me that he had played for Accrington in the first team that was made up entirely of non-English players, when 11 Scots represented the team long before Arsenal's 11 players from across the globe turned out for them some 50 years later.

What he didn't tell us, and we only found out some time later while looking through a record of the players from that bygone era, was that Bill, or Willie White as he was known as back then, as well as playing for Accrington Stanley – 18 league appearances, as well as two more in the Lancashire Senior Cup and a couple of friendlies against East Fife and Third Lanark in front of crowds around the 10,000 mark, the latter commemorating the official opening of Stanley's first set of floodlights – also worked as a miner at Huncoat Pit as part of his National Service. Bill would fit his training with Stanley between long shifts in the mines. If that wasn't astonishing enough, his record revealed that it hadn't been the first time he had combined the job of goalkeeper and miner. He had turned out for Motherwell while working in a Scottish colliery, and indeed his career had been cut short after only three matches at Mansfield, when a mine he was working in collapsed and he suffered a broken back.

We left Bill to his rugby, and Keil and the lads to the fruit machine; another great day with the Stanley family having been spent, and that family a little larger thanks to our time in the pub and the club shop. I'd come to find comfort in the inspirational Kal Naismith, but I'd left having seen the equally inspirational Lottie, and having met some more lovely people along the way.

Just another day following the Stanley.

23

4 April 2015. Lydd Town v Lewisham Borough
Kent Invicta League

I HAVE REMEMBERED another reason why you need football, and especially football in the lower reaches of the pyramid, in your life.

When I was a shy, introverted school child I was once confronted by two boys from a couple of years above me who were notoriously cruel and violent bullies.

'What football team do you support?' one of them challenged as they blocked my path.

I stuttered, knowing the wrong answer would be potentially very painful. Even though we were less than 15 miles from The Dell in Southampton, I knew the question wasn't that simple. Liverpool were also very popular, as they were winning almost everything at the time, and so too were the Ricky Villa FA Cup wonder goal inspired Tottenham.

'What team?' the second bully shouted at me, getting impatient for a kicking. Frozen with fear, it just came out, and stopped them in their tracks.

'Salisbury,' I said meekly.

Silence.

'What?'

'Salisbury, I support Salisbury.'

Limited cogs began whirring behind their mean eyes, and then after what seemed like an age one of them laughed and scoffed, turning to his partner in hate and motioning him leave, probably in search of another victim with a more satisfactory answer:

'Salisbury? What league do they even play in?' he said mockingly. 'Salisbury?'

Their laughter echoed down the school corridor after them.

That was the first time football saved me in my life, quickly followed by a second when a particularly brutal and pyromaniacal monster of a boy decided he was going to set fire to my trousers while I sat and watched the school team play. Even though I was a couple of years younger than the majority of the team I often got picked to play, but on this occasion I was injured.

I could see him in the corner of my eye, looking toward me, then ambling across. He seemed enormous, and as he took out a lighter and told me he was going to set fire to my trousers I just sat there frozen in fear. He crouched down and tried to get his lighter to work, leaning over my legs, focusing on one particular frayed strand of fibre dangling from the hem of one trouser leg.

I closed my eyes and tried to weigh up whether being set on fire (my cheap polyester school trousers would have gone up in a flash) would be more or less painful than running away and enduring countless beatings because of it.

'Oi!'

I looked up. It was one of the team's substitutes who had come across to see what was happening. He too was a feared member of the school population, and he shook his head at the fire starter.

'Leave him alone, he's alright, he plays for the team.'

The look of disappointment on the first boy's face at the thought that a bigger fish had prevented him from immolating a fellow pupil will remain with me forever. Once again, thank you non-league, thank you football.

Hopefully in your walk of life you no longer need to meet the more twisted elements of humanity, but to be honest, why would you even take that chance? If you value your health (and your slacks) then heed this cautionary tale and get yourself into football at the less glamorous end of things. You never know when it may come along and save you. With that advice ringing in my own ears, I felt it time to pay a respectful visit to the lower reaches of the football food chain, as a kind of offering of thanks.

Usually with football travels it is the team you want to see that determines the location you get to explore. This chapter however is all back to front, with our destination of the Kent Invicta League match between Lydd Town and Lewisham Borough chosen because geographically it is the closest club and match to one of my favourite places in the country, Dungeness.

Dungeness, in my experience, is a place you either love or hate, its isolation and bleakness either beautiful or depressing, with little variation in emotion between those two extremes. Its infinite skyline of miles and miles of flatlands due to a treeless nature reserve behind it, and the beach before it feels almost otherworldly. Shingle built up to protect the low lying and unique looking beach houses means you can't see the shoreline from them, and it seems like the beach stretches on forever. It feels like there is far more sky than land, and is quite unlike anywhere else on earth that I have been. The only man-made constructions large enough to register in this vast open space, and help remind you that you aren't wandering on some alien landscape, other than the old lighthouse and the newer foghorn/lighthouse nearby, is the imposing Dungeness nuclear power plant.

Yes, nuclear power plant. To some that can be an instant turn off when it comes to a beauty spot. Me, I think it looks fascinating, a dense tangle of pylons stretching out from its enormous bulk, on and away, hugging the coast as they slip into the far distance of the flatlands.

The small beach houses, some of which have been constructed using old railway carriages, appear to be either smart looking holiday homes or more ramshackle, lived-in homes for the committed recluse or artist. The odd shed with art on display huddles next to a house, looking out on little beach gardens made up of hardy plants, driftwood, and rusting parts from the old fishing boats resting on props in the distance.

It is a wonderful place to just wander about with your thoughts, and it became even better when I realised that the old lighthouse was open. My previous couple of visits had been during the week, when it was shut.

'I'm going up that!' I informed Emma, who didn't do heights. I left her to it.

I am still the boy that used to visit Victoria Park to see Salisbury play with my grandfather in more ways than one!

Lydd is a small town four or five miles away from Dungeness. The Lindsey Field, home of Lydd Town, is a beautifully tended ground on the outskirts, close to the Dungeness road, and surrounded by miles of ploughed fields and what looks like a mostly disused crop of aged warehouses. A small row of old terraced houses look out onto the pitch, cowering from the bitter wind whipped in off the English Channel.

For the Easter weekend it was unseasonably cold, perhaps explaining why there appeared to be no more than 30 paying punters for a second v bottom clash in the sixth tier of the non-league pyramid. A fair number of those punters were hurrying to the clubhouse for a tea before heading back to their cars (which can be parked to look out on the pitch), to watch proceedings from there.

Like the ground at Corinthian, the Lyndsey Field looks like a homage to Kevin Costner's baseball ground from *Field of Dreams*. As in the movie, Lydd's pitch looks almost out of place among the vast expanse of flat farmland that surrounds it; a lovingly kept pitch in the middle of nowhere that, under the newly erected floodlights, during hot summer nights of pre-season when the fields of crops (I am imagining tall, thick corn stalks as in the movie) close in on it, mosquitoes flitting beneath the lights, you could almost imagine the crack of ball on bat, Costner sat in the bleachers looking on, so idyllic, almost magical a spot it appears.

We paused a while in the clubhouse to take it all in, looking at the rows of old pictures on the wall; founded in 1885, the same year as

Southampton, Lydd Town have played a vital little role in the social and sporting history of this small town on the coast of Kent. Generation upon generation of the town lined the walls, proudly wearing the green and red of this little club. Just like at Downton in December, clubs like this aren't measured in trophies won, but in its importance to the small community it serves. While Lydd is slightly easier to get to than Dungeness, it is still far from anywhere, and the loss of this club would be profound on the town's sporting and social outlets. It is, like Downton, a lifeline for a small number, who rely on it for company, friendship and purpose on a Saturday afternoon.

Thankfully, judging by the wonderfully kept clubhouse, the painstakingly painted railings around the pitch, the Lydd Town FC flag whipping furiously about its pole in the wind, the lovingly produced programme and remarkably pristine looking pitch, Lydd Town FC is being looked after by its current custodians very well indeed, and the town needn't worry about life without it.

One of the glorious peculiarities of non-league football, that supporters that have never darkened its door will have missed, is the ceremonial displaying of the match day teams on a board outside the clubhouse. Back in the Victoria Park days it was a blackboard with the names etched in chalk, at Lydd, like at most lower non-league grounds these days, it was a whiteboard with marker pens. But no matter what the means, and which generation, it always attracts attention, with those that need to know carefully transcribing the teams onto the backs of their programmes for future reference.

I just took a picture of it on my phone in case I needed it, trying to get a decent view behind an old man jotting it all down. He smiled and nodded, explaining that he had to do it the old way because he used to be a teacher, and, although he had retired more than 20 years ago, he couldn't not write it all down, and properly, because that was what he had always told his pupils to do: write it down, slowly, and properly.

'And what if one of them saw me today, all those years later, not heeding my own words? Well that wouldn't set a very good example, would it?' He laughed and smiled, then once done he hurried back inside the clubhouse to keep warm before the match.

From the off it was clear who were second and who were bottom. Lewisham, though with a number of exciting attacking players on show, didn't seem to have the complete team package as Lydd did. Too often their attacking wingers drove forward, trying to link up with the strikers, only for it to break down, leaving the defence and one sole holding midfielder outnumbered against a far more disciplined home side.

Having only notched their fourth win of the season the previous Saturday, and being five points adrift at the foot of the table, Lewisham were still an entertaining team to watch, with impressive centre back Gary Linton and holding midfielder Moussa Traore trying to shore up the back while Stefan Beckford, Orin Boreland, Junior Kumbi, and Jamal McNamee used their undoubted skill to try and find a way through the Lydd backline.

It was refreshing to see a team at the bottom of the table attack with such vigour a side so far above them in the standings. However the gaps left at the back began to tell, and Lydd's superior team ethic began to bear fruit: a penalty, a close range finish, and a great strike from Matt Collins saw them cruising before half time. To their credit, Lewisham stuck together and kept on at it, forcing the issue in the second half, even though neither side added to the score line.

The grass bank that ran the length of the pitch was a glorious spot to watch a game of football, even in the cold. Beyond the miles of flat, patchwork fields, the Dungeness power station stood in the distance in sharp relief. As the odd spell of sunshine lit up one side a brilliant white, the opposite was cast in shadow. Further on, the old lighthouse looked out to sea.

If Dungeness was my go to spot for beauty, peace and contemplation, then Lydd Town would always be my team for watching football near a place of beauty, peace and contemplation. I am sure other football fans that travel the country have favourite stop off spots on the way.

I find it hard to believe, for example, that every long distance supporter doesn't have a favourite dead poet's grave to visit to break up the journey there or back again. I mean, that's just standard, right? No weekend trip to see Accrington Stanley would be complete without a small detour to Heptonstall, near Hebden Bridge, to visit Sylvia Plath, and now, after our time here, no visit to Dungeness would be complete without an afternoon's football spent in the company of the good people of Lydd.

Maybe one day even a summer trip to watch a pre-season match under the lights, and get the full flavour of this wonderful field of dreams would be in order. I hope so.

The players and the managers may possibly not agree, but watching this match, it didn't really seem to matter where the teams were in the table. It didn't matter that one was near the top, and the other at the foot. For community clubs like these, just being is enough for the small band of supporters that hold them dear. Promotion, relegation, neither would affect how they felt about their team, neither would encourage nor discourage them to visit more, or less.

Like the spirit of Costner's field and team, Lydd Town win every week if they put in their all for the supporters, if they express themselves as best they can in the moment, for the moment, regardless of league or opposition, as all their forefathers lining the clubhouse walls once did. Ultimately that endeavour, that drama, in the moment, transcending the context of a match or a season, is what makes football, and indeed baseball from across the Atlantic, so special to play and magical to watch. It is what has the old-timers coming back week after week, programmes neatly folded in back pockets, looking out for familiar faces in the clubhouse and flowing passages of play out on the pitch.

As the game came to an end, I couldn't help but feel happy to have seen such a spirited display of attacking football from Lewisham in the face of such steep odds, and such a complete performance from their hosts; a match worthy of and well befitting the staggering beauty of its surroundings.

I'd also managed another match without my trousers being set alight, which, for me, can only be a positive.

24

6 April 2015. Accrington Stanley v Carlisle United League Two

TRADITIONALLY, FOOTBALL SPANS the generations and is handed down through those generations, with one young child being taken by a family member or friend to their first match, invariably becoming intoxicated by the sights and sounds of the bustling crowd, stepping out onto the terraces or into the stands to see the pitch for the first time (if they are particularly lucky, illuminated a vibrant, brilliant green by the floodlights of an evening match), the players in their kit, the cheers and chants of the supporters, a fast and entertaining match.

That's how it was for me. A family friend, now sadly passed away, took me to The Dell on a warm afternoon for an early season match. I remember the Saints kit seeming even more vivid in the flesh than in pictures, the bright sun making it and the pitch pop, the rich smell of some kind of tobacco drifting about the thick mass of bodies high up on the old Milton Road terrace, the crowd roaring and shouting in unison while Kevin Keegan and Mick Channon worked their magic below.

I loved The Saints before I went, but seeing the players on the pitch, the shirts I hoped for on my birthday and Christmas in action, the sights and sounds, the excitement of the match, well, it ensured a life-long love affair with my club and all the unimaginable highs and unbearable lows that went with it.

So great was my obsession that during the summer holidays, if we were going into town I would beg my mum to go by the ground so I could spend a few minutes peering through the locked gates and turnstiles, trying to catch a glimpse of the pitch, a groundsman drifting in and out of view, carefully pushing a mower up and down to create pristine, sharp strips of mown grass between the empty stands that basked in the hot sun. I remember the distant sounds of children playing somewhere among the maze of terraced streets beyond, the drone of cars rumbling lazily by.

I remember spending every last penny of my pocket money in the club shop that was mostly empty, waiting on the new season's stock, pouring carefully through the player pictures from the season just gone. Discounted to clear, I would pretty much collect them all through the course of the summer.

My parents, my family friend, they knew what would happen in taking me to my first match, in opening my eyes to the spectacle of it all. They knew they were creating a monster, just as someone had once created a monster in Colin, our family friend, and the person that took the person who first took Colin. And so on, and on, back through the generations.

I have been lucky enough to feel that thrill, that belonging, more than once. Everything I felt at The Dell, I also felt at Victoria Park with my grandfather watching Salisbury, because Salisbury were Grandad's team, and just as I looked up to him, so too I looked up to his team.

Just because the ground was smaller, and the crowds a fraction of what you could expect at The Dell, didn't mean that I loved life at Victoria Park any less.

The white strip of Southern League Salisbury when they ran out gave me just as big a rush of adrenalin as when Division One Southampton ran out, a goal for either was met with ecstasy. Victoria Park, though comprising just one small stand and a couple of thin strips of covered terracing running one length of the pitch was held with equal reverence as The Dell.

Despite its smaller stature, the honking of horns from cars parked behind one goal every time Salisbury scored, the cheers and cajoling of a few hundred hardy souls made a match there seem just as magical as one at The Dell, and it was visited just as regularly through the school holidays whenever we went up to stay with my grandparents.

Just like the tobacco smoke at the Dell, it is the glorious, rich smell of freshly printed programmes that, more than 30 years later, hits me so vividly whenever I think of that lovely old ground, as though we had been sat in the stands, programme tucked safely under our legs, watching a match there only yesterday. I felt I belonged at both equally, loved both equally, existing as they did at opposite ends of the football food chain.

Some days I would fret about what would happen if Salisbury ever managed to battle through to the third round of the FA Cup, and somehow contrived to draw Southampton; who would I support? What would I do if either team scored? These were impossible questions that I never could answer.

So when Salisbury, my last connection to Grandad, folded in the summer of 2014, the loss was like a sucker punch. Though the pain had been great, and the eternal balance of my personal football equilibrium ('big time' Southampton 'small-time' Salisbury) had been shattered, it really had never been my intention to find a replacement.

At the age of 41 those feelings; of falling in love with a club, of stepping out onto a terrace and almost immediately feeling at home, well, it just can't happen, can it?

There had been the odd small-time precedent, of people falling for football in adulthood, having missed out as a child; Emma for one, Effie another. But what happened when I first went up to Accrington Stanley was neither expected, nor sought. It just happened.

The club's warm and welcoming feel, its friendly supporters, their combined togetherness in the face of greater economic foe, its place as the soul of the community deeply rooted, all these things helped me have 'a moment' by the time we walked out onto the Clayton end terrace for the first, second, third time.

It may not be as big as the Dell, or most grounds in the Football League, but looking up at all the banners draped along the back of the stand, at the hills beyond the away end, the pitch drenched in sunlight, activity slowly growing in the main stand. It made me feel ten again, hurrying to keep up with Colin through the bustle outside The Dell, taking my first look out from the top of the Milton Road terrace.

I've kept my falling for Accrington no secret, in fact I've told anyone that would listen about my epiphany, so my sister knew what she was potentially letting herself in for when she agreed to let her eldest son, 11-year-old Sam, who still hadn't discovered a club that he could call his own, but had grown curious about this club his uncle kept on about, come up with me during the Easter holidays. My sister knew the potential risk of infatuation her son could experience, just like my mum had when she let Colin and Grandad take me, and those who let them go for the first time.

Both Sam and his younger brother George had been to St Mary's, George being the family's youngest ever season ticket holder, when he got a free one with mine when he was less than three! But both had found it a little intimidating, being much younger than when I first went, and it being more than twice the size of The Dell. After a number of years of not going, however, both found themselves enjoying matches at AFC Totton in the Southern League, and Salisbury in the Conference, and they started to tag along to a few matches this season at Lymington, Eastleigh and Newport.

This handing down of the game from one generation to the next has been in the back of my mind since the morning of Sam's birth back in June 2003, when I found myself outside the Saints store getting a tiny shirt with his name printed on the back. It is something, like all uncles, I am sure, that I took very seriously, understanding the importance of doing it right.

Never did I think, however, 11 years ago, that my handing down of the game to my nephew, that moment when he got it, or it got him, would possibly come so far from home as standing on the terrace at Accrington Stanley.

This Easter Monday match against Carlisle came a day after Burnley, a couple of miles to the east, played at home to Tottenham in the Premier League, and two days before Blackburn, a couple of miles west host Liverpool in an FA Cup Quarter final replay.

With the average football supporter's pockets stretched to the limit, it was easy to see how some prefer to give up the opportunity of an afternoon of Fourth Division football in favour of these bigger matches, both of which are on TV as well. Whether some consider it apathy, or simply the financial reality of the day, it is Accrington whose crowds suffer from stay-at-home supporters, who have to carefully monitor the money they spend on tickets for what many consider to be their second team, or on satellite sports subscriptions, or both.

Fundraising initiatives through the club and the supporters' club are cranking up in order to improve spectator facilities to try and give the neutral, away fan, or fair weather Stanley supporter more incentive to visit the Crown Ground. To the hard-core supporter however, run-down simply translates as full of character, and it is that character that got us to the ground with plenty of time to spare.

It was good to bump into Keil again in the club shop, who was busy preparing for six coach loads and God knows how many cars full of Carlisle fans, and all the ticket stock that would require over at the away end. He took some time however to say hi to Sam and admire the Stanley shirt that I bought the trip before, and smiled as Sam's dad gave in to the temptation of buying a 'Keep the Faith' Stanley t-shirt.

'Brilliant,' he said, 'have a great time Sam. We need all the Stanley fans we can get.'

If Sam had not already been excited about his first Accrington visit, a member of the Stanley staff saying hi, then finding that he got in for free from a cheery old man at the turnstile, then also getting a free Easter egg from an even cheerier bloke tending a stall on the other side, having already bought a programme and two pin badges for his collection, he was buzzing before he even stepped out into the sun by the corner flag on the Clayton end. He took a big deep breath as he looked out, then smiled and looked up at me.

'Uncle Mat, this is the best ground I've ever been to!'

And there it was. It wasn't just me, and Emma, and all the local, faithful Stanley support that slowly began to wander in that knew there was something special about this place. A young boy, having spent close to five hours in a car to get to this point; a small terrace in a small ground in a small town he had never been to before, appeared to be experiencing his 'eureka' moment while looking out at the Crown Ground.

What it was for him may have been different to what it was for you or I; that jumble of experiences that make you come alive. It's a personal moment, after all, but something was most definitely happening, helped no doubt by the warm and friendly faces that welcomed him from the programme seller, to Keil in the club shop, via the turnstile, to the Easter Egg stall.

Even his dad seemed to be taken in as we explored the back of the stand, checking out all the different banners.

'Mate,' he said, 'this place is amazing.'

We don't necessarily get to choose when we find that revelation, and it doesn't necessarily need to be at the first ground we visit, but when it does happen, when that tangle of sights, sounds, smells and feelings come together in someone's imagination, to those who have been there before, it is plain to see, and it was wonderful, watching Sam take it all in.

It is at this moment that I finally lay to rest the only bug bear of my Stanley experience so far. It's fair to say that I am a little afraid of mascots. I just don't trust the way they walk, or lurch. Maybe I've seen too many zombie films, but either way I'm wary of them. I was extremely wary of Winstanley, the Accrington bulldog mascot, when I first saw him, with his bulbous amphetamine tweaked eyes seemingly picking me out among a crowded terrace.

But with Sam and his dad waving at him and beckoning him over for some photographs I realised that Winstanley, despite his intense stare, was just another friendly mascot dog that loves to moonwalk in front of the away goalie as he's trying to warm up, or dance clumsily to the delight of the children at the front of the terrace. Winstanley; like all of us, just wants to be loved!

With the away end close to bursting, and the home stands filling up nicely, including us tucked in behind the goal after Sam asked if we could stand with the ultras, he turned to the programme and the team sheet, studying the Accrington players' names.

'Who should we look out for?' his dad asked.

'Piero Mingoia. Sam, keep an eye on him. I think you're going to enjoy watching him play.'

And enjoy it he did as the teams come out onto the sun-kissed pitch.

Carlisle were in trouble; only a couple of points above the drop zone and with games running out, they needed points and they needed them fast. I'd always had a soft spot for Carlisle, especially after the warmth and humility of their fans after Saints beat them 4-1 at the Johnston's

Paint Trophy final in 2010. The amount that stopped and congratulated us as we celebrated in the car park afterwards, chatting for a few moments before their stupendous journey home, was more than enough for me to always hope that they did ok.

As for Stanley, they were clear from the bottom two, but not far enough clear to not need the three points just as desperately. The bottom of League Two, with that potential drop into the non-league, is a treacherous place, and every season seems to suck a team that appeared well clear of it right back into the heart of the storm.

Last season, Bristol Rovers found themselves in the bottom two only once, but it just so happened to be after the last match, and they were gone. There seemed to be a steely determination about the ground that Accrington were not going to be that team this season, especially with safety for another year signalling the milestone of ten seasons back in the Football League.

No, Accrington needed the points just as much as Carlisle did, and the match reflected that in the first half, with United pressing hard, whipping in crosses and taking shots whenever and wherever they could, while Stanley tried to force a passing game on their opponents. Things were tense, edgy, until the 25th minute when Piero Mingoia, right in front of where Sam was standing, decided to take on the Carlisle defence single handed from way out by the touch line, running at the left back, then both centre backs, dribbling past and between them before dinking the ball past the keeper and into the net.

The ultras, and Sam, went wild. Piero Mingoia had just become his hero.

It was a piece of skill and endeavour that made the long trip worthwhile all on its own, and Sam was still talking about it long into the half-time break.

'I think that's the best goal I've ever seen,' he said, with some certainty.

If that was the best individual goal he had ever seen, then Stanley's second, which broke up a sustained period of Carlisle pressure where it looked like an equaliser was the far more likely outcome, must surely have been the best team goal he had witnessed in his short football viewing life. Left back Adam Buxton sent a long free kick across the field to Argentine Gerardo Bruna, who had been growing into the game after a slow start. He took the ball and drove a few paces before whipping in a great cross that Josh Windass ran on to, smashing the ball into the bottom right hand corner. 2-0!

Before we could fully take in the spectacle of that second goal, Stanley sensed that Carlisle had been stunned by the sucker punch and went for the knock-out blow that came only a couple of minutes later; Séamus Conneely prodding home to make it 3-0 and effectively game over.

To their credit, Carlisle kept trying, but they knew they were beat, and had to suffer long periods of Stanley passing the ball around them for fun as their dejected fans turned nervously to their mobile phones to check scores elsewhere.

A consolation goal three minutes into added time did little to cheer up those long suffering supporters, nor dampen the mood in the home end, knowing that 50 points with five games still to play was a healthy position that a number of clubs beneath them could only dream of, and at the full time whistle the sun seemed to shine that little bit brighter. The atmosphere on the terraces was brighter still as the Stanley faithful began to drain away, happy after a strong Accrington display.

It had been a good day all round, the only pity being that we had to head back to Southampton straight away, so neither Sam nor his dad got to experience The Crown after a home win; something that I hoped to rectify in the not too distant future, at least as far as Sam is concerned who, after glancing back to take one last look out at the Crown Ground while we filed out, looked up at me and asked:

'Uncle Mat, when can we come back?'

Sam crashed out on the back seat of the car not long after dinner at Keele services, but the fact that he did it still wearing his Stanley shirt, his bag with programme, badges and Easter egg safely stowed by his head, suggested that it wouldn't be too long before we would find ourselves coming up again.

From one generation to another, the magic that is Accrington Stanley and life in League Two.

On Stanley On!

25 April 2015. Dagenham & Redbridge v Accrington Stanley
League Two

IT HAD BEEN a long season.

It seemed a lifetime since we set off on our first trip for the book to Bangor in the middle of July, and it seemed an age since our first trip of the season to see Accrington kick-start their campaign with a first win of 2014–15 against Tranmere back on 6 September.

Not only had it been a long season for us, criss-crossing the country all in the name of football, it had been an even longer season for Stanley, with so many twists and turns along the way.

The break in at the club in August that left the players borrowing boots for a mid-week away match at Shrewsbury; the sudden departure of James Beattie and subsequent return of John Coleman and Jimmy Bell in September. The astonishing 5-4 away win at Northampton, and the good run of form that saw the team threatening a play-off push in November. The agonising late defeat in an FA Cup second round replay at Yeovil that saw the club miss out on a home tie against Manchester United, and the tragedy of Kal Naismith's girlfriend passing away suddenly that put such a defeat into perspective. The loss of the influential Tom Aldred to Blackpool and John O'Sullivan back to his parent club after an impressive loan, followed by a poor January and February that saw the team flirt too close to the relegation zone for anyone's comfort, followed by a steadying of the ship that saw Stanley safe with three games to spare. The almost *Spinal Tap*-esque way in which Stanley kept losing goalkeepers to injury; as the band did drummers to spontaneous combustion (is one team using eight different goalies in one season a record?). This season had been long and winding, exhilarating and frustrating, littered with moments of ecstasy and despair for every Stanley player, board member, and fan.

But here, at the last away match of the season, the club could look back on another year spent outperforming clubs with far greater financial backing and support, a feat highlighted by the outstanding display in December in front of more than 14,000 spectators, where the team whose budget was based on attendances a tenth the size beat Portsmouth at Fratton Park 3-2.

That survival this season meant the next will be the tenth back in the Football League and makes the achievements of player, board member and fan even sweeter.

And with games to spare, the nucleus of a really good side coming together, and the hope that a close season of player wheeling and dealing can go well, preparing for pre-season friendlies and the release of a new fixtures list, there is a real belief that maybe a push for the play-offs isn't too unrealistic a target for this anniversary season. Either way, after the drama of this season, that vital first win against Tranmere courtesy of a brace by James Gray, at this point out on loan at Northampton, seemed so long ago that it felt like it must belong to a different page of history.

I can only imagine how it must feel to those familiar faces that we had seen at every away fixture we had been at; those hardy souls who were there for the delirium at Northampton and Portsmouth, the numbing drudgery at Wimbledon, the heartbreak at Yeovil, and the countless other emotions and experiences, bad motorway services, tedious car and coach journeys, late nights home and early starts the following morning that they undertook all in the name of Accrington Stanley and their love for their club.

To the hardy few that made it down to Plymouth and Southend, and up to Hartlepool and Carlisle, and all the other away matches in between, their reward for another season of undying loyalty: an away trip to Dagenham! Safe in the knowledge that this last away day for a few months could be enjoyed like no other before it, knowing that Stanley are safe, and all that was riding on this fixture was pride and the desire for a good end to a good season. It is somehow fitting that this end of season away day celebration was being shared with a club that could, to all intents and purposes be described as the Accrington Stanley of the south, in Dagenham & Redbridge.

They too operate on one of the smallest budgets in the league, and are also surrounded by much larger clubs with a greater pull, which keeps their average attendances to around the same as Accrington's. And like Stanley, the fact that Dagenham were safe with games to go, and could relax on their final home game of the season while far bigger clubs continued to fight for their lives, indicates what a decent season both had had. And in Dagenham there is a blue-print for Accrington to follow for play-off success, because they have proven it can be done.

In Southampton's promotion season from League One, I remember clearly the match between a side featuring Adam Lallana, Rickie Lambert, Alex Oxlade-Chamberlain, and Morgan Schneiderlin and a fearless Dagenham team who, though well beaten, constantly took the game to their hosts.

That away day to St Mary's was one of a great many big days out that season, with League One littered with larger clubs on hard times, and is the just rewards for small, well-run clubs like Dagenham and Accrington if they can find themselves in the promotion mix come May.

Every season the football community will write both teams off, pencilling them in for relegation, and every season they both prove that community wrong; so why not Stanley, like Dagenham before them for promotion at the end of next season? They already overcome huge odds every year.

Given all the joy that criss-crossing the country for this book has brought me this season, it seems very apt that this penultimate chapter should bring together some of the best memories of that long journey: Ade Yusuff, one of many inspirational characters in the lower reaches of the football pyramid, League Two, the real heartbeat of football in this country, and Accrington Stanley.

This final chapter was to be played out at Dagenham's Victoria Road ground, as close as I would ever get to the name of Salisbury's old ground (sadly I couldn't fit in a trip up to Victoria Park, Hartlepool, this season), which means that there was also a little poignancy to this final trip.

With Salisbury's demise at the beginning of the season, I felt a real need to find a way to reconnect with those wonderful memories of afternoons spent with a wonderful man, now sadly passed on, and with the equally wonderful memories of football far from the glamour of the top flight, memories as rich and important as anything that I had experienced with Southampton.

Flicking through football programmes of old, despite helping to recapture bygone sights, sounds and smells, could only take me so far, and never as far as stepping out on an old terrace somewhere, steeped in history and memory.

So here we were, at Victoria Road, Dagenham, waiting to enjoy an end of season match between two shining lights of community football, that are ensuring future generations of grandparents will have somewhere to take their grandchildren, their teams littered with good, honest pros you would want your children looking up to, waiting for Accrington Stanley.

The London Borough of Barking & Dagenham stadium is sandwiched between cramped residential streets one side (I dread to think how team coaches manage to squeeze through those narrow, car choked back roads) and a park the other, where we watched some guys having a kick about, the sounds of an ice cream van echoing around the streets beyond. After an hour-plus journey by train, foot and tube across central London, this part of the capital at least had a more suburban, small town feel to it.

As the sun came out and bathed the pitch a brilliant billiard green, a small band of 91 Stanley supporters congregated in the away end, most full of smiles at another season successfully dealt with, but some making the most of this last-day-of-school feeling by raising the stakes.

A small band of familiar faces, who made all the noise at every away match we had been to, had decided that staying in the league for a tenth season warranted more than just smiles; it demanded a balls out drunk blend of delirium, laughter, singing and dancing you only normally find at the closing stages of a wedding reception.

Like the Wimbledon fans at the last match of last season up at the Crown ground, these lads' dedication to the cause clearly warranted a lager based party that had probably started with some early morning tins on the journey up, and would possibly end by making last orders at The Crown back home much later that night. It was good to see such an outpouring of happiness and love for their team, an expression of just how much Accrington Stanley and staying in the league for a tenth season means to them.

In fact, those lads turned out to be the highlight of the entire match, but not before the sobering commemoration of the 30th anniversary of the Bradford City fire disaster that claimed 56 lives, and physically and psychologically injured hundreds, if not thousands more that were there that day. Just like the Stanley and Dagenham fans here today, those poor souls had simply gone to see their team, to take part in an end of season celebration after a successful season, never to return home.

A minute's silence was impeccably observed, the sounds of birdsong from the trees behind one stand making the hush feel even more emotionally charged and poignant, a beautiful sonnet for the fallen. I couldn't help glance about at the 91 Stanley supporters around us, those happy, smiling faces now sombre, and try to imagine the horror of well over half of them not making it out of this stand, the laughter, beaming faces, and hugs of the noisy, drunk, band of brothers at the back, gone, in one terrible moment. Another reason to feel thankful for everything we have; everything we are.

One thing however that we didn't have, as Stanley fans, was a good match! It's almost irrelevant, as the real action, the real magic of this trip, came from the stands, but for the record, Stanley slipped to a 4-0 defeat.

It was a game where nothing came off, and every mistake was punished. Clearly, Dagenham wanted to finish their home programme on a high for their own dedicated supporters, and Accrington really didn't have any answers. Perhaps the relief of being safe subconsciously had them thinking of their summer holidays, or perhaps a long season had caught up with some of the team, either way they were second best for much of the game, conceding from a corner, free kick, defensive mix up, and a decent goal by a young player called Jodi Jones, who not only scored on his full debut, but also picked up man of the match. Ade Yusuff played his 19th game of the season and threatened up front before limping off with an injury after half an hour; a decent first season in the pro ranks. May there be many more to come for him.

The only positive for Stanley was the impressive display by Danny Whitehead, who looked a decent prospect. Other than that the real highlights came from the small band of Stanley Ultras at the back of the stand, determined to have a great day out no matter what. Quickly tiring of their usual batch of Stanley songs, the ultras started singing and dancing to anything they fancied, by far the best being *Twist and Shout* by the Beatles, where they eventually had a group of Dagenham supporters a little further along the stand up on their feet dancing as well!

Into the second half, and a few of the Dagenham kids realised the real party was over by the Stanley end. They crept closer to sing and dance with the Ultras, who didn't let up with their repertoire that ranged from The Kaiser Chiefs to Rick Astley. The only breaks from the singing came when they announced to the ref that, having missed Dagenham's second goal at the start of the second half due to excessive propping up of the bar, the goal didn't count as they hadn't seen it. They then celebrated like Stanley had just won the FA Cup when Luke Joyce hit Accrington's first shot on target deep into the second half.

Amongst all that, among all the jokes, chants, and songs, came a moment that was quite possibly the best that I have ever seen at a football match. It's hard to know how many of the 2,000 strong crowd even saw it, and if it didn't get caught on film for posterity then I guess it will have to join the ranks of glorious lower league mythical moments, passed down from supporter to supporter in lieu of the multiple angles it may have been captured on if it had happened in the top flight. But for those who did see it, well I hope it lives in their memories as long as it will in mine!

On a rare Stanley attack, and with yet another rendition of *Twist and Shout* in full swing, Shay McCartan volleyed a shot high and wide up into the stand we were sat in. It hurtled toward the ultras, one of whom instinctively launched himself at it, planting a diving header high up into the rafters before tumbling over the empty row of seats in front of him.

Silence. One second, two.

Then up he stood, arms stretched, and belted the first line of his favourite The Beatles song out at the top of his voice, imploring all that could hear him to shake it, then to twist and shout as if their lives depended on it!

The ultras, arms raised behind him joined in, while those Dagenham fans who saw it rose to their feet in awe and admiration, cheering, laughing, joining in on the singing.

I'd lost count by then, but I think Stanley were three down at that point. It didn't matter. Legend had been created for those who witnessed it, and Stanley were safe, and there was a whole lot more lager to be drunk before the amazing day would be over.

The game meandered to a lazy end like only an end of season match with nothing riding on it can, drenched in late spring sunshine, and at the final whistle, as the ultras sang their way out of the ground, the Dagenham supporters gave them a standing ovation. It was the least they deserved! Who else could have turned a long and tiring journey up to and then across London to see your team lose 4-0 in a meaningless match into one of the most enjoyable days of the season?

As Emma and I made our way back to the tube station, our thoughts started to turn to next Saturday, and the final home game of the season. It would mark one year exactly since we caught the Stanley bug, having come up for the final match of last season against Wimbledon.

Memories started flooding back of why this club from Lancashire, at the end of a nine/ten hour round trip, had become so important to us. Friendly faces in and around the ground, the welcome at the Crown pub, at the Sparth House Hotel, Keil and the guys in the club shop, the supporters who embraced us as one of their own, who made my 11-year-old nephew feel so welcome when he came up recently. The players who had responded so positively to our coverage of their club. Good, honest pros such as Luke Joyce, Tom Aldred, James Gray, Piero Mingoia, and most importantly the inspirational and brave Kal Naismith. The combination of all these elements creating a single, unified, unstoppable whole that is more valuable, more powerful than money: that is Accrington Stanley.

Last season, as the Wimbledon fans drank and sang themselves hoarse, and as the Stanley players filed into The Crown for a pint with the supporters after the match, we knew we had stumbled onto something special. Everything that has happened following Stanley since that day has only proved that notion right, and if the feeling at the Mansfield match on the last day of this season is half what it was last season against Wimbledon, then the arduous car journey to get there will be irrelevant.

I can't wait to find out, I can't wait for one more taste of Accrington magic standing on the terraces of the Crown ground, and already I can't wait for next season.

26

2 May 2015
The End of the Road

VICTORIA PARK, ON Castle Road, Salisbury, is still; the sounds of cars drifting by, a few children playing on some swings echoing about the old oak trees that used to tower over the main stand.

Now they look out on a council pitch, a prefabricated set of bleak changing rooms on the spot where Grandad used to sit; the only signs that Southern League football used to inhabit this place are the old barrier and a narrow strip of hard standing that line the pitch.

It is a strange feeling to be in the park these days, especially if you have a photo of Salisbury's old ground with you, taken by a young boy a long time ago. Standing in the rough spot where it was taken, holding it up so that the trees behind the stand match up, the past and the present overlap for a couple of glorious seconds. The ghosts of Victoria Park spill out around the place one more time.

Up the road, the newly reformed Salisbury are fresh from playing a couple of end of season friendlies, looking forward to their only season at the Raymond McEnhill Stadium before their lease is up and they have to move on. Where to no-one knows, but for now all that those who were there really care about is that football in Salisbury has returned. Still unsure of what league they will be playing in next season, those forlorn faces that mourned the loss of Salisbury City FC last summer have at least something to look forward to this close season.

Me, I'm not there. My mind is lingering around Victoria Park, while my body is undertaking one last road trip of the season up to Accrington, to enjoy an end of season party that will celebrate exactly one year since our first taste of Stanley magic; that wonderful day last May with the drunken Wimbledon fans that became the genesis for this book.

Since then we have used planes, trains, boats, and taxis, as well as my trusted old car, to travel the length and breadth of the country in the search for that 'Victoria Park feeling' I experienced as a child. That feeling that makes standing on a terrace somewhere, programme in your back pocket, cup of tea in hand, looking on expectantly, feel so special; the atmosphere charged with endless possibilities. Along the way I have seen others experience their own version of that Victoria Park feeling; Emma at Bangor last July, my friend Sarah at Wimbledon in November, another friend Rich in the away end at Fratton Park in December, and possibly most importantly my nephew Sam at Accrington on Easter Monday.

And as we drove up for this last match of the season, I couldn't help but think back on their mini-revelations; experiencing lower league and non-league football for the first time, or the first time in a long time, for some. As we drove, on roads we had used so often this season, stopping at the same services trip after trip, mile after mile slowly ticking away, I found myself thinking of that old photo that I took of Salisbury's old ground. I found myself drifting back among those idyllic, nurturing ghosts of Victoria Park. I found myself weaving between the groups of supporters leaning up against the barrier, laughing and joking with one another, wandering past the cars parked behind one goal, popping my head into the programme hut to watch my younger self pouring over piles of treasure, Cyril Smith smiling and standing by his little booth taking gate money, the old-timers gathering in the stand, waiting for the mighty whites.

And there, in the corner, in our usual spot, waiting patiently, is Grandad. He is staring wistfully out onto the pitch at the floodlights flickering on, growing in strength, lost deep in his thoughts. Then he spots me, and his trademark smile comes to life, and he shifts along a little for me to sit down, offering me a homemade cushion to make the old cold concrete slab seats more comfortable.

'It's been a great season,' I tell him. 'Stjarnan, remember they were Bangor's opponents in the Europa League? Well they went on to beat Motherwell and Lech Poznan, before being beaten by Inter Milan at the San Siro in the final qualifying round. They also won the Icelandic league for the first time ever, so it will be the Champions League qualifying rounds for them this time Grandad.

'Bangor had a tough year, only avoiding relegation with a game to spare. So it will be a while before we get to check out another European adventure on the banks of the Menai Strait.

'Sarah Wiltshire, the Yeovil Town and Wales International who had lit up the Wales v England World Cup Qualifier in August, well she didn't make it to the finals herself Grandad, Wales missed out right at the very end of qualifying. But she did get a big move to Manchester City, and though it didn't really work out for her there, I'm sure we'll be hearing about her again before too long.

'For Sarah, like with Stjarnan, I think the future looks bright.

'Jared Wetherick, the Cowes Sports forward that Emma was fascinated by at an FA Cup preliminary match in late August, due to him being not the slimmest player you will ever see, well, he scored a hat-trick on the last day of the season which meant they got promoted to the Wessex League Premier. They'll be going to Lymington and Brockenhurst just like we used too.

'You would like Cowes' ground Grandad. It feels just like here.'

He smiles, nods.

'Two of the inspirational characters that we met along the way, and I am sure you would have really liked; Kelly Smith and Dan Seaborne, they had their seasons ended early through injury. For Dan at least he played 22 times and cemented himself as a vital part of the Partick team. For Kelly, the Women's Super League had only just begun when she was the victim of a horrendous tackle that ended any chance of her playing again this year.

'She has come back before. Hopefully she can again, the world needs a few more years of her genius out on the pitch. She's the kind of player you loved to see in a Salisbury shirt, Grandad. Kelly had already retired from international football so her injury didn't prevent her from going to this summer's Women's World Cup in Canada, which England had qualified for with ease.

'More inspirational characters like Fara Williams, Casey Stoney, Fran Kirby and the heroic Laura Bassett helped make it the second most successful tournament ever for an English team. They did the country proud, Grandad, it really was something to see.

'Downton managed to escape relegation with a few games to spare, no doubt much to the relief of the evergreen Mars bar salesman in the tea hut, and your mate Bobby Andrews. Meanwhile Amesbury faded away from the promotion spots right at the end, though they did win the district cup to help cement this season as one of the best in the club's history.

'Bury's Barcelona-esque play helped them win automatic promotion to League One on the very last day of the season. You would have loved to watch that one.

'And Bhutan, football's international minnows, having beaten Sri Lanka, were drawn in a really tough group against China and Qatar among others in the next round of qualifying for the 2018 World Cup. It will be an amazing adventure, and one that Karun Gurung, one of the young Druk United boys from that photograph that I showed you, taken on that rough scrap of land high up in the Himalayas, well he will be a part of it. 'Even Southampton had a great season.'

All those fears of a mass player exodus on that blissful Susan Sarandon summer evening back in July in Swindon turned out to be unnecessary, with Ronald Koeman confounding everyone's expectations by building a team that spent the entire year near the top of the league.

'They may even qualify for Europe, Grandad!'

But of all the stories from this season, Accrington is the one that Grandad smiles at the most; the warmth, friendship, humility of this club proving that that Victoria Park feeling that he showed me all those years ago can be found in lots of places, if you are prepared to look for it.

He beams as I tell him about his great grandson Sam and his first trip, and that after the last match of the season his new hero Piero Mingoia signed him an autograph on the front of a programme and asked after him.

In fact it's just happened, I tell him, as Emma and I stand in the Accrington clubhouse watching the end of season awards ceremony after a hard fought 2-1 win over Mansfield Town, a victory that ensures a happy ending to a great season.

I open up my bag and show him a Stanley shirt.

'I want to try and get the players to sign it, as a memento of a wonderful season.'

Grandad nods and smiles, ushering me on, so I don't miss out.

He waves as I stand up and walk away; Victoria Park, the old-timers, the cars behind the goal, Grandad slowly fading away as I step further into the room, and as it slips, into focus comes groups of friends laughing, mingling with players, the manager, the board, raising a glass or two to everything that makes them proud to be where they are.

By the bar the Stanley Ultras are still singing, carrying on the party they started down in Dagenham a week before. Elsewhere familiar faces from other trips, old-timers who had seen this club die, come back to life, then slowly rise through the non-leagues to where they are now drink to the thought of a tenth season back in the Football League.

Excited children look on as the players mill about, in awe that their heroes are just there; fiddling with a pen and their programme as they try to summon up the courage to ask for an autograph, just as I am trying to do.

The one player I would have loved to have signed my shirt was Kal Naismith, but he left early, quietly, clearly ill at ease in such a large social gathering. I understood entirely why he felt that way. I had once felt like it too, still do some days. May the coming months and years help ease the pain a little. With friends like team-mate Shay McCartan you can't help but feel he is in good hands. I left a space on the shirt for him. Maybe one day, when things don't seem so overwhelming, he might be able to sign it.

On the far side of it all meanwhile, Emma has been roped in by the chairman of the supporters club to help hand out sandwiches; laughing and joking she dishes them out to supporters and players alike, completely taken in by the warmth of the Accrington Stanley family. In one tiny moment you have a microcosm of an entire season, a season that has proven that real football, the soul of football, the football I came to love as a young boy, is still alive and battling on against all the financial odds.

For as long as these gatherings continue, as long as clubs like Accrington intertwine club and community so seamlessly that you can't tell where one ends and the other begins, as long as people like Emma feel that in supporting a team, in falling in love with it, they have become a part of one big family, then we truly have something to treasure. Even if attendances are down, the soul of football soldiers on; the old men on the gate and in the tea hut at Downton, Keil in the club shop at Stanley, the shoe-wielding Bangor fans, the Corinthians of Kent, and so many more besides, they remain the custodians of everything that makes this game make sense on every spare spot of land across the globe. Where Victoria Park is gone, they are the living embodiment.

It's time to stop mourning, because it is all still here in spirit. And because of that it's time to celebrate, to shout from the rooftops at all that we have had, all that we still have, and thanks to the wonderful, selfless and hard-working souls we have met along the way this season, all that we will always have.

Bring on the summer, pre-season and those wonderful, balmy, Susan Sarandon afternoons.

Bring on next season and all the adventures it may bring.

Postscript

UNTIL THIS BOOK, the idea of a spiritual home had always been married with the realities of actual home. For me a homecoming, spiritual or otherwise, was always Southampton, where I was born and still live, or Salisbury where my grandparents lived and where I spent many a happy summer – with The Dell and St Marys in Southampton, Victoria Park and the Ray Mac in Salisbury being the footballing equivalent of my grandparents' house in a tiny village just north of Salisbury, or the fresh smell of sea air that hits you in Southampton after a long car ride or time away. They were home.

Despite finding places of great beauty that spoke to me in a language far greater than words on family holidays as a child, or whilst travelling as an adult, places like the Alps, the Highlands of Scotland, the Faroe Islands, they would always remain distant aspirations, dreamy reminiscences to while away dreary days at work, the thought of returning helping to keep boredom at bay. They were a kind of spiritual home, but without any kind of tangible or physical connection that you need for a place to really seem like home.

Never in a million years did I think that 'home' could be added to, that another place, another football club could assimilate itself into who I felt I was as deeply as Southampton had after my first adventures at The Dell, or Salisbury had after sitting in the stand at Victoria Park alongside Grandad, no matter how many amazing adventures and clubs I visited. But somehow one club has.

Everything I had come to love about football that had first captivated me as a young boy at The Dell and Victoria Park, I found once more on the terraces at Accrington Stanley. It was a football club rooted in the community, for the community, where fans, players, club staff and board members were all in it together, fighting against the greater financial odds of every other club in League Two.

For me the eight chapters on Stanley are the backbone of *Another Bloody Saturday*, the narrative rudder that underlines all that is great about football far from the bright lights and media frenzy of the Premier League; the enjoyment of standing on the Clayton End terrace also highlighting the sadness and loss at Saturday upon Saturday of still, deserted stands a five-hour drive away in Salisbury.

Among all the other adventures in the book, Accrington is the moral, the emotional weight that for me explains why smaller football clubs matter, possibly more than the larger ones. And through all the Stanley chapters, and the devotion and belonging of its supporters, I hope I have been able to detail why a club like Salisbury folding had such a debilitating effect on a community, its identity, on me.

A lot has happened since my first game at Accrington back on the last day of the 2013/14 season: this book has been published, my love affair with Stanley has grown stronger, Salisbury has reformed, and my grandmother and my last physical link to the city has passed away, leading me to 12 March 2016, a pivotal day it would seem for everyone.

For Accrington it was another in a string of do or die matches that would define their season. Against all odds and expectations, John Coleman, Jimmy Bell and players amassed on the smallest budget in the football league, had produced some of the best football League Two had seen in many a good year, keeping them in the play-off spots for the entire season. Defeat against Portsmouth the Tuesday before had dented their chances of automatic promotion, but victory against Plymouth Argyle would help set them back on track for what most people (other than the small band of Stanley fans who knew how good their team really was) would consider to be the most unlikely of promotions.

At the same time the newly reformed Salisbury FC would be playing the first leg of their FA Vase semi-final away at another phoenix team in Hereford FC. Just two games from a Wembley final, Salisbury would travel with as many fans as Plymouth (sitting just above Accrington in the table) would take to Stanley, and play in front of a crowd just shy of 5,000. It was an amazing turnaround from the shambles left by the previous incarnation, and I was really rooting for them, but it didn't seem quite right to be there in person.

Going to watch Salisbury play again had been tough. The loss of a club that had been a warm, nurturing place as a child, a club that was a unique and special bond between me and Grandad, that had been a focal point of our relationship and friendship, a talking point even in his later years when dementia was taking hold. A place that became a way to connect with happier times after he passed away, standing on the terraces letting memories drift among the present, that loss had been awful, the club gone, the stadium locked and bereft. Not only had there been the pain in losing what had been the one thing that symbolised my relationship with Grandad, but also my Nan passed away before the new Salisbury kicked a ball in anger, making it tougher still to drive up to watch them. However, drive up I did one cold night in February when fate offered up a rematch of the very first game Grandad ever took me to back in Easter 1985, for a local derby against Andover.

From the old timer taking payment for the car park, to the people behind the turnstiles, to the people slowly congregating on the terrace, you couldn't help but see familiar faces that dated back to those Victoria Park days. It was reassuring that they were still there. It was a connection back to happier times and the old club, as was the voice of another old timer over the tannoy – these were things that Grandad would have recognised had he been here. He would also have recognised my scarf, knitted by Nan for a birthday or Christmas long since lost to the fog of time; a lovingly made scarf in Salisbury colours with 'Salisbury FC' stitched carefully across the middle. This cold winter night had been its first outing for many a year after I had wrongly decided that I was too cool to be wearing home-made football scarves anymore!

Salisbury ran out comfortable winners that cold night. And among the roar of the crowd as each goal went in, I could almost hear the car horns of those parked behind the goal at Victoria Park, the cry of 'Tally Ho!' by one old timer that used to quickly follow every goal back then; the ghosts of the past slowly trying to return to validate the club of the present. It was great to see, but it was still hard work, knowing that now Nan was gone too, there was nowhere nearby to call home to head back to for a warming cup of tea and a chat. Though lots did feel the same, things were different.

No, my rehabilitation back to Salisbury will be slow and bittersweet, and will ultimately be a different relationship to the unconditional love of before.

Piggy-backing on their new-found FA Vase success now they are on the brink of something special just didn't seem quite right, not after only one match back. For me, 12 March 2016 would represent a shifting in the sands of my spiritual homes, it would represent a making way for another, the opportunity to hold a book launch of *Another Bloody Saturday* with the people of Accrington Stanley, who had done so much to inspire and fuel it too great a draw for anything else.

Two previous attempts at an Accrington book launch had been postponed due to torrential rain in December, and then frost in January, but as Stanley was the only place where I wanted to launch the book in England, it was a case of 'if at first you don't succeed...'

The Scottish launch at Partick Thistle and the Welsh launch at Bangor City had been great fun, and I had met some great people and like-minded souls. Both had been humbling experiences as both clubs had thrown their full support behind the book. Up at Firhill, Glasgow, little had changed, other than that their mascot Jaggy McBee had been replaced by Kingsley, a David Shrigley creation that had gone viral around the world when its spiky insanity was released on an unsuspecting public! It had been a real pleasure to stand among the Jags fans once again, trying to find an explanation for the publishers as to why a lone man stood among a sea of empty seats in a massive inflatable Santa suit! When Thistle scored and he started jumping around like a lunatic, the suit bulging and bouncing like some unstable matter that threatened to envelop his head, it looked like some drug fuelled out-take to a New Order or Daft Punk music video! I had no explanation, and in a way I am glad, for some things don't really need explaining; you just enjoy them for whatever the hell they are.

After the match, it had been great to meet up with Dan Seaborne, another pivotal character in the book, almost fully rehabilitated from his terrible head injury in Glasgow with Thistle. It felt great to hand him a copy, an acknowledgement of everything he had done for Emma, me and the book.

At Bangor we were treated to Matt, one of the volunteers who manned the club shop, showing us all the framed shirts and pennants, posters and pictures of past European nights that lined the walls of the club house; from great matches against Napoli and Athletico Madrid to their latest, and the first chapter in *Another Bloody Saturday*, against Stjarnan of Iceland.

Sitting in the stand looking out over the beautiful Menai Straits, marvelling at the four Port Talbot Ultras who had made the long journey up from the south of the country for this Welsh Premier League fixture, having crammed themselves, their drum and banners into a car, singing from start to finish, it felt great to be back where it had all started.

As with the launch at Thistle, it had been a wonderful experience to once again witness some of the characters that had made writing the book so enjoyable, as well as discover some more like our inflatable Santa and Port Talbot Ultras. And to meet people who had connected with the book, who believed in it the way I did, was an overwhelming experience to say the least.

But for me the book wouldn't truly be out there, wouldn't truly be 'launched' until I had been able to do it at The Wham Stadium (as it is now known) and thank the people that had inspired it, that had saved my football soul. Over the course of the book I got used to the anonymity of travelling about to different clubs, of blending in quietly with the locals so as to experience what each club was really like. It is, I think, one of the reasons why it ultimately worked so well.

Anonymity for me at Accrington however isn't quite so easy these days, as Nick, the chairman of the official supporter's club and the first person I bumped into after my long drive, summed up with a warm handshake and a smile. 'You're one of us now', he said 'a part of the fixture and fittings.'

For a small club in a small town, sandwiched between much bigger teams in Burnley and Blackburn, and only a relatively short drive away from bigger teams again, it is hard to get people on their own doorstep interested in the Stanley. So to find a complete stranger that lives hundreds of miles away falling for their club, and then writing about it must be as strange an experience for them as it has been for me!

Either way, the warmth and friendship that has developed meant that a trip up to the Wham Stadium isn't complete without a wander round, finding and chatting to people like Nick who were a part of the reason why I fell for the club. Keil in the club shop and ticket office, despite busily printing out tickets for the match had time for a catch up while his mate sold programmes to a queue of Plymouth fans just off one of the away coaches that were pulling up. Marc Turner, club secretary, who had sorted out a couple of free tickets to an away match after the first Accrington chapter had been posted online, wandered past with handfuls of paper.

'Alright Mat', he said, a little distracted as he went off to try and find solutions to this fistful of problems.

Adam and Julie, a mother and son operation that I had seen at every Stanley game I had been to, both home and away, stopped me at half time to talk; it was great to chat like old friends, with a genuine warmth that a common bond often allows.

Meeting all these people soon made my aching back and stiff legs from the near five-hour drive melt away; a small price to pay to feel a part of something as special as Accrington Stanley.

And Accrington Stanley *are* special. Not only does the club operate and survive year on year on the smallest budget in the football league, with the smallest fan base in the football league, but during the 2015/16 season it had also been playing some of the best football you could see anywhere in the football league.

The club that wouldn't die, whose togetherness and spirit has overcome their financial shortcomings to outperform far wealthier and better supported teams for ten seasons, was also mounting a promotion bid. Since the season began, Stanley had been in or around the play-off spots and had been consistently hitting well above their financial weight.

Portsmouth, a side whose attendances are ten times that of Accrington, had struggled to keep up with the neat passing style that John Coleman had crafted out of his small band of players, players that other clubs had deemed surplus to requirements. And now, by mid-March, Stanley were looking up rather than down, gunning for Plymouth who were in the third and final automatic promotion spot and who, like Portsmouth, have resources way beyond the reach of Accrington.

Before the match, in the sports bar, Andy Holt, the new owner of Accrington Stanley, bought a copy of the book for his son Joe, a young lad still at school who clearly had developed the Stanley fever. His enthusiasm was infectious as he excitedly talked about how good he thought the team was, the adventures he had had going to away matches with his dad on the team coach, though he said with a disappointed tone that he wasn't able to go the games where the team stayed overnight because of school.

'They go up on a Friday, and I can't miss school,' he said, not sounding entirely convinced at his dad's wisdom! 'But if we are in the play-offs then I will be allowed to go. But I still think we'll go up automatically.'

Like Partick Thistle and Bangor City, Accrington have done all they can to help me and the book: devoting a page in the programme to it, and having the PA announcer mention it a number of times. As if that wasn't enough both Bangor and Stanley had been selling it through their club shops.

And like at Thistle and Bangor, the people that I get to talk to, that show an interest in the book are the very sorts of people that inspired it in the first place; their self-deprecating love of their club, far from the bright lights of the Premier League and the mainstream media being the reason why I felt the need to write it, to show them and their devotion, the true soul of football, in all its glory.

These three book launches have been some of the most rewarding experiences of my life, being able to meet and connect with people who see the world and football as I do, who have their own childhood memories similar to mine at Victoria Park and The Dell, and as kick-off approached we all made our way into the Wham Stadium in the hope of collecting some more. And, as always, Stanley did not let us down.

In league Two Accrington play football that teams just can't cope with. Their fast, passing style, probing down the wings, then through the middle, then in the channels beyond the defence, has been consistent since day one of the 2015/16 season back in August. And since day one most teams hadn't found a way to combat their attractive and enthusiastic play. Plymouth were no exception, rarely touching the ball for the first 20 minutes or so as Stanley dominated, so obviously it is no irony that with their first real attack Plymouth took the lead! A looping header eluded Etheridge in the Stanley goal and the 600 or so Argyle fans that had made the stupendously long trip go crazy. But this is Stanley: the club that wouldn't die, and despite this set back they kept on plugging away with their passing style, even as the match ticked down into the final ten minutes they refused to panic or to resort to the long ball. And with minutes to spare their faith was rewarded when a neat pass into the box set Billy Kee goal side of the last defender, who brought him down to prevent a shot.

Red card! Penalty to Stanley!

The Clayton End, behind the far goal, who had been cheering the team on relentlessly the whole match held their breath, then exploded with joy as Kee put the penalty away as the game slipped into five minutes of added time. The relief at equalising was palpable around the stands, but Stanley weren't done. As soon as the ball hit the net Piero Mingoia ran to retrieve it and raced back to the half way line, placing it on the centre spot; faith, belief, determination that this season would be one to remember meant that even now, at such a late stage in the game, Stanley's players weren't thinking of a draw.

And the match didn't end in a draw. Four minutes into the five added, and yet another attack saw right back Matty Pearson drive in a wicked cross into the Plymouth box. Shay McCartan, who had looked lively ever since he had come on half way through the second half, threw himself at it, planting a brilliantly placed header past the keeper and into the goal! Delirium! they had done it! Players went nuts, the bench went nuts, the fans went nuts. And among it all, I went nuts, because after everything that had happened, that had brought me to this point, Stanley had become my team.

Since the last day of the 2013/14 season, this little club had saved me from footballing oblivion. And since that end of season match two seasons ago I had been privileged not only to meet the characters that were the soul of this club, but I had got to see these players develop into a side to be feared. The togetherness that kept this club above the dreaded relegation zone year after year was now the togetherness that was fuelling a historic tilt at promotion to League One.

For what the devoted fans and club staff represent, the true soul of football, for the players that had mostly been thrown on the scrapheap by other teams yet have bought in to the spirit of Stanley and resurrected themselves, it really would be the least that they deserve.

But despite the romance of the underdog, the romance of the Accrington Stanley story, there would be no fairy-tale ending, at least for this season.

It is a story for another chapter in another book, however Stanley's future involved a last day draw that saw them finish out of the automatic promotion spots on goal difference only. This was quickly followed by play-off heartbreak against AFC Wimbledon, the eventual winners of that coveted fourth spot in League One. But such heart-ache was still a couple of months away in the bright sunshine of early May. For now, in a breathless sports bar on a cold March day, fans and players mingled over a pint and talked in excited tones about their last gasp win over Plymouth. Joe, the owner's son and a new found friend at Stanley talked excitedly about the match, shouting out well done whenever a new player came in the room. And as it was time to leave to head back home, I couldn't help but feel a tinge of sadness, jealousy as I looked through the windows of the Crown pub at the Stanley fans inside, at the table where I had sat a number of times sipping a pint of Pride of Pendle, talking to Bill White, a former Stanley goalkeeper who sadly passed away just before this book's publication, the chatter in the beer garden that had been a welcome sun trap that very first trip up. It felt like a tinge of home-sickness, and it was as much motivation as the football on display to make sure it wouldn't be too long before I came back up. And let's hope that when I do it will be to take part in another promotion push, and maybe, just maybe, one hell of a promotion party.

On Stanley! On!

This book is small time, unapologetically so. It deals in the passion and love that truly belonging to something can yield. And the fans of Accrington Stanley, Bangor City, Cowes Sports, Dagenham & Redbridge, Corinthian, HB Torshavn and all the others truly do belong. Without them their clubs couldn't survive, and without their clubs their community, its identity would struggle and fade. Each fan is valued, and understood to be an important part of their club, something that an ever growing number of disenfranchised supporters of English Premier League clubs no longer feel. And no matter how small time, how precious is that? To feel as you did when a child going to your first match? How precious it must be as an exiled Tibetan to represent your homeland, even if it is only in front of a handful of people? Or to score a goal for Bhutan in a World Cup Qualifier?

There is a wealth of stories and adventure beneath the big money leagues.

It is there that you really can find the soul of football; the idyllic notion of football that you first fell in love with when a small child. It exists in a world where almost every top flight league in the world can be beamed into your front room, where the world's best players are only a subscription away. And while that is fine, travelling far and wide for this book has proven one thing: that that is only one small part of what makes football the most popular game in the world. Beyond your remote is a vibrant world of humour, passion and lower league magic. It has taken writing this book to truly fathom just how rich a place it is. And now I've found it, there is no going back!

Bring on next season, and the season after that, and the season after that.

Bring on the soul of football!

Some other books published by **Luath Press**

Stramash: Tackling Scotland's Towns and Teams
Daniel Gray
ISBN 978 1-910745-70-0 HBK £14.99

Fatigued by bloated big-time football and bored of samey big cities, Daniel Gray went in search of small town Scotland and its teams. Part travelogue, part history, and part mistakenly spilling ketchup on the face of a small child, Stramash takes an uplifting look at the country's nether regions.

Using the excuse of a match to visit places from Dumfries to Dingwall, Stramash accomplishes the feats of visiting Dumfries without mentioning Robert Burns, being positive about Cumbernauld and linking Elgin City to Lenin.

… a must-read for every non-Old Firm football fan – and for many Rangers and Celtic supporters too. DAILY RECORD

Daniel Gray's volume is in another league. THE SCOTSMAN

I defy anyone to read Stramash *and not fall in love with Scottish football's blessed eccentricities all over again…*
THE SCOTTISH FOOTBALL BLOG

Should've Gone To Specsavers, Ref!: Wickedly funny tales of a referee, booze, Bovril, pies and prejudice
Allan Morrison
ISBN: 978 1 908373 73 1 PBK £7.99

The Cowdenbeath goalkeeper had let in seven goals and was clearly distraught. As Erchie gave him a sympathetic pat on the back the goalie groaned. 'Whit a day. Imagine losing all these goals an' noo ah think ah'm going doon with the cauld.'
'At least ye were able to catch something,' consoled Erchie.

Featuring the antics of wisecracking referee 'Big Erchie' as he faces match-fixing, love and everything in between, *Should've Gone Tae Specsavers, Ref!* is about those people who hate football but go along to games to ruin them for everyone else – the referees!

Interweaving humour with a history of football in Scotland and featuring every team from Scotland's four divisions, this book is a must-read for every football fan.

Details of these and other books published by Luath Press can be found at:
www.luath.co.uk

Luath Press Limited

committed to publishing well written books worth reading

LUATH PRESS takes its name from Robert Burns, whose little collie
Luath (*Gael.*, swift or nimble) tripped up Jean Armour at a wedding
and gave him the chance to speak to the woman who was to be his wife
and the abiding love of his life. Burns called one of the 'Twa Dogs'
Luath after Cuchullin's hunting dog in Ossian's *Fingal*.
Luath Press was established in 1981 in the heart of
Burns country, and is now based a few steps up
the road from Burns' first lodgings on
Edinburgh's Royal Mile. Luath offers you
distinctive writing with a hint of
unexpected pleasures.
Most bookshops in the UK, the US, Canada,
Australia, New Zealand and parts of Europe,
either carry our books in stock or can order them
for you. To order direct from us, please send a £sterling
cheque, postal order, international money order or your
credit card details (number, address of cardholder and
expiry date) to us at the address below. Please add post
and packing as follows: UK – £1.00 per delivery address;
overseas surface mail – £2.50 per delivery address; overseas airmail –
£3.50 for the first book to each delivery address, plus £1.00 for each
additional book by airmail to the same address. If your order is a gift,
we will happily enclose your card or message at no extra charge.

Luath Press Limited
543/2 Castlehill
The Royal Mile
Edinburgh EH1 2ND
Scotland
Telephone: +44 (0)131 225 4326 (24 hours)
email: sales@luath.co.uk
Website: www.luath.co.uk